DEALING WITH DICTATORS

To Cella

Dealing with Dictators

The Destruction and
Revival of Europe
1930–70

Frank Roberts

Weidenfeld & Nicolson
London

First published in Great Britain in 1991 by
George Weidenfeld & Nicolson Ltd, 91 Clapham
High Street, London SW4 7TA

Copyright © Frank Roberts 1991

British Library Cataloguing in Publication Data
(available on request)

ISBN 0 297 81197 5

Typeset at The Spartan Press Ltd,
Lymington, Hants
Printed and bound in Great Britain by
Butler & Tanner Ltd, Frome and London

Contents

Illustrations

The Queen's visit to Germany in 1965 (*Stern*)

The Queen's visit, 1965: German dinner in Schloss Bruhl

Arrival in Bonn with HRH the Duke of Edinburgh, President Lubke, members of the German Government, Michael Stewart, British and Commonwealth diplomats (*Bundesbildstelle, Bonn*)

The author and his wife in the Embassy residence, Germany 1965 (*Camera Press*)

The author in Germany in his Embassy office, 1965

The author with Chancellor Erhard and George Brown (*Camera Press*)

Farewell in Berlin: with the governing mayor, Klaus Schutz, 1968 (*Landesbildstelle, Berlin*)

Farewell in Bonn: with the President and Frau Lubke, 1968 (*Bundesbildstelle, Bonn*)

Anglo-German Königswinter Conference in 1968, with Lilo Milchsack DCMG and Sir Robert Birley (*Foto Sachsee*)

Acknowledgements

This book is my own personal commentary on those major international events between 1930 and 1970 in which I was directly involved, and on outstanding personalities at home and abroad with whom they brought me into contact. Perhaps unwisely I have not burdened friends and colleagues with requests to read and advise.

I am therefore mainly indebted to the Foreign and Commonwealth Office for giving me such interesting although not always easy postings, and to the great men at home and abroad with whom I worked. I think first and foremost, and I leave out those still living, of Churchill, Bevin, Eden and Neville Chamberlain at home, and of de Gaulle, Sikorski, Adenauer, Spaak, Nehru, Tito, Khrushchev and, in a very different sense, Stalin and Molotov, abroad. But any opinions expressed are my own, and do not necessarily represent those of the Foreign and Commonwealth Office at the time or now.

I want to thank my wife Cella, who not only made such a valuable contribution over so many years to our joint activities at home and abroad, but whose regular letters to her mother in Cairo have helped to replace the diary which I never kept myself. Sadly, she did not live to see the book published.

I am most grateful to Dr Anita van de Vliet, on whom has fallen the main task of preparing this book for publication, for her good advice and hard, effective work.

Last but not least my thanks are due to colleagues who served with me in Foreign Office departments and posts abroad, too numerous to mention individually, who ensured that these were efficient and 'happy ships', as also to many foreign colleagues, more especially in NATO, the Soviet Union and Germany, posts where close cooperation was so important.

1 | The Way to the Foreign Office

1930

When I retired from the Diplomatic Service in April 1968, I was encouraged to write by several publishers. I had had an unusually interesting career, in posts where things were happening and in contact with a number of outstanding people at home and abroad. But I was then starting a second career in business, with Unilever and with Lloyds of London, and for over a year I was also extremely busy as a member of the Foreign Secretary's Committee of Three on Overseas Representation, better known as the Duncan Committee, on which I shall have something to say later. And then I got involved in so many other activities that there was always a good reason to postpone writing.

The reason that I am at long last putting pen to paper is that so much has happened since 1989 in those countries with which I was most closely concerned, above all in Germany, in Poland and in the Soviet Union under Gorbachev, for which I can provide some background from what I had myself seen in Russia under another reformer, Nikita Khrushchev, and before that under Stalin; from my experience with the Poles during the war; from my years at NATO; and above all from my close involvement with German affairs from Munich in 1938 to today. Andrei Gromyko, who must have been the longest serving Foreign Minister of the century, would not be my model for many things, but I was encouraged by his belated decision to write his memoirs not because he expected them to make 'very interesting reading' but because he felt he should describe events and individuals seen by few other living people, without any pretensions to overall analysis, and in my own case, still less to write the history of the past half-century.

1

Diplomatic

I was, I suppose, a rather unusual entrant into the Foreign Service, as it was called in 1930. I was born in Buenos Aires in 1907, because my father had gone out to start what would now be Unilever in South America. By Argentine law I was an Argentine citizen. However, on both sides of my family I was pure English. My father came from Preston, and his ancestors would in those days have been called 'gentlemen'. They were mainly lawyers, or doctors, or in the case of my paternal grandfather, a civil engineer. Although the great Victorian Liberals, John Bright and Richard Cobden, were friends of the family, most of them would I think have voted Conservative. Basically my father's was a Lancashire middle-class family, no member of which had to my knowledge gone to London to join even the Home Civil Service, still less the Foreign Service.

My mother's family came from Blackburn, and they were very different. Her father was a man of many new ideas. He was one of the first people in the country to get involved in the cinema at the start of this century – in his case, Pathé news reels. He also invented rather improbable things like a new water closet and a special kind of composition cricket ball, but he never bothered to patent his inventions. He had something in common with my paternal grandfather, who was a civil engineer with very firm ideas of his own who had lost all the family fortune through his determination to build the Preston ship canal. It was afterwards built, but not by him. He always maintained that the House of Lords had been wrong to turn down his project, and when my mother asked him, 'But what is the other side of the story?' he replied simply, 'My dear, there is no other side.' I hope this is a characteristic that I have not inherited, as I have had to spend most of my life explaining the other side of the story, either to foreign Governments or to British Ministers sometimes reluctant to hear it.

My mother's family were active Liberals. One of their friends was the editor of the local Blackburn paper, who afterwards became the editor of the *News Chronicle*, then the leading London Liberal paper. So in many ways, my mother and my father came from different political and even social backgrounds. My father had joined Lever Brothers at Port Sunlight in its early days because, with seven younger brothers and sisters, he had to rebuild the family fortunes. He founded what is now an important Unilever business all over South America, retiring in about 1930 after building factories in Buenos Aires and Sao Paolo. I was in Argentina until I was seven but we travelled home every year to Britain. The large and important

2

British community in Buenos Aires was rather close-knit, and we did not have many Argentine friends.

Then I went to school in England, first to Bedales, which was already the leading co-educational school. It was a remarkable school under a very remarkable headmaster, John Badley. I was there through the war until 1921. My mother stayed in England most of the time, taking a senior student's course at the London School of Economics under R. H. Tawney, whom she much admired. She also saw a certain amount of Bernard Shaw and the Fabians, with whom she did not agree because, unlike the rest of her family, she was rather to the right in many ways. But she was also a keen suffragette, and she would probably have preferred to stay in England before the war, supporting Mrs Pankhurst (also from Lancashire) if she hadn't married my father and gone out to Argentina.

My time at Bedales, where I was doing rather well, already in a high class and in the cricket XI at thirteen, came to an end because Bedales, as a 'progressive' school, did not have an Officers Training Corps, membership of which would in those days, when so many Anglo-Argentines had served in the First World War in Europe, have made my military service in Argentina, had I returned there, much easier. So I went to Rugby, for which John Badley, who had been at Rugby himself, still retained a certain loyalty. I was quite alarmed about going to Rugby. I had read *Tom Brown's Schooldays*, and thought that the minute my fellow schoolboys learned I had been at school with girls I was bound at least to be tossed in a blanket. This was a great mistake, and when the deadly secret came out, I became the centre of interest for some days.

I was lucky at Rugby because I was again under another great headmaster, W. W. Vaughan. I also had a stimulating housemaster, John Bruce Lockhart, with wide interests, who was the brother of the well-known Robert Bruce Lockhart who had been in Russia at the beginning of the First World War and whom I got to know well during the Second World War. And I had a very good history teacher in C. P. ('Tiger') Hastings. W. W. Vaughan wanted to make modern languages a better educational discipline, comparable with the classics. This experiment was tried out, much to our benefit, on me and Richard Hare, who also later joined the Foreign Service. I was Head of my House and of the School and in the rugby and cricket teams for two years, and have happy memories of Rugby, from which I went to Trinity Cambridge with a Rugby leaving Exhibition and a Trinity History Scholarship.

3

None of this would normally have led me to the Foreign Service, had it not been that history and modern languages, which had been my subjects at Rugby and Cambridge, were appropriate subjects for the Foreign Service examination. It was, I suppose, this, together with my childhood experience abroad, which led me after a brief and belated flirtation with medical studies to prepare for this examination in 1930. It was then a very different Foreign Service from today. Languages, very rightly, played a big part, but the general way we learned our languages (I had been lucky, having been very well taught at Rugby) was to take a year or two after university going around families in Germany and France learning their language. I did not do it that way: after getting two Firsts in the History Tripos, I stayed on a fourth year at Cambridge, doing some tutoring in history, and I went to two of these families during the vacations. There was one family in France, that of Professor Martin, in Paris and, during the holidays, either in the Alps near Chamonix or at Wimereux near Boulogne. His establishment was the original for Terence Rattigan's successful comedy, *French Without Tears*, without being quite so glamorous. In Germany I went to a Catholic family in Bonn, that of Frau Justizrat Menzen. I arrived there during Lent, and was at once asked if there was anything I gave up for Lent. Feeling that the honour of England was at stake, I decided to give up smoking, and I have never smoked since. This decided my life, because my wife, who suffered from migraines, would never have married me if I had smoked. So I am eternally grateful to Frau Menzen. I was lucky enough to come out top in the Foreign Office exam, and second in the wider Home and Indian Civil Service examination, entering the Foreign Office in October 1930.

Within a few weeks the question of my second Argentine nationality came up unexpectedly. In those far-off days, Britain kept a naval squadron on the South American station, and a cruiser, HMS *Glasgow*, was to visit Buenos Aires. The Admiralty asked what would happen to one of their midshipmen who, like myself, had been born in Argentina but had not done his military service there. The official answer was that, if he set foot on shore, he might be arrested as a deserter. Someone recalled my background and it was decided to take up the two cases together. I at once suggested that I would ask my father, who had by this time returned to London, to write to friends in Buenos Aires to settle matters, as was then possible, 'out of court'. The idea that a young Foreign Office recruit with three weeks' service and his father could solve the matter better than through the normal official channels was rejected by shocked officials, and the case went on for eight years. An elegant solution was then found by the Argentines, who discovered that I had applied for permission to perform my military service with a view to becoming an officer of the reserve but that since in that year the candidates were not called upon to serve, I was free from service and not guilty of any infraction of the law. Fortunately, by the time of the Falklands War in 1983, I was a little old to be called up either to seize the Malvinas for Argentina or, recalling my days in the Rugby Officers Training Corps, to recover the Falklands for Britain. The only serious result was that I could never be appointed as a British diplomat to Argentina and, by a natural if not necessarily logical extension, to any other Latin American post.

Since I shall be writing later about the Diplomatic Service, upon which I was called as a member of the Duncan Committee to report in 1968–69, I should perhaps say a little more about the very different Service which I entered in 1930. The differences went beyond the question of foreign languages and the fact that almost our first obligation was to purchase not only a diplomatic uniform but also Court Dress, including knee breeches for Palace Levées and a special Household Evening Coat for dinners with Royalty present. All this, with the attendant gold lace, ostrich feather hat, evening shoes, a cloak and overcoat could then be purchased with a grant of £100! They went beyond even the generous although also, for poor swimmers like myself, alarming practice of the then Permanent Under-Secretary, Sir Robert Vansittart, of inviting new entrants to breakfast and a swim at the Grosvenor House pool. The Foreign Office 'clerks', who had never been posted abroad, had only relatively recently been joined to the Diplomatic Service, whose members had never served at home. The Consular Service was entirely separate, as was the Commercial Diplomatic Service which, under the Department of Overseas Trade, had two controlling Departments, the Foreign Office and the Board of Trade. There were therefore three quite separate services, separately recruited, with the diplomats at the head of the pile, preserved from contact with commercial and consular work. There was even a separate Passport Control Service.

Within but rather separate from the normal Consular Service, there were specialist consular services, whose duties were basically political, and whose members became special advisers to their less expert Ambassadors. There was a special Middle East service, whose members were trained in Arabic, Persian and Turkish. There were specialist Chinese, Japanese and Siamese services, also with experts and linguists. When I went to Egypt in 1935 on my second overseas posting, the Oriental Secretary at that time, Walter Smart, a Persian as well as an Arab scholar, had great influence as the senior member of the Middle East service. His position was more important than many Embassies.

Before the 1939 war, we had only some forty diplomatic posts around the world. Today there are about 150. The continents of Asia and Africa consisted largely of British, French, Dutch and Belgian colonies. Ethiopia and Liberia were the only two fully independent countries in the whole of Africa. South Africa was then a British Dominion. Egypt, although it had its own King and was in the League of Nations, was in effect under British occupation. The League of Nations membership count was under fifty states: this reduced the number of diplomats considerably.

I started work in the Foreign Office – rather prophetically, in view of later events – in the Northern Department, and dealt with Russia, with whom we had only recently entered into diplomatic relations. I did not speak Russian and was not encouraged to learn it by my Head of Department unless, he said, I particularly wanted to be sent to the Soviet Union, not then a much sought after posting. It was then discovered that another new entrant had good Russian, so I changed places with him and spent the next two years dealing with, or more correctly, learning about China in the Far Eastern Department. Important things were happening in China in the early Thirties. Chiang Kai-shek had recently broken with the Communists, with whom he had been working closely. The Japanese were moving into Shanghai as well as Manchuria. We still had big interests in China, above all our settlement in Shanghai. In the Far Eastern Department it was in fact a former Consul-General from Shanghai, Sir John Pratt, who, although technically an adviser with no executive authority, really ran our relations with China. Apart from authorizing Sir John Pratt's proposals when no one more senior was available, I cannot claim to have made a significant contribution myself.

One subject I was allowed to handle was individual claims against the Chinese Government, which were numerous, usually with a long history and little prospect of success. Going through one of these cases, it seemed to me clear that the Chinese would never pay and that the kindest thing I could do was to make this clear to our claimant and prevent him borrowing more money in pursuit of his claim. Having done this, as I thought, sympathetically, I was one day summoned to the presence of Hugh Dalton, then the only Junior Minister in the Foreign Office. He handed me a copy of *John Bull*, a more popular predecessor of our *Private Eye*, with a circulation of about two million, with my letter published under the headline 'Unsympathetic Foreign Office Official Dashes Hopes of British Claimant!' Dalton's booming voice added to my embarrassment. Good intentions are not enough for a diplomat.

With Sir John Pratt and some others taking most of the strain, I was not overworked in my first Department and even managed to play squash at the RAC with one of my senior colleagues on many mornings, arriving at the office at about ten o'clock. It was not quite as bad as the story that used to be told against the pre-1914 Foreign Office, that its officials played like the fountains in Trafalgar Square from ten till four. But this was not typical of the Foreign Office as I got to know it later, working very long hours indeed.

My first years in the Foreign Office coincided with a major world economic crisis, in the course of which sterling broke its longstanding link with gold. My only economic studies at Cambridge had been medieval economic history, which was hardly relevant. So I went along for evening lectures at the London School of Economics under some outstanding economists, including the late Lord Robbins and Professor Hayek, who is still around and has been one of Mrs Thatcher's gurus. Prophecy was dangerous in what was a rapidly changing situation. I learned the useful lesson that economics was not an exact science.

2 | Paris

1932–5

My first overseas posting in 1932 was Paris, which was very lucky for me. It brought me into what was then the main stream of British policymaking. America was still isolationist and on the whole reluctant to become involved in anything outside the Americas and to a lesser extent the Far East, more especially as she was still recovering from the Great Depression. The Soviet Union, which only reached Super-Power status after the Second World War, was then in serious internal trouble and of little international account, apart from the ideological threat of Communism. There were some strange, rosy ideas around from such visitors as Bernard Shaw, H. G. Wells and the Webbs, who should have known better, about what they considered to be the real democratic nature of the Soviet Union under Joseph Stalin, quite regardless of the horrors inflicted by agrarian collectivization, the murder by Stalin of up to two-thirds of the members of his Central Committee and, a little later, of the vast majority of the senior officers in the Red Army.

So the two major world powers at that time were Britain and France. Germany had not yet recovered from the First World War, although under Hitler she was pushing back to the centre of the stage. Italy under Mussolini was embarking upon the creation of a mini-Roman Empire in the Mediterranean and Africa. In the Far East, Japan was pursuing an expansionist policy in China. But Britain and France were the only two powers with worldwide interests and responsibilities and active foreign policies. Our relations with France were very close, although we were by no means always in agreement, and France played the same kind of role in British diplomacy that

America did later on. So the Paris Embassy was really our key Embassy. France had the biggest army and was still the most important country in the Continent of Europe. She regarded herself as the guardian of the Versailles settlement after the First World War, which in the West had given her back Alsace-Lorraine and authorized the occupation of the Saar and the Rhineland, and had set up in Eastern Europe a 'Cordon Sanitaire' which was the reverse of that organized by Stalin after the Second World War. Through France's alliances with Poland and the Little Entente, comprising Czechoslovakia, Roumania and Yugoslavia, Germany was contained in the east as well as the west, and the Soviet Union sealed off from infecting the rest of Europe with dangerous Communist theories.

The French priority, never shared and increasingly disapproved in Britain, was to keep Germany down. But under the Weimar Republic, which was very successful in the late Twenties (1924 to 1929 are still known in Germany as the 'Golden Years'), and under a remarkable Foreign Secretary, Stresemann, Germany changed its international role from that of an outcast to positive membership of the Western European grouping led by France and Britain, whose outstanding Foreign Ministers, Aristide Briand and Austen Chamberlain, established a special personal relationship with Stresemann. The Locarno Treaty of 1925 signalled a new era of cooperation in Western Europe. Locarno earned the Garter for Austen Chamberlain, the half-brother of Neville and at that time considered a much more important political figure. As an undergraduate at Trinity Cambridge I met him in the mid-Twenties, when he returned to his old college to celebrate the Locarno Treaty. It was a colourful and even romantic occasion, reflecting the new confidence in the future of Western Europe.

The 'Golden Years' in Germany meant even more to the Germans. Inflation was at an end, and the economy recovering. There was genuine optimism about the stability of the new Weimar democratic structure. The arts flourished, with Berlin as a major artistic centre. But then came the world economic crisis of 1929–30, which affected Germany more than any other great power – six million were unemployed at that time – and the feeling was revived that the Versailles Treaty had not been fair to Germany. The Weimar Republic collapsed under Communist, Nationalist and Nazi pressures, and Hitler, with Nationalist help, became Chancellor in 1931.

Hitler was already more than a name to me. When I was learning German in Bonn for the Foreign Service examination, I had met a young student from Bonn University who thought he was a Communist and therefore strongly opposed to Hitler. He was certainly no Nazi, and once he whisked me into a side alley at night to avoid both of us being beaten up by Bonn University Brownshirts. He took me for my education to a typical Nazi rally, with banners and trumpets and Brownshirts, and Hitler began speaking. I understood German well by this time, and was not impressed by what I thought demagogic ranting. His audience was wildly enthusiastic. I noticed that my Communist friend became as enthusiastic as everybody else. As we were leaving, I took him to task. He shook himself like a dog coming out of a pond, and said that he had been told that Hitler had this effect upon Germans, who developed collective hysteria under the influence of his oratory.

When I arrived in Paris at the end of 1932, Britain and France were more than ever the joint guardians of the Versailles settlement, with, however, increasingly different views on how to handle Hitler's Germany and Mussolini's Italy. The defence of our interests as the two leading colonial powers added to the importance of the Paris Embassy. The French had managed the recession better than some other countries and the French franc remained on gold, when the pound had tottered. Laval, the Minister of Finance, later executed for his role in the wartime Vichy Government, was most helpful in supporting the pound.

We had an outstanding Ambassador in Lord Tyrrell. He had been Private Secretary to Sir Edward Grey before the First World War, and Permanent Under-Secretary at the Foreign Office after it. He knew Germany well and had made a major contribution to the prevailing climate of opinion in the Foreign Office, which was suspicious of Germany, either under the Kaiser or under Hitler, and therefore favoured the maintenance of the Anglo-French Entente. He was regarded very much as a friend of France, and had a great position in Paris, so much so that French Ministers would often come to see him instead of the more normal reverse procedure. His daughter's wedding in Nôtre Dame was even compared to that of Mary Queen of Scots to the Dauphin of France.

He was a remarkable figure. He never wrote official despatches or recorded even his official interviews, preferring to recount them to one of his staff for the report to London. He did, however, write letters in his own hand with no copies to the Prime Minister, Stanley Baldwin, who was unfortunately not much interested in foreign affairs, despite annual visits to Aix les Bains for the cure. In the Foreign Office Willy Tyrrell rarely if ever did more on papers submitted to him than write his initials, 'W.T.' And he is rarely if ever on record with decisions or even opinions. On one occasion an Under-Secretary in despair returned a file to him with the arguments for and against a particular course of action carefully rehearsed, and concluded, 'This, P-U-S [Permanent Under-Secretary] requires a decision.' Even then, Willy Tyrrell confined himself to writing, 'Yes, it does.' He infinitely preferred discussion, and he was a great conversationalist.

He had a great contempt for our then Foreign Secretary, John Simon. John Simon was a great lawyer and, I believe, a good Lord Chancellor, but he approached foreign affairs like legal cases: you fought the case, won or lost it, and that was the end of the matter. But foreign affairs are not like that; little if anything is finally put to rest. And he got very irritated when what he regarded as a case which had been settled suddenly popped up again. John Simon had to attend meetings of the League of Nations in Geneva, and sat behind the pilot in an open RAF plane, breaking the journey to stay overnight in Paris and occasionally staying long enough for a game of golf. On one such occasion I missed a put which gave him the game on the eighteenth green, and never lived down the incorrect critique that I was currying favour with the Foreign Secretary. One evening after dinner he was talking at great length, when the Ambassador put a hand to his mouth to stifle a great yawn, walked out, and never came back. The next morning his staff reported that we had not quite known what to do with the Foreign Secretary, to receive the reply that he could not waste his time on John Simon, since he had discovered that 'you could load him, but he never fired'.

Willy Tyrrell liked playing golf and bridge and going to the cinema. I was one of the few young secretaries in the Embassy who played golf and bridge. I was often invited to join him, and so got to know him well. In this I was very lucky since, although no modern Ambassador could ever conduct the affairs of his Embassy as he did, he was a considerable personality and ready to share his wide experience and good judgement with a young colleague like myself. We saw a great deal of him in London before and during the war, and as a young diplomat I benefited greatly from his fascinating 'table talk' and diplomatic gossip, in the best sense of the expression.

Games indeed helped me in Paris. I played hockey for the Racing Club de France, visiting many provincial centres and meeting a wider cross-section of the French younger generation than a foreign diplomat would normally have done. Rather oddly, I even became a French international, because I also played cricket, and we had an annual match against Belgium – the British in France against the British in Belgium. French sport was so organized that you could not play even for the British in France against the British in Belgium at so unimportant a game for the French as cricket without becoming part of the French international structure.

The French situation internally and internationally deteriorated considerably during my three years there. Indeed, in 1934 the Government very nearly broke down. There was a neo-Fascist movement called the Croix de Feu, which staged a mass demonstration in the Place de la Concorde against the politicians of the Third Republic, when I was representing the Embassy in the Chamber of Deputies. There had been a bad scandal centred on a French financier called Stavisky, who was reputed to have given money to French politicians and who was found dead in the Alps in suspicious circumstances. The demonstrators repeatedly tried to break through the police cordons holding the bridge over the Seine, and the situation became extremely dangerous. A leading figure then was Herriot, and there were loud shouts of '*À l'eau! Herriot! Herriot! À l'eau!*' I and an American colleague (I appreciated the special relationship that night!) finally got out of the Chamber by underground passages, collecting my small car from the front with the help of the police, who were impressed by my American colleague's insistence that I was the British Ambassador, also a small man, although they must have thought it odd that the British Ambassador had so small a car. The rising, for such it had become, was suppressed that night. There were many casualties and the well-known Café Weber in the Rue Royale had been converted into an emergency first aid station. The immediate crisis was met by the creation of a Government of all the talents under well-known elder statesmen, to be followed later by the Front Populaire.

On the international front one of these elder statesmen, Barthou, set out as Foreign Secretary to maintain the Cordon Sanitair in Eastern Europe and to breathe fresh life and confidence into France's alliances in the East. King Alexander of Yugoslavia was invited to France. He came by boat to Marseilles, where Barthou met him, and both were murdered by the Croatian Ustashi. The story was that the police in Marseilles had not heeded warnings from the police in Paris, with the result that France lost its best Foreign Minister for many years and its toughest ally in Eastern Europe.

The resulting scandal spread to the British Embassy. There were two police forces in Paris, one headed by the Préfet de Police, in the centre, and the other by the Préfet de la Seine, who looked after the Paris region. The former, Chiappe, told us that he was on the tracks of the Croatian murderers and that these tracks seemed to lead to a British diplomat who had been seen travelling with a girl thought to be one of the Croatian group. Could we help by bringing our man, who was posted in the Far East but had been on holiday in France, from where he had gone to Scotland, back to Paris for questioning? Our Ambassador at this time, Sir George Clarke, agreed on Chiappe's assurance that he would be allowed to leave immediately afterwards but also on our assurance that he would not be told in advance why the French wanted to see him. My own role in this strange affair was to meet our man at Le Bourget airport and bring him to Chiappe in the centre of Paris. But Le Bourget was under the authority of the Préfet de la Seine who, Chiappe insisted, must not be allowed to discover what was going on, so my small car was preferred to an official Embassy car. I got a puzzled colleague away from Le Bourget, but as ill luck would have it, while I was still in the territory of the Préfet de la Seine I was hit by a car from a side street (my only accident in France!). Luckily, I could still drive on without any police intervention, and successfully delivered my colleague at the Préfecture de Police on the Ile de la Cité. My difficulties arose later in explaining to my insurance company why I had not stopped to take the other driver's number! As we had expected, my colleague was able to prove that he had not been travelling with a beautiful Croatian terrorist but with a British friend from the Paris Embassy of similar appearance.

Delightful though life was in Paris for a young British diplomatist, invited to the best houses and more or less automatically made a member of the best golf and other clubs, in the two and a half years I spent in Paris until the spring of 1935 the French position in Europe was weakening against not only the menace of Hitler's Germany but also of Mussolini's Italy. Worst of all, the French, not yet exposed to the pressures of the Spanish Civil War or Hitler's reoccupation of the Rhineland, were already losing their self-confidence, although their British friends, including Churchill and the Paris Embassy, comforted themselves with the thought that the French Army was the best in Europe and that in a serious crisis the French would pull themselves together and show their traditional spirit.

In Britain we were still recovering from economic recession, and Stanley Baldwin was healing the wounds left by the General Strike. There was certainly greater self-confidence than in France, to some extent fuelled by underestimation of the German danger. The Prime Minister's interest in foreign affairs was minimal, and he did not believe the country would accept a serious rearmament programme. So it was not only Anthony Eden who was looking forward to the prospect of strong Government under the obvious successor, Neville Chamberlain. I had a personal experience which illustrated our underestimation of Hitler's actions. Baldwin's Parliamentary Private Secretary, Geoffrey Lloyd (later Lord Lloyd), had the task of keeping in touch with French politicians, and one of my tasks was to keep in touch with him. He invited me to visit him in the House of Commons, where he could arrange for me perhaps to meet the Prime Minister. I had the opportunity during a big debate in the House of Commons on air rearmament. I was taken to the PM's room just after he had made a speech dismissing alarming statistics on the speed and scope of German air rearmament produced by Winston Churchill – incidentally, supported by the private researches of a colleague in the Foreign Office, which turned out to be nearer the mark than those of the Air Ministry. I was asking myself whether the Government really believed their own case or were just pushing aside Winston's accusations. I found everyone congratulating Baldwin on his speech, and there was no doubt that he and they were convinced that Winston had been completely wrong. We simply did not realize how fast the Germans were rearming at that time; and Neville Chamberlain also got it wrong later on.

3 | Cairo and Marriage

1935–7

I was equally lucky in my next posting to Cairo, above all because I met my wife in Egypt. Egypt in the spring of 1937 was a key centre in British diplomacy. To a great extent, we ran Egypt. It was not part of the British Empire, and its status was that of an independent kingdom. But we had very special rights there, with large British forces stationed in the country and with the Sudan, theoretically an Anglo-Egyptian condominium, under British control and administration. The British High Commissioner's role was far greater than that of a normal diplomat, marked by his special train for his longer journeys and by motor-cycle outriders around his car. Our original purpose of ensuring control of the Suez Canal and the route to India now extended to protecting growing British oil interests in the Middle East and to maintaining our dominant position in the Arab world. There were three sources of power in Egypt, the other two being the Palace and the Wafd (the main political party set up to gain independence). The British position in Egypt was, however, increasingly anachronistic at a time when negotiations had started with the goal of independence for India itself. Not only the Egyptians, Palace and Wafd alike, but also successive British Governments had been trying for many years to arrive at a mutually acceptable treaty relationship which would still protect our interests and ensure security in the Suez Canal Zone and in the Sudan. Fortunately for us, the King and the Wafd were rarely in agreement, and our constant problem was the choice of one or the other as the more promising negotiating partner at the time. As Private Secretary to the High Commissioner I was closely involved in all this, as I was also in his important relationship with the British Commanders-in-Chief and with the four senior British advisers to the Egyptian Government, responsible for Finance, Justice, Public Security and the Police. I also had a special subject of my own, the overdue promotion of British influence in cultural and educational affairs.

The Egyptian situation was transformed by the Mediterranean ambitions of Mussolini and above all by his seizure of Abyssinia, giving Italy partial control of the head waters of the Nile, on which Egypt was absolutely dependent. For the first time there was a real community of interests between Britain, determined to maintain control of the Suez Canal, and the Egyptians, fearful of encirclement by an Italian empire in control of Abyssinia and Libya. King Fuad, an intelligent monarch but one educated in Italy and surrounded by an Italian camerilla, might have been a difficulty, but following a false alarm in 1934 he died in 1936. His son, Farouk, was only sixteen, and the way was clear for negotiations with the Wafd. We were fortunate enough to have in Sir Miles Lampson (later Lord Killearn) an impressive and forceful – but also shrewd – High Commissioner well suited to making the most of this opportunity, and with strong backing from Anthony Eden at home. He came to Cairo from Peking, where he had also exercised a rather dominant pro-consular role. He was a big and normally jovial man, not only physically, at his best in critical situations, even though he must often have appeared overbearing to many Egyptians. He enjoyed life, and especially his privileged position with his duck shoot at Ekkiad and his racehorses at Gezira. He had recently remarried a much younger wife, Jacqueline Castellani, who had come out to Egypt with his niece. She rapidly settled into running her side of the High Commissioner's duties with great efficiency. But there was an embarrassment in that her father, Sir Aldo Castellani, an outstanding specialist in tropical diseases with a big practice in London, was an Italian, and was called upon by Mussolini to advise the Italians in Abyssinia. It must have confused many Egyptians, with whom we were negotiating on the basis of the Italian threat, and at a time when the Royal Navy were in strength in Alexandria, to find that the High Commissioner and Lady Lampson, usually accompanied by me as their Private Secretary, were exceptionally well entertained at the Italian Legation, manned by three brilliant young Fascist bachelors, of whom the youngest was the Minister, Ghigi, in order to meet Sir Aldo on his way through the Suez Canal to and from Abyssinia. In fact, however, Sir Miles leant over backwards in emphasizing to London the Italian danger and in playing down the even greater threat from Hitler's Germany, although he had himself handled our relations with Germany shortly after the First World War.

Although negotiating with the Wafd, the High Commissioner gave much thought to the training of the young King Farouk, who was highly intelligent, slim, good-looking and very popular. However, his education had been neglected by his father, so much so that when he was to be sent to the Military Academy at Woolwich very late in the day, he first needed private tuition at a house on Kingston Hill, unfortunately interrupted by his father's death. On his return to Cairo he was then given a good young British Private Secretary, Edward Ford, who later became one of the Queen's Private Secretaries. He served with a very nice young Egyptian, Amr Bey, then the world squash champion. An older and outstanding Egyptian, Hassanein Pasha, became a sort of Tutor. The High Commissioner, I think, hoped that Farouk would also turn to him for advice. But all these plans were frustrated by King Fuad's Egyptian and Italian courtiers, anti-British and anxious to preserve their own influence, and by the growing wilfulness of the young King Farouk himself, who was much spoilt by his mother, Queen Nazli, reputed to have taken Hassanein as her lover.

However favourable the climate, the Anglo-Egyptian negotiations were not easy and had their ups and downs. We wanted Egyptian agreement for several battalions to remain in the Canal Zone, and we also needed several airfields, too many in the Egyptian view. At the height of the crisis we had a large part of the Royal Navy in Alexandria and thought we might remove any doubts he might have about our capacity to defend Egypt by inviting the Prime Minister Nahas Pasha to a day at sea with the Royal Navy. They of course put on a very good show – too good, as it turned out. On the train returning to Cairo, Nahas told me that, much as he had enjoyed his day at sea, he could not understand why we had organized such a convincing display of British strength, since he could no longer understand why we needed so many airfields as well. However, the treaty was duly signed in 1937, and Nahas Pasha and his rather domineering wife were entertained by Anthony Eden in London in celebration. It stood us in good stead in the Second World War.

Cairo, like Paris, was a most enjoyable posting. And I enjoyed it all the more because I met my wife within a few days of my arrival.

Her name was Celeste (Cella) Shoucair. Her family on both sides was Lebanese (Greek Orthodox). They had come to Egypt, as many Lebanese had done, in the days of Cromer, who set up the British authority at the turn of the century. Her father, Said Shoucair, had been a young professor at the American University in Beirut, where he became a Presbyterian, although I think he must have been a natural agnostic. He came to Cairo in a Government posting, which took him to Suakin, the only Sudanese centre not overrun in the Mahdi's uprising. Her mother was a daughter of Dr Yacoub Sarruf, who had started the *Mouktataf*, the first popular scientific magazine in Arabic. He was in close touch with Nimr Pasha and Takla Pasha, also Lebanese, who started the first Arabic newspapers, the *Mokkatam* and the *Ahram*. Dr Sarruf, like his future son-in-law, was a considerable scholar as well as man of affairs. When Kitchener reoccupied the Sudan after the Battle of Omdurman, where Churchill had charged with the Lancers, he needed an official to reorganize its finances. His choice fell upon the young official in Suakin, who succeeded so well that after a few years he moved to Cairo as Financial Adviser to the Sudan Government, eventually becoming an Honorary KBE and an Egyptian Pasha. He was highly regarded by his British colleagues and throughout the Arab world. After the First World War, on British initiative he acted as an adviser to Feisal, first in Damascus and later when he became King of Iraq.

So my wife grew up at the centre of Cairo social and political life, in close touch with the British in Egypt as well as with the Egyptians and the Lebanese and other foreign communities. Among her close friends were Amy Smart, the brilliant Lebanese wife of the Oriental Counsellor at the High Commission, in whose house we first met, and Mary Lampson, daughter of the High Commissioner. It was lucky for me that her father had died shortly before my arrival in Egypt, as he would probably never have agreed to his daughter marrying a penniless young diplomat. In those days diplomats, especially those who were Private Secretaries, were not expected to marry young. Since there were also family problems on both sides we agreed to postpone our marriage until shortly before I was to leave Cairo in the autumn of 1937.

This agreement was well understood in the Foreign Office, whose approval was necessary for marriage with a foreign national. Cella and her family were so well known in British circles that this clearly presented no problem. We were to be married by the Bishop in the Anglican Cathedral in June 1937 before Cella's mother and grandmother left Egypt to escape the heat. Two days before the wedding a new regulation came into force requiring the Foreign Secretary's personal written approval. Luckily his Private Secretary, Oliver Harvey, was an old friend of mine from the Paris Embassy, to whom I could explain the impossibility of postponement. So we went ahead, and lived together most happily until her death in 1990. We were kept very busy before and since retirement from the Diplomatic Service in 1968. So it was perhaps a prophetic prelude that I went back to my office on the afternoon of our marriage and that our honeymoon in Greece and Turkey only came several weeks later.

Since most of my subsequent career was concerned either at home or abroad with events in Europe and with the Soviet Union and the United States, it was valuable to have the experience of Egypt at such an interesting time.

An unusual feature of Cairo was that the High Commissioner conducted nearly all his Egyptian business with the Prime Minister and left the Foreign Minister to deal with the other lesser diplomats. For the Private Secretary there was also much internal British diplomacy with the four major British advisers to the Egyptian Government, with the British military advisers to the Egyptian Armed Forces, with senior British educational and cultural figures, and with senior officers in the British Forces in Egypt. There were also key Egyptian officials and personalities who visited the High Commissioner, one of them, Amin Osman, acting as a link with the Prime Minister. He had an English wife, and some years later he was murdered by anti-British terrorists.

Normally relations were good between the British and the Egyptians, despite Egyptian resentment over what amounted to a British occupation. But there had been excesses from time to time, the worst having been the murder in 1924 of Sir Lee Stack, the Sirdar (or Commander-in-Chief) of the Egyptian Army, which at that time had units in the Sudan. He was on his way to visit my wife's family. At a garden party at the Palace I found myself placed at a tea table with two well-known Egyptian politicians, Ahmed Maher and Nokrashi, each of whom became distinguished and by no means anti-British Prime Ministers but who had been associated with Stack's murder. I found them very interesting. But some British at the garden party criticized me for sitting with 'the murderers', who were themselves later assassinated partly because they were regarded as pro-British.

The abdication of Edward VIII took place during my time in Egypt, and there was much talk about Mrs Simpson in the British community. I saw a lot of the British Army at all levels. Whereas the officers by and large were prepared to accept the King's choice, the other ranks would not hear of the King marrying a divorced American. Stanley Baldwin correctly sensed that this was the view of ordinary people throughout the Empire, and he handled the abdication crisis with the same skill that he had shown in healing the social wounds left by the General Strike in 1926.

While most of my official work lay in my duties as Private Secretary, I also looked after cultural relations, previously much neglected by British Governments worldwide and especially in Egypt. The French had, since Napoleon's expedition to Egypt, been in charge of Egyptian Antiquities and had good schools, secular and Catholic, in Cairo and Alexandria. French was the leading European language. We had one very good school for boys, the Victoria College in Alexandria, whose pupils covered the Arab world, and an English Day School in Cairo, but little else. We did, however, have British professors and teachers in Egyptian universities, and there were many distinguished British Egyptologists. The time had come to increase our efforts. The British Council had just been established and we in Egypt were lucky that its first Chairman was Lord Lloyd, who had not forgotten his years in Egypt. The High Commissioner set up a special Committee, of which I was the Secretary. On my next visit to London I put our case to Lord Lloyd, who undertook that Egypt should have priority and was to receive two-thirds of British Council funding for a start. It seems almost incredible today that this meant a total amount of only £25,000. When I went back to Cairo, the Committee nearly resigned *en bloc* because of its inadequacy.

However, we started a successful English Girls' School in Alexandria and another English school in Cairo, and supported some British archaeology. Gradually English took over from French as the main foreign language, helped by the American University and by the growing international authority of the USA. At a very early stage I accompanied the High Commissioner to persuade the British community in Alexandria, which was much richer than that in Cairo, to help fund the new English Girls' School, which was intended to attract pupils from all over the Middle East. Sir Miles put the case to about a dozen major British cotton merchants, who within a few minutes guaranteed between them about £200,000, a very large sum in those days. We then had a dinner with the Finneys, one of the wealthiest families, which compared favourably with the grandest parties I had recently attended in the best houses in Paris. Victoria College and the

English Girls' School in Alexandria have served not only British interests but also Egypt and the rest of the Middle East well. Although 'nationalized' in the Fifties under Nasser, I understand they have continued to give a good account of themselves and to meet a real need.

Egypt had been all-absorbing. Hitler's growing strength and boldness, shown in the 1936 reoccupation of the Rhineland, the Spanish Civil War and the weakening of France's position all seemed far-away events. It was really only Mussolini's actions in Africa and the Mediterranean which reminded us of the importance and danger of developments in Europe. But this changed for me in the autumn of 1937 with the news that we were posted to London, where I was to start my long connection with Germany.

4 | Munich

1938

We left Cairo in October 1937, with Cella's grandmother, to whom she was devoted, dying of cancer, so the farewell was tense. We came home through Germany, stopping first in Munich, where we saw Hitler's two great art exhibitions, one devoted to approved Nazi art and the other to so-called 'decadent' art. The 'decadent' pictures were intended for destruction but many of them we later found, to our great pleasure, in museums and private houses throughout Germany when I returned as Ambassador in the Sixties. Some were in the 1988 Royal Academy Exhibition of German Art of the Twentieth Century. In Berlin we stayed with my old friends and colleagues from Paris days, Christopher and Catherine Steel, in a lovely flat which was completely destroyed in the war. We were later to follow the Steels at the NATO and Bonn Embassies.

Our visit coincided with one which Lord Halifax, then Lord President of the Council, was paying to Germany. The Prime Minister, Neville Chamberlain, had wanted some contact at ministerial level, but it was not then considered appropriate to send the Foreign Secretary, Anthony Eden. The solution was found in an invitation from Field Marshal Goering, the 'Number Two' man in Germany despite the position of Hess as the Fuhrer's Deputy and regarded as 'moderate'. Insofar as he did not want his luxurious lifestyle jeopardized by a prolonged war, he was to that extent more 'moderate' than most other Nazi leaders. He had laid on a great hunting exhibition, under cover of which a visit by Lord Halifax in his capacity as a master of fox hounds (and so nicknamed 'Lord Halalifax' in Berlin) could be arranged. Halifax also saw Hitler and other Nazi leaders at Berchtes-

22

gaden, and recorded that he had been most impressed by Goebbels, no doubt because of his obvious intelligence. I found Berlin much more orderly and on the surface changed for the better since my last visit in 1930, when there had been conflicts on the streets between Hitler's Brownshirts and left-wing groups.

We reached London in a cold winter, but soon found a nice modern flat in Cornwall Gardens, where we lived happily through the war years, including the 1940 Blitz and 1942–43 minor air raids and the V1s and V2s of 1944, without even a pane of glass broken, although we spent many nights in the cellars. My salary then as a Second Secretary was around £500 a year, half of which went on our rent. But with the help of Cella's small private income we could still afford a live-in servant, and lived on much the same scale as when I was a Deputy Under-Secretary in the Fifties. I was a junior member of the Central Department of the Foreign Office, so-called because it dealt basically with Central Europe and more especially with Germany. Insofar as Germany was the main problem with which the British Government then had to deal, it was also central in policy formulation and was fortunately well staffed. I found myself working with present and future Permanent Under-Secretaries Lord Vansittart, Sir Alec Cadogan, Sir Orme Sargent, Lord Strang and Lord Sherfield. I was brought into close contact with Anthony Eden and Lord Halifax as Foreign Secretaries and with Neville Chamberlain and Winston Churchill at No. 10 Downing Street.

The immediate problem was Austria, Hitler's first target for integration within the Reich. Increasingly threatened by Nazi and German pressures though it had been since the assassination of its Chancellor, Dolfuss, in 1934, Austria had been protected by Mussolini's mobilization on the Brenner as well as by French and British moral support. But Abyssinia and the Spanish Civil War had strained this 'Stresa' front to breaking point and pushed Mussolini into Hitler's arms. Without effective external support, undermined by a weak economy, and faced with a very strong pro-Hitler opposition, the Austrian Chancellor, Schuschnigg, a weaker character than Dolfuss, was summoned to Berchtesgaden in March 1938 to become the first of many central European leaders to be subjected by Hitler to an ultimatum, accompanied by his special brand of bullying and browbeating. Shortly afterwards, German troops entered Vienna, where they were so well received that, even if a genuine referendum had been taken in Austria as proposed by Schuschnigg, a large majority would probably have approved.

When I returned to London, the German Ambassador was still Ribbentrop, who had persuaded Hitler that he was a great expert on the British scene. None of the other Nazi leaders had any experience of Britain, and Hitler trusted Ribbentrop far more than he did his earlier 'career' Foreign Minister, Baron von Neurath, which was hardly surprising since few professional German diplomatists favoured the Nazis and many of them were members of the Resistance to Hitler.

The German armed forces presented Hitler with greater problems and opportunities. In 1934 Hitler's coup against the Brownshirts and his old comrade the SA leader, Röhm, had also provided an opportunity to murder General Schleicher and some other senior officers. Schleicher, however, had been a very 'political' general – he was Chancellor in the last days of Weimar – and the German officer corps had not reacted to this. Its attitude to Hitler was ambivalent. Most professional soldiers were happy to benefit from Hitler's rearmament and the increase in the size of the armed forces. But many, especially in the top ranks, thought his policies adventurous and dangerous. Since many of them came from good families in Prussia and elsewhere, they were not natural supporters of 'Corporal' Hitler and his Nazi band. In 1936, at the time of the reoccupation of the Rhineland, the German Army was still very weak, and the Generals realized that, had the French opposed them, they would have had to withdraw. Many would have welcomed this as providing an opportunity to get rid of Hitler. But lack of British support provided the French with a welcome excuse for inaction. Hitler then felt strong enough to dismiss two successive Commanders-in-Chief, Von Fritsch and Blomberg. The most distinguished of the German Generals, the Chief of Staff General Beck, was so disturbed by what he knew of Hitler's future plans of aggression that he established secret contacts with London in the hope of persuading the British and the French to stand firm against Hitler's expansionist policies and so enable the German Army to remove him. His messages, supported by those from German diplomats like the Kordt brothers, some of which I took personally to the Prime Minister, were dismissed by him as part of a Foreign Office campaign to make him change his policies of appeasement. He was on stronger ground, indeed sharing it with many in the Foreign Office, in his scepticism about the capacity of Beck and his friends to stop Hitler, who was extremely popular with the German people and indeed with the junior and some senior ranks in the armed forces. Beck's position was also weakened by his resignation in 1938.

However, he and those who shared his views throughout the old non-Nazi German establishment did not give up, and formed the core of the German Resistance Movement before and during the war.

The occupation of Austria changed the whole situation in Central Europe. England and France were left without Italian support, and a shudder of apprehension went down the Danube Valley into the Balkans, undermining France's alliance system in Eastern Europe. Clearly this was only the beginning of Hitler's moves to change the Versailles system. Czechoslovakia, with its large Sudeten German minority, was the next target. Its powerful defences to the north and west could now be turned from Austria. These developments only strengthened Neville Chamberlain in his policy of appeasement. This was based mainly upon two considerations. The first was that in 1938 British rearmament, especially in the air, was not yet far advanced, and this applied equally to France in the air. For the first time in British history, there was the fear of air bombardment of our civilian population, on a major scale, without any effective defence. It was thought – rightly, as it turned out – that in a year or two British air rearmament would have made such progress that these fears need not have a decisive influence on policy. The Chiefs of Staff were also concerned about Japanese encroachments in the Far East and the resulting requirement to send a large part of the Royal Navy and other forces there. They also had to consider a nearer, if lesser, threat in Mussolini's declared aim of re-establishing a new-model Roman Empire in the Mediterranean, including claims against France for Corsica, Nice and Savoy.

But, I think, more important even than the strategic position was the political consideration, which played a large part not only in Chamberlain's thinking but also with majority British and Commonwealth public opinion, that the Treaty of Versailles had been unfair to Germany. One of its main principles, self-determination, had, it seemed, been denied not only to the Austrians but also to the three and a half million Sudeten Germans in Czechoslovakia, as well as to the German cities of Danzig and Memel and to Germans in the Polish Corridor. There had been attempts, before I returned to London in 1937, to meet the Germans half-way. The first was the Anglo-German Naval Agreement of 1935, which had strained our relations with the French. Secondly, there were plans, which fortunately came to nothing, to give back to Germany some of her old colonies in Africa or to 'compensate' her for their loss, mainly at the expense of our

Portuguese allies. These were not among Hitler's priorities, which were centred upon extending Germany's 'living space' in Europe at the expense of the Poles, the Ukrainians and the Russians. Even in *Mein Kampf* he had written of the Germans and the British as the two great Aryan races, concluding that if only he could persuade the British to let him have a free hand in Europe to deal with what he considered its 'lesser' peoples, particularly the Slavs in the east, then he would be happy to see Britain continue to carry the burdens of Empire throughout the rest of the world.

The general climate of opinion in Britain, and also in Canada, Australia, New Zealand and South Africa, which formed the then British Empire, was certainly behind Chamberlain's policy of appeasement, a word which did not have the same pejorative connotations as it has since earned. It really meant the prevention of war, and the solution of existing problems by peaceful means. The '*Anschluss*' with Austria was accepted as the legitimate union of two German peoples, however regrettable the way it had been achieved, a dangerous conclusion for the future but one endorsed by what seemed to be the enthusiastic support of the majority of the Austrian people.

From March 1938 I had to concentrate on the problems of Czechoslovakia, long considered a major success story of the Versailles settlement. Of all the newly independent countries in Central and Eastern Europe, Czechoslovakia was the only one which had developed a genuinely democratic system, under such well-known leaders approved in the West as Thomas Masaryk and Edward Beneš. But Czechoslovakia was also an amalgam of nationalities. In the Austro-Hungarian Empire, the Czechs had played an important part in the Austrian administration, whereas the Slovaks had been dominated by the Hungarians. In independent Czechoslovakia they did not get on well with each other. Sub-Carpathian Ruthenia was ethnically more akin to the Soviet Ukraine, which eventually took it over. But the main problem for Czechoslovakia, once Hitler embarked upon expansionist policies, was that of the three and a half million Sudeten Germans on the northern and western frontiers with Germany. They had never been part of any purely German state but always of Bohemia, which had been an important Kingdom in the Holy Roman Empire. They were not an oppressed minority but they had found it difficult to adapt themselves to a subordinate role. There were minor grievances for Hitler to exploit, by expanding the modest demands of the Sudeten leader, Henlein, for a degree of autonomy into an insistent call to 'return home into the Reich'.

The French were much more closely involved than we were with Czechoslovakia, to whom they had treaty commitments under the Little Entente Alliance which Barthou had tried to invigorate. Another great asset, denied to the Poles, was the good relations President Beneš had built up with the Soviet Union, also committed by treaty to support Czechoslovakia, but only after the French had acted themselves. The Soviet Union was not a neighbour of Czechoslovakia, as she was of Poland. Beneš went out of his way to ensure effective Soviet support, but without effect. Britain, unlike France or the Soviet Union, had no treaty commitments to Czechoslovakia, described later by Chamberlain as a far-away country of which few of us had heard. But we had treaty commitments to France, which would have led to our involvement in any major European war. The French were ready to allow Neville Chamberlain, who never lacked firmness and conviction, to take the lead. He was motivated by a strong desire to avoid war and therefore to find some solution which would relieve the French of any obligation to fight for Czechoslovakia.

To complete the general background to the Munich crisis some six months later, as I saw it, Eden was no longer Foreign Secretary, after disagreements with the Prime Minister over Italy and the possible involvement of President Roosevelt in the European crisis. His successor was Lord Halifax, which left foreign policy firmly in the hands of the Prime Minister, supported by an Inner Circle of Lord Halifax, Sir Samuel Hoare and Sir John Simon, relying also very much on his senior adviser at Number 10, Sir Horace Wilson, a highly efficient Civil Servant but with little experience of foreign affairs. I recall throughout the summer months 'feelers' from German visitors to London, not all of them loyal supporters of Hitler, and similar 'feelers' by British visitors to Berlin, often under the guise of trade talks.

The Prime Minister's objectives were twofold, first to convince Dr Beneš that he could maintain Czechoslovak independence only by making some sacrifices to Hitler over the Sudeten German minority, and secondly, to persuade Hitler, who we now know actually wanted to achieve his aims by war, that his requirements could be satisfied by peaceful means and by international agreement. Neither of these tasks was particularly easy or pleasant. In London, there was an outstanding Czechoslovak diplomatic representative in Jan Masaryk, the son of the first President, Thomas Masaryk, who had excellent contacts and was extremely popular in all circles. He had been regarded as something of a playboy, and was not always taken as seriously as he should have been. But he could expect under-standing and even support from leading Conservative politicians outside Chamberlain's circle, Churchill and Eden in the first place, and of course in the Labour Party.

Within the Foreign Office itself, Vansittart had been side-tracked to the post of Chief Diplomatic Adviser with no executive func-tions, and Alec Cadogan, more acceptable to the Prime Minister, was Permanent Under-Secretary. With Orme Sargent and William Strang in charge of European affairs, the prevailing mood was con-cern about where Chamberlain's appeasement policies might lead us, and the conviction that at some point we must stand up to Hitler, while at the same time there was acceptance of Chamber-lain's policy of avoiding war, if possible, and of the desirability of gaining time for rearmament. Number 10 and the Foreign Office often differed on the best tactics to deter Hitler and above all in assessing Hitler's long-term aims. The Czechoslovak position seemed to us entirely different from that of Austria, in that here was an independent, basically Slav country created by the Allies at Ver-sailles, which was a democracy, and by and large behaved as such. With the possible but by no means certain exception of the Sudeten minority, it was, unlike Austria, determined to preserve its indepen-dence. The obvious advantage of having a stronger British Air Force within a year or so had to be balanced against the danger of losing the well-supplied Czechoslovak Army (Czechoslovakia had a strong armaments industry) behind strong fortifications, conscious though we were that these fortifications could be turned from the Austrian side.

There were those, and they included Churchill and Eden, who felt that the Soviet Union, with its treaty commitment to Czechoslova-kia, should be brought into consultation. On the other hand, Stalin was anything but a desirable ally. He had been responsible for the death of millions of Soviet peasants in his collectivization of agricul-ture, for the mock trials and execution of many of his own col-leagues in the Politburo and the Central Committee, and above all, in this context, for executing the great majority of the senior officers in the Red Army. All this convinced Chamberlain, naturally hostile to the Communist Soviet Union, that it could not be an effective ally. These doubts seemed confirmed by the difficulties the Red Army experienced shortly afterwards in its war against 'little Finland'.

The Foreign Office tended to share the view held strongly outside the Foreign Office, by Churchill, Eden and many others, that France was stronger than in fact she proved to be. We thought that the French Army, still on paper the strongest in Europe, would give a good account of itself 'on the day' and, despite our justified doubts about French resolution, we hoped all would be well in a crisis. On this the Prime Minister's judgement proved better than ours, but his actions had themselves contributed to weakening French self-confidence. One of the factors which affected French resolution very much had been the building of the Maginot Line, which gave the French a general defensive attitude with the feeling that they were safe against German attack. So, of course, they might have been, had the Maginot Line been continued to the sea. But it did not cover the Low Countries, through which France was invaded.

As the summer progressed, it became increasingly clear that the Czech leaders were in no mood to abandon the Sudetenland. They argued, with much justification, that the treatment of the German minority in no way justified Hitler's complaints, which however only increased his impatience and determination to bring matters to a head. The result was increased British pressure on Beneš for concessions without equally effective balancing pressure on Hitler for greater moderation. Chamberlain forced Beneš to accept the special investigation mission of Lord Runciman, a British ship-owner and politician with no experience of Central Europe. His report was considered by the Czechs, in my view correctly, to have exaggerated and even perhaps unwittingly encouraged Sudeten dissatisfaction, and also to have increasingly and dangerously brought out the lack of harmony between Czechs and Slovaks.

At home, *The Times* and the Cliveden set played an influential role behind Chamberlain's appeasement policy, on occasion undermining with leading articles, known to have been written after contact with Number 10, Foreign Office press guidance and even messages sent to Hitler through diplomatic channels and so increasing unduly the Anglo-French pressures on Dr Beneš for major concessions. Chamberlain's pressure on Hitler was not for concessions but only to persuade him that he could get the Sudeten areas by peaceful means. But Hitler was set upon military action, and met any concessions forced out of Beneš by Chamberlain with new demands. Chamberlain was equally obstinate in his pursuit of peace, but it was Czechoslovakia which had to pay the price. This took him to Godesberg in mid-August. Chamberlain was housed on the Petersberg above the British Embassy Residence, while Hitler stayed at the Hotel Dreesen on the other side of the Rhine. Chamberlain therefore had to come across the river to meet Hitler. During the first talks, the manner in which Hitler refused to accept the concessions prised out of Beneš by Chamberlain, which met his previous demands, was so outrageous that the Prime Minister felt he could not cross the river again. Finally Hitler climbed down to the extent necessary to persuade Chamberlain, always in the interests of peace, to return to Beneš for further concessions, under what amounted to an ultimatum from Hitler. Within a few days, Hitler, longing for military action, went back even on this, and finally Chamberlain had to accept the prospect of war.

It was in this mood of deep disappointment and anxiety that on 28 September Chamberlain opened his speech to a packed and tense House of Commons to explain the failure of all his efforts to arrange a peaceful settlement and to announce the probability of war. At that point in the middle of his speech I passed from the officials box a note for the Prime Minister, enabling him to announce a message just received from Mussolini that he had persuaded Hitler to meet with himself, Daladier and Chamberlain in Munich. It was a most dramatic moment, with members wildly cheering the Prime Minister and the prospects of peace saved after all. None of them worried very much about the price to be paid, above all by Czechoslovakia, which was not even to be represented at the Conference, but also in terms of honour, prestige and diminished influence throughout Central and Eastern Europe by Britain and France.

At Munich, Chamberlain had another objective, going beyond a peaceful solution of the Sudeten problem. Even within his limited perspective of Hitler only wanting to bring Germans into the Reich, there still remained the problem of Danzig and the Polish Corridor. So he arranged a private meeting with Hitler, at which he got agreement, all the more easily since Hitler had always wanted an agreement with the British, that there should never be war between the two countries, and that whenever difficult problems affecting our relations arose in

30

the future, there would be consultation between them before resort to action. This was basically the famous piece of paper which Chamberlain brought back from Munich, as Disraeli had in 1878 brought back from Berlin an agreement with Bismarck.

In the Foreign Office we had been working immensely hard throughout this period. The differences between us and the Prime Minister were over the right steps to avoid war, not only then but later, and over the Prime Minister's refusal to accept that Hitler's ambitions went far beyond bringing Germans from Austria, Czechoslovakia and Poland into the Reich. We shared the general sense of relief that immediate war had been averted. But there was also a strong sense of shame over our treatment of Czechoslovakia and of regret that we and not the French were mainly responsible. Nor had we much confidence in the viability of the truncated Czechoslovakia and the duration of the agreement imposed upon her at Munich.

The Foreign Office was also sceptical about the piece of paper on Anglo-German relations. Despite the enthusiasm with which the Prime Minister had been greeted when he held it up to the cheering crowds, an action which had horrified Orme Sargent who was present at Number 10, I think our mood was nearer to that of Walpole two centuries earlier on a very different occasion, when public pressures had forced him into war and when he had said, 'They are ringing the bells now. They will soon be wringing their hands.' Chamberlain himself realized almost immediately that he had made a mistake in playing up the piece of paper so much. Daladier, also welcomed back in Paris by cheering crowds, realized better what had happened, and expressed his amazement that he had not been pelted with eggs and tomatoes. However, it was only Duff Cooper, First Lord of the Admiralty, who resigned from the Government and spoke his mind in the House. Even today, the question remains open whether, had we stood firm, had the French stood firm, had the Czechoslovaks been allowed to defend their country, had we tried to secure Soviet support, it would have been better to have fought a weaker German Army at that point, or to gain more time for our own rearmament. There were strong arguments each way, political and military. Since one of the main considerations in Chamberlain's mind was the public reluctance, at home and in the Empire, to go to war, as it seemed, to prevent self-determination for Sudeten Germans, it can be argued today that without Munich and without Chamberlain's obstinate pursuit of appeasement, there would not have been such a high degree of national unity when the war came a year later. But it can also be argued that, had different policies been followed at an earlier stage, we need not have found ourselves in this shameful predicament.

5 | The Road to War
1939

After Munich I continued to deal with developments in Czechoslovakia, where there was increased tension between Bohemia and Slovakia, and of course with Germany itself. But my main priority soon shifted to Poland, since Hitler's next target was clearly Danzig and the Corridor. Danzig was a 'free city' under a League of Nations-appointed High Commissioner, a highly intelligent Swiss called Burkhardt. Roger Makins (now Lord Sherfield) knew him well and therefore handled Danzig's affairs. The population was largely German, and it was historically a German Hansa port. It was only a matter of time before Hitler stirred up a popular demand for return to the Reich on the Sudeten model. He soon created a precedent in the return of Memel with Lithuanian acquiescence. There remained the Polish Corridor, a very artificial Versailles creation separating the heartland of Prussia from the rest of Germany.

Poland differed greatly from Czechoslovakia. It was much bigger, the size of Spain with a population of about thirty million. It was not a country 'created' at Versailles, although it was through Versailles that it regained its independence. The Poles recalled the days before partition in the eighteenth century when the Polish 'Commonwealth', uniting Poland with Lithuania and much of the Ukraine, had been a Great Power in Eastern Europe, occupying Moscow and saving Vienna from the Turks. They saw themselves in the twentieth century as the main buffer for Europe against Communist Russia and as a balance between Germany and the Soviet Union. If forced to make a clear choice between the two, they might well have chosen even Hitler's Germany. Unlike Czechoslovakia, Poland was not a democracy, but rather a relatively mild form of military dictatorship under Marshal Smigly-Rydz. Its Foreign Minister, Colonel Beck, was a soldier, self-confident and clever, but he did not inspire confidence. All this meant that the Poles were not amenable to the same kind of pressure that Neville Chamberlain and the French had exercised on the Czechs and required more careful diplomacy, more especially as the Soviet Union was so much less well-disposed to Poland than to Czechoslovakia. In the last resort, as we discovered in September, the Poles, who lacked the Czech defences and defence industries, were not only prepared to fight the Germans but even thought that they could beat them.

Just as the run-up to Munich started with the German troops entering Vienna in March 1938, the run-up to the Polish crisis and war started in March 1939 with Hitler sending his armies into Prague, a pleasure of which Chamberlain had deprived him at Munich, after the Czech President Hacha had been bullied as Schuschnigg had been. Hitler turned Bohemia into a protectorate. Slovakia became an independent state. The Munich agreement was torn up and the piece of paper signed by Chamberlain and Hitler was ignored. This was a personal blow to Chamberlain, shattering his illusions about Hitler's limited aims and, to use a modern term, about the possibility of 'doing business' with him. Like St Paul on the road to Damascus, Chamberlain turned from one extreme to the other. Still determined to work for peace, he substituted for appeasement the modern concept of deterrence, which had always been our preference in the Foreign Office. The basis for this new policy remained the Anglo-French alliance, although we did not yet realize the debilitating effect on the French themselves of so many retreats, so often, alas, under British pressure.

Chamberlain did not have to wait long to show how much he had changed. Within a few days of the Nazi seizure of Prague a British journalist in Berlin, Ian Colvin, reported that the Nazis were preparing to move into Poland and/or Roumania. The story, which was not checked, proved to be quite wrong or at least premature. But Chamberlain moved at once to deterrence, with a guarantee of British assistance to both countries. It was our first such commitment in Eastern Europe. We had no effective means of carrying it through, if Hitler ignored our warning. Deterrence was I am sure the right policy, but this was not the best way to start down this new path. In effect, we reduced our bargaining power in future negotiations, not only with Poland but also with the Soviet Union, who in practice received a unilateral Western guarantee for themselves against any German aggression.

After the false alert of March, it soon became clear that Hitler's first, although not quite so immediate target was Poland, and our priority was therefore to transform our unilateral guarantee into an Anglo-Polish alliance. Roumania, with its oil wells at Ploesti, was of great importance to Hitler, but not first on his list of conquests. Our negotiations with the Poles were complicated by three main problems. The first was that Colonel Beck was naturally cautious, and wanted to keep his lines open, if only to a limited extent, to Berlin. The second was the frontier question. The eastern provinces of Poland were very largely inhabited by Ukrainians, White Russians and Lithuanians, and in the Versailles settlement the British had advocated the 'Curzon Line' as Poland's eastern frontier, which would not have included within the new Poland these large and important minorities. But the fighting between the Soviet Union and Poland after the First World War, which had at first brought the Russians to the gates of Warsaw, had ended with victory for Pilsudski, with Weygand's help, who pushed the Polish frontiers far to the east and included such important and largely Polish cities as Vilna and Lvov, surrounded though they were by non-Polish populations. In the negotiations for the Anglo-Polish Alliance we therefore had to insist, against strong Polish opposition, that the British guarantee covered Polish independence but not the integrity of her 1939 frontiers.

The third and insoluble problem was how in practice Poland could be helped in the event of a German attack, by British or even French forces. Poland was beyond the range of the Royal Air Force, and the Royal Navy could not operate in the Baltic. The French, despite their long-standing alliance, had the same problem, with the important exception that the French Army was strong enough to respond to a German attack upon Poland with a French advance into Germany. Chamberlain was therefore faced with the problem he had put on one side before Munich of involving the Soviet Union in deterring a German attack upon Poland. In contrast with the Soviet relationship with Czechoslovakia, there was not and never had been any love lost between the Catholic Poles and the Orthodox and now Communist Russians. Bringing the two together would have been a major task even for Churchill or Eden. Chamberlain had not only to overcome his strong prejudices against 'the Bolsheviks' but also to set aside his conviction that Stalin's Soviet Union, with the Red Army High

Command almost completely eliminated and its political and econo-mic structure under great strain, could not be a reliable and effective ally. There was, however, no better alternative in sight, and he was in no mood to return to his earlier appeasement policies. So he was persuaded to instruct the British and French Ambassadors in Moscow to open negotiations with the Russians. To help them, William Strang was sent to Moscow in June. He took me with him for the first of many contacts with the Soviet Union, although only a brief one as I returned to London after a week or ten days of slow-moving talks.

One welcome result of these major changes in British policy was an easier relationship between the Prime Minister and the Foreign Office, with both broadly on the same tack. Two personal experiences illustrate how tense they had been. The first was when I had to take to Chamberlain in the House of Commons the latest secret report from the German General Beck, pressing for a firm British attitude towards Hitler. While I was waiting outside a door the PM did not realize was open, I heard his Secretary announce my arrival and the Prime Minister's dismissive comment to the effect that the Foreign Office were no doubt sending yet another unreliable report to persuade him to change his policy. The second concerned the answer to a Parliamen-tary Question which I had to prepare for the PM. Attlee, then leader of the Labour Opposition, was reverting to a question he had asked some time before which we had hoped he had been persuaded not to press. I had to write a minute explaining this previous history, concluding with the phrase that 'the PM having failed to persuade Mr Attlee to withdraw his question' we were now faced with the problem of how best to answer it, to which the rest of my minute was addressed. I was asked to go over to Number 10 by the Private Secretary, whom I knew quite well, to be shown my minute with the word 'failed' circled in red ink and in the margin the words, 'Another insult from the Foreign Office'. Lord Halifax, by then Foreign Secretary, wanted to take this up with the PM on my behalf. But, young though I was, I dissuaded him, since I felt no good would come to me from such a high-level exchange on a minor matter.

Returning to the Strang Mission, there were clearly many problems facing us in Moscow, in addition to the one we had set up ourselves by our unilateral guarantee to Poland. The first was the climate of mutual suspicion between London and Moscow; the second, the rebuff Stalin had received by exclusion from the negotiations over Czechoslovakia; the third may have been, one cannot be sure, the choice of a relatively junior official rather than a senior politician such as Anthony Eden, who was ready to go to Moscow. Strang, on the other hand, knew Russia well, having recently been Counsellor at the Embassy in Moscow at a difficult time in Anglo-Soviet relations, that of the show-trial of the British Metropolitan Vickers engineers. The fourth was the discreet reopening of contacts between the Germans and the Russians, although we could not judge how far either of these hitherto deadly enemies were prepared to develop what were ostensibly commercial talks. Just before our arrival in Moscow there were two important warnings which could also be interpreted as raising the negotiating stakes. The first was the replacement as Foreign Minister of Litvinov, who by Soviet standards stood for an 'international' Soviet policy, more sympathetic to the League of Nations and the Western powers than to the Nazi and Fascist dictators, by Molotov, the senior Communist leader after Stalin, hitherto Prime Minister and Stalin's right-hand man. This indicated a harder line as well as closer high-level attention to foreign affairs. The second was an important speech by Stalin himself, of which the key phrase was that the Soviet Union was not going to 'pull the chestnuts out of the fire for other people'.

Our major problem therefore was to persuade Stalin that he had more to gain from joining Britain, France and of course Poland in order to deter Hitler from attacking Poland than he might gain from remaining neutral. One of his main concerns was the possibility of pro-Nazi coups in the Baltic States, which he compared to traditional British concern with the Low Countries. Strang discussed our instructions with the French Embassy. They did not cover the Baltic States. The French representative, commented that we should be wasting our time if we could not offer Stalin control of the Baltic States. In diplomatic terms, this meant agreement on our part to the Soviet Union guaranteeing to protect these States against Nazi intervention or internal subversion, balanced by Soviet recognition of a similar Anglo-French concern with the independence of the Netherlands, Belgium and Switzerland. Unfortunately the Baltic States themselves were – rightly, as it turned out – as frightened of Soviet as of Nazi intervention. We did, however, after hard bargaining, agree with the Russians on a respectable formula meeting their legitimate concern over Lithuania and Latvia.

Then and only then, at the end of July, Molotov agreed to an Anglo-French military delegation joining in the Moscow talks to discuss the basic problem of Soviet military assistance to Poland. The Russians had logic on their side in proposing military talks with the Poles to plan the entry of Soviet troops into Eastern Poland to help in repelling a German attack. In the light of their historical experience and of the Soviet claims upon the eastern provinces of Poland, this was, however, entirely unacceptable to the Poles. The Anglo-French military delegation took its time to reach Moscow by sea in the second week of August, which lent itself to subsequent cricitism but did not in my view have a decisive influence on the failure of our negotiations. Marshal Voroshilov, the senior Soviet General and close to Stalin, received the delegation well, but naturally concentrated upon the issue of Polish agreement to the entry of Soviet troops into Poland.

Meanwhile, Soviet talks with the Germans continued, and on 22 August came the staggering news of Ribbentrop's visit to Moscow to conclude the Ribbentrop–Molotov Pact, thus freeing Hitler's hands to attack Poland in the confident expectation that in these circumstances Britain and France would not go to war. Then and later the Pact was represented in Moscow and in Berlin as intended to prevent and not to trigger off a European war. This was no doubt Hitler's intention, provided of course that he could polish off Poland on its own. But it was certainly not Stalin's. The secret protocols attached gave him a free hand in the Baltic States, in the eastern provinces of Poland, in Bukovina and Bessarabia (re-christened Moldavia) and in parts of Finland, restoring to a considerable extent the frontiers of Tsarist Russia. But he could only hope to digest these vast territories if Hitler were otherwise engaged in what Stalin must have expected to be a prolonged repetition of the 1914–18 war in the West, bleeding dry France and Britain as well as Germany and leaving the Soviet Union time to recover and dominate Europe.

In these circumstances the Strang mission was doomed to failure. The prospect of such great territorial gains with German acquiescence and without the immediate risk of war for the USSR was obviously more attractive to Stalin than that of joining Britain and France in a deterrent policy which offered no such prizes and which, should it fail, would involve the Soviet Union bearing the main brunt of war with Germany to protect a most unwilling ally in Poland. In the short term Stalin's choice, however amoral, must have seemed to him the right one. But he made the mistake of over-estimating French military strength and under-estimating Hitler's. Within less than a year the French Army had collapsed, and only a year after that an ill-prepared Soviet Union was overrun by the German invasion.

The firmness of the British reaction to the Ribbentrop–Molotov Pact must have surprised those who still suspected Chamberlain of hankering after a return to appeasement. The Anglo-Polish Alliance, still under negotiation, was at once and most demonstratively signed, followed by diplomatic action in Berlin to convince Hitler that an attack upon Poland would still mean war with Britain and France. On the other hand, Chamberlain still wanted peace, and therefore tried to persuade Hitler and the Poles, even at this late hour, to enter into discussion, always however against the background of what were now British as well as French treaty commitments to Poland. Official approaches were made by HM Ambassador Sir Nevile Henderson to Ribbentrop. The emphasis throughout was upon making quite sure that Hitler understood that the Ribbentrop–Molotov Pact had in no way changed the British determination to fulfil its commitment to Poland, and that this time we would fight. There was also an unofficial line to Goering through a Swedish businessman, Birger Dahlerus. He and Henderson have each written their own accounts of events, to which, however, I might add the following comments based on my personal experience at the time.

Nevile Henderson was a distinguished professional diplomat who had been a good Ambassador in Yugoslavia in the early days after Versailles and the First World War. He had a good relationship with the King and with the rather tough people who ran Yugoslavia at that time. He had also been in St Petersburg as a young Secretary, where he got on well in important court circles. Then somehow his career changed, and he went as Ambassador to Buenos Aires, which removed him from what in those days was the European 'Inner Circle'. Oddly enough, it was Vansittart and Eden, not Chamberlain and Halifax, who picked Nevile Henderson for Berlin, on the grounds that he might cope better with the Nazi leaders and talk more frankly with them, if necessary, than his more 'intellectual' predecessor, Vansittart's brother-in-law Eric Phipps, who would be more at home in Paris. Henderson, thus unexpectedly brought back from a distant post to the centre, not unnaturally regarded his mission primarily as one of support for the Chamberlain appeasement policy, and took his lead much more from Number 10 than from the Foreign Office, with the result that in the Czech crisis he always seemed to be criticizing the Czechs and defending the Nazis. He had, however, moved with Chamberlain after Hitler's occupation of Prague in March 1939, and in the last days of August he was commendably firm with Ribbentrop, even if sometimes inclined to press his Polish colleague, Lipski, unduly hard to meet the Germans half-way. In this he was unsuccessful, since Lipski shared the Polish conviction that their forces could resist a German attack.

With Birger Dahlerus my relations were closer, as I had been his original official contact in London. He had come to know Goering through family connections. He had lived for many years in Britain and had business connections with some British financiers and industrialists interested in Danzig, through whom he was put in touch with me in London. We did not take him very seriously at first and thought him rather naive on the political scene. But it soon became clear that he had Goering's ear, and that he was as ready to put the British views frankly to Goering as he was to bring to us Goering's professions of peaceful intentions. He was a man with the self-appointed mission of trying to prevent war. As the situation grew more dangerous, Goering's role as a relative 'moderate' became more interesting to us. Dahlerus's contacts in Whitehall became more important, and I found myself taking him through the back garden entrance to Number 10 to see the Prime Minister from time to time. He proved a reliable carrier of messages in each direction, and in my experience acted correctly and with sincerity throughout. In the light of hindsight, we probably overrated Goering's moderating influence on Hitler, but this was the best high-placed channel we had. Dahlerus was particularly active during the last days of peace, and even rang me from Karinhall with Goering at his side, late at night, after our ultimatum had expired, begging me to tell the Prime Minister that in Goering's view peace could still be saved. As we had already delayed our entry into war for a considerable time after Hitler's invasion of Poland and thus created major trouble for the Prime Minister in Parliament, my reply had to be that this was too late, since we were now at war.

The delay had created the impression in the House of Commons that the Prime Minister was perhaps reverting to his old appeasement line. In fact, we had most reluctantly agreed to a request from the French, who needed more time to complete their preparations and in the end timed their ultimatum five hours later than ours. This created some suspicion even in the Foreign Office. There was strong anti-war feeling in France and a potential anti-war leader in Marshal Pétain. There had been placards, 'To die for Danzig! Never!' And Georges Bonnet did not inspire confidence at the Quai d'Orsay. I did not, like

40

Harold Nicolson in 1914, have the tragic task of taking a British ultimatum to the German Embassy. Ours was delivered in Berlin. But I was among the small group of officials closely involved in the run-up to war sitting in the Foreign Secretary's room on the evening before our ultimatum was to expire at 11 am, still waiting for confirmation from Paris that their instructions had also gone to Berlin. It did not arrive much before midnight and was received with great relief by all of us, from Lord Halifax down to myself.

6 | The Phoney War
1939–40

The war started for us with some surprises. The first and most tragic was the speed with which Poland was overrun in little more than three weeks despite courageous resistance. Then came the not unexpected Soviet occupation of the eastern half of Poland on the pretext of safeguarding its Ukrainian and Byelorussian populations, shortly followed by Soviet entry into the Baltic States, Bessarabia and Bukovina and the winter war against Finland. Such Poles as could escape through Roumania found their way to France to create a new army in France under Sikorski. At home we had prepared for German air raids and were evacuating women and children from London. I took my Egyptian mother-in-law to friends in Oxford and my wife to Berkshire. But no German bombers came. My wife was back in a few days and never left London again, and my mother-in-law soon returned to Egypt by boat through the Mediterranean. We were also made to look rather foolish over the arrangements for sending diplomatic personnel home from London and Berlin. Fearing rather rigorous Nazi measures in Berlin, our measures in London were on the harsh side, only to be confounded by very correct behaviour on the German side. Much more shaming, however, was British and French inaction in the West and failure to involve the Germans in war on two fronts. The French stayed behind the Maginot Line, and the British could do little more than prepare and despatch our few divisions to France, while concentrating on air rearmament and the war at sea.

Hitler's victory in Poland was immediately followed by peace feelers to Britain and France. These at least were firmly rejected, and we settled down to the prospect of a long war. To help us on our way a

Supreme War Council was set up under the two Prime Ministers, and my own most vivid memories of the phoney war months are evoked by my additional work as a Secretary to the Council working, on the French side, with Roland de Margerie, who had been at the Embassy in London. The Council did useful work in coordinating British and French purchasing programmes in the USA. I first met Jean Monnet in this context, and recall his conviction that the war could only be won with full US support. Otherwise its time seems to have been largely taken up with British proposals for action near at hand, for example dropping newly invented contact mines in the Rhine to interfere with Germany's important river transport, rejected by the French as likely to provoke German air attacks on French cities, which could not then be defended, or with French proposals for action as far away from France as possible, which depended mainly upon the British naval or air forces. Among these ideas were bombing the Soviet oil wells at Baku to deprive the Germans of Soviet oil, and interrupting the flow of iron ore to Germany from the north of Sweden. Neither was an easy operation, and each would logically have involved us in war with important neutral countries. An even more startling idea, which came from British as well as French sources, was support for the Finns in their war against the Soviet Union. Fortunately the winter war ended before such a decision could be taken. Plans were, however, laid for what seemed a less difficult operation given Allied superiority at sea, the occupation of Narvik and Trondheim in northern Norway. In the event, we were preceded in April 1940 by Hitler's successful seizure of Denmark and the main centres of Norway in the south, which at least relieved the Allies of the onus of being the first to breach Norwegian neutrality, but resulted in our having to beat a hasty retreat from Norway ourselves. The last Supreme War Council meeting which I attended on 26 April discussed this deterioration in the Allied prospects in Norway, held to be due largely to German superiority in the air.

These reverses in Scandinavia soon faded into relative insignificance with Hitler's victories against Belgium, Holland and France itself in May and June. The last six meetings of the Supreme War Council were all held in France, the last three, as the French Government retreated to Bordeaux, at Briare and Tours, with Churchill now Prime Minister. The collapse of France was again followed by peace feelers from Hitler, as always on the basis that if Britain left him in control of Europe, he would be happy to see us remain the great imperial power overseas. Churchill was in no mood to accept this, and although Halifax himself and even more Rab Butler seem to have at least listened to approaches made through Sweden and Switzerland, there was never any suggestion at official level in the Foreign Office that consideration should be given to the possibility of peace negotiations. In my department our immediate task was to welcome and settle in Britain Allied leaders and military forces from the countries now occupied by Hitler and to continue our preparations for a long war.

7 | The Foreign Office in the War: Germany

1940–44

Germany remained the main responsibility of the Central Department, although in war conditions German affairs did not take up as much time as those of the Iberian Peninsula or the Allied Governments, and more especially the Polish Government, in London. They fell under three main heads. The first was planning for the future on the assumption of an Allied victory, which, perhaps surprisingly in 1940, we took for granted, even before the Soviet Union or the USA had been brought into the war. The second was contacts with the German Resistance, and German peace feelers, for example from Hess, coupled with overt and covert propaganda to Germany, conducted in close consultation with our Department. The third was war crimes. Planning for the future, and also war crimes, eventually became topics of such a special character that they could not be handled by a busy operational department, and were given departments of their own. But for two or three years they took up much of our time, and we continued to be consulted about them throughout the war.

It was, I suppose, the first time that so much attention was given at an early stage of a war whose result was at best uncertain to what was to be done when it ended. One reason was no doubt the nature of the Nazi regime and the need to 're-educate' the German people. There was also a strong conviction that for this purpose and to avoid a repetition of the 1918 myth that the German Army had been stabbed in the back and never really defeated, there should be a total occupation of Germany. Here we came up against the difficulty, after the Soviet Union became our ally in 1941, that the British and

Americans had very different ideas on the future social structure of Germany from those of Stalin. We used the same terms, such as 'democracy' and 'free elections', but meant very different things by them. All this created problems for our propaganda to Germany, which also had to overcome the decision, influenced by the American Civil War experience, to insist upon unconditional surrender. Goebbels naturally used this to convince the German people that they had to fight to the bitter end. I doubt myself whether this made very much difference. Western commitments to their allies, above all to Poland and the Soviet Union, would in any case have prevented us from suggesting peace terms likely to detach the German people from Hitler, or even to attract the German Resistance, whose leaders were thinking in terms of Germany's pre-war frontiers. The fears of Soviet victory and occupation were probably far more effective than any surrender slogan. These were some of the considerations which guided the European Advisory Commission, consisting of the American and Soviet Ambassadors, Winant and Gusev, with William Strang from the Foreign Office, in planning the Allied occupation of Germany.

War crimes had been an issue in the First World War, but there was no precedent for the enormity of German war crimes under Hitler. While there was no secret about Hitler's plans to get rid of the Jews, and his persecutions had begun well before the war, it took a little time, not only at the Foreign Office but also in Jewish circles, to realize that, even when conducting a major war, he would devote such a large part of the German war effort to exterminating the Jewish race throughout the whole of Europe. It took many months before the scale and horror of what was being done was understood. The stories that reached us first came through the Allied Governments in London, more especially the Poles, on whose territories so many of the atrocities were committed. After the German invasion in 1941, the anti-Jewish campaign extended into the Soviet Union. I recall one of my German friends (later Ambassador in London), Baron Hans (Johnny) von Herwarth, telling me after the war of the horror that was felt in his regiment in Russia, when one of their officers came back from an expedition with a white face, saying that he had been with the SS when they had lined up Jews outside one of the villages and shot them, after ordering them to dig their own graves. Then came information about the first Jewish extermination camps. And it was not only the Jews who were the victims.

Pressure grew from the Allied Governments in London and from Jewish organizations for effective action going beyond declarations of condemnation and post-war punishment. The problem was to agree upon an effective course of action, a problem made more difficult by the presence at the conference table of Stalin, with his own record of atrocities. The only military action open to us at that time was to bomb Germany. The Royal Air Force, and later on the American Air Force as well, had the task of bringing the war to an earlier end by destroying key elements in German production like ball-bearing or synthetic oil plants, or by weakening German civilian morale by raids on big cities. The suggestion came from Jewish organizations that extermination camps and the communications to them should instead be bombed, but these camps were distant and difficult objectives, and in the view of the Royal Air Force this would have prolonged the war and resulted in heavy losses without stopping Hitler's anti-Jewish atrocities.

Turning to the future and the issue of legal retribution, international law had previously been based upon the principle that their own Governments should take up the issue of offences against their own citizens. But Hitler had turned millions of Jews into stateless persons. A whole new chapter of international law had to be written, and in such a way that the delicate balance in Palestine and the Middle East was not destroyed, with all that this meant for the Allied war effort. Sir John Simon, then Lord Chancellor, took a major part in this.

The pressure in 1941 and 1942 came mainly from the Allied Governments in London because they could at least speak for their own nationals on the subject. In the case of Poland, this involved many ethnic Poles as well as large numbers of Jews. This applied to a lesser degree to all the occupied countries. It was therefore decided, on General Sikorski's initiative, to hold a high-level conference in January 1942 at St James's Palace, which I had to organize, to discuss the whole question of how to handle war crimes. All the Allied Governments in London were there, and the UK and the USA were observers. The Prime Minister and the President committed their Governments to firm action against those responsible for war crimes. As fast as possible international law was modified to meet these new needs, and this led on to the Nuremberg trials, which were unique in history, and to the subsequent arrest and prosecution of war criminals, which goes on to this day. But during 1943 a special Department had been set up to take over this major issue from the Central Department. In the light of hindsight, we in the Foreign Office, in common with most others concerned, were mistaken mainly in failing to realize at the outset the scale of Hitler's atrocities. But I cannot even today see what more effective measures could have been taken. Indeed, it could even be claimed that the Nuremberg trials, with one of Stalin's judges on the Bench, went too far in the direction of subjugating the defeated to the law of the victors. Churchill had more than once expressed a preference for summary execution.

Contacts with the German Resistance and German peace feelers remained the responsibility of the Central Department. I will begin with the flight of Rudolf Hess to Scotland in the summer of 1941, which aroused the greatest interest at the time and since the war, although it was not in my view the most important. It could, however, have caused such dangerous misunderstanding at home and among our allies, and also with the USA and the Soviet Union, not yet in the war, that the Hess papers had to be kept in my office safe. Hess was still officially Hitler's Deputy, although his role had become relatively unimportant after the outbreak of war in 1939. He was born in Egypt, and shared Hitler's admiration for the British Empire as well as his contempt for the Slavs in Eastern Europe. Knowing of Hitler's plan to invade the Soviet Union in July, and seeing the British in trouble in Iraq and North Africa, he took it upon himself to carry out a peace mission with the double aim of restoring peace between Britain and Germany and of enabling the occupation of the Soviet Union to proceed without a second front in the west. He had met the Duke of Hamilton at the Berlin Olympic Games in 1937 and chose him as his intermediary, executing a remarkable solo flight from Bavaria to Scotland through a massive German air raid.

The first reaction of the Duke himself, of Number 10 and of the Foreign Office was complete scepticism, to be followed by great caution when Hess's identity had been confirmed by Ivone Kirkpatrick. The potential embarrassment caused by this self-appointed but still very senior would-be intermediary seemed at first equally great for Hitler and for the UK. The last thing we wanted to encourage at that time of isolation and relative weakness, tempered however by firm resolution to continue the war, was the idea that we were open to peace feelers. It was Hitler who broke the news, disowning Hess completely and correctly. We were thus left with a disowned but still very high-ranking Nazi on our hands, deeply disappointed by the reception he had received, although honourably treated under guard in a country house not far from London. His behaviour became at times very odd, and he attempted suicide by flinging himself down the well of the central staircase. Doctors and psychiatrists, including the disguised Lord Chancellor, Sir John Simon, could not decide whether he was deranged or only feigning madness. Interest in the Hess case soon subsided. He remained a prisoner for the remaining years of the war and his sanity was no longer in question when he was tried at Nuremberg and condemned to life imprisonment for his share in the planning and preparation of the war.

This was not the end of the Hess story for me. He was one of the three remaining prisoners in Spandau prison in Berlin, with Speer the architect and Von Schirach the Austrian youth leader, when I became Ambassador in Germany in 1963. I found that Hess behaved very strangely, as he had in the UK. He would have nothing to do with his fellow prisoners, and would not even join them in looking after the prison garden. When I visited Spandau and 'inspected' the prisoners, Hess alone had nothing to say for himself, no complaints on the model of Von Schirach, nor intelligent conversation on the model of Speer. On one wall of his cell there hung the aviation cap and overalls in which he had accomplished his great feat of solo navigation in 1941.

By the Sixties, and more especially after Speer and Von Schirach had completed their prison terms, there was German and international pressure for the release of Hess, suffering increasingly from bouts of illness, and for the closing of Spandau. The Russians consistently vetoed this. My own impression was that Hess had cast himself for the role of silent martyr, acting it with the same skill that he had played another part in England during the war, and that he was relatively indifferent to any prospect of liberation. Legends have grown up around him, including the final story that his death was not suicide but assassination, although for what motive or by whom remains unclear. One of his British surgeons, Mr Thomas, has written a book with much circumstantial evidence to show that the man who parachuted on to the Duke of Hamilton's estate and died in Spandau more than four decades later was not the real Hess, but a substitute trained by Himmler, while the real Hess was shot down on his flight by the Germans. I find it hard to accept that such a substitute could have maintained conviction for so long, deceiving his own wife and family, but the whole Hess story is so strange that there may be a case for the Scottish verdict of 'non-proven'.

There were, however, more important if less unexpected approaches from the German Resistance, continuing those of pre-war days. These came mainly from soldiers and diplomats. Hitler's victories in the west and in the east still left some serving officers as well as the retired Chief of Staff, General Beck, convinced that Hitler had embarked Germany on a very dangerous course. Many of them were shocked by the excesses of the Nazi regime. Their guiding principle was, however, to preserve Germany within its pre-war frontiers from Soviet Communism. Despite their high traditions and honourable intentions, this made it difficult if not impossible for a British Government allied to Poland and the Soviet Union, and almost as strongly opposed to German nationalism and militarism as it was to Nazism, to respond to such feelers, even when, as frequently happened, they came through Church channels, in particular through the Bishop of Chichester, and even though there were important Socialists like Julius Leber or distinguished independent personalities like Goerdeler also involved. Many members of the Resistance were in Military Intelligence or even high up in the Secret Service, like Admiral Canaris. This tended to lessen the credibility of the Resistance in the eyes of Eden and Churchill, and it was indeed remarkable that for so long they plotted rather openly without any apparent reaction from the Gestapo. Another remarkable feature of the Army Resistance was that even when senior officers refused to support the Resistance, it was never betrayed. Among civilians, the Kreisau circle met frequently in the home of so great a Prussian family as the Von Moltkes. At the head of the Foreign Office, Baron von Weizsäcker, father of the present German President, was a strong opponent of Hitler, and clearly did not discourage diplomats like Adam von Trott from fomenting opposition to Hitler at home and abroad. This would have been impossible in Stalin's Soviet Union.

Among the Resistance supporters were the Von Haefften brothers, one of them a diplomat, my old friend from Cambridge and Paris days. His brother was in the Army, and they were both involved in the July 1944 plot to kill Hitler. His brother was ADC to Stauffenberg, and they were shot together after the plot failed. My friend, Hans, had an even worse fate. He was eventually arrested, tried with the maximum humiliation and strung up on a meat-hook in the Ploetzensee Prison, as so many members of the Resistance were in 1944. He behaved with great dignity and courage. Knowing him as a man of honour and courage helped me in the Foreign Office to respect the motives of the

German Resistance, in spite of some doubts, unjustified as it turned out, about Adam von Trott, arising from the great freedom with which he travelled abroad with the avowed aim of undermining the Nazi regime. My real problem in the Foreign Office was to convince myself and then to convince my sceptical masters, Eden and Churchill, that the German Resistance had any hope of undermining the Nazi regime while it was victorious throughout Europe and which later, when the tide had turned, could so easily convince the German Army and people that their only hope lay in the stoutest resistance against the Red Army, intent on revenge for the horrors inflicted by Germany in Eastern Europe. It was not until July 1944 that Stauffenberg could launch his heroic but ill-fated attempt upon Hitler, which resulted only in the destruction of the German Resistance and the deaths of so many of its members. One of the most heroic, Axel von dem Busche, escaped and is now living in Switzerland. He had volunteered to kill Hitler and himself at a military review. Twice he prepared himself for death, and on each occasion Hitler failed to turn up.

There were many brave left-wingers in the Resistance, including many Communists. Among them was Willy Brandt, who survived because his work as a courier took him to Norway. We heard less of these in Whitehall, since for the most part they did not have the communication facilities available to the soldiers, diplomats and churchmen. Also, their possibilities of effective action in Nazi Germany were less. The late Richard Crossman, with whom I was in close touch over propaganda to Germany, once told me that this should in his view be concentrated on the Generals and the Bishops. I had to remind him that this might not be welcomed by his friends in the Labour Party, quite apart from the unwillingness of Churchill and Eden to meet German soldiers with strong national sentiments even half-way.

Another consideration also counselled caution. This was the fact that Stalin had already done a major deal with Hitler in 1939 and was capable of doing another, whereas we were only in contact with Hitler's opponents. Until the Battle of Stalingrad, the Russians were under terrible pressure and suffering very great losses in men and territory. If Stalin had got the impression that we were in contact with German Generals, whose main aim was to protect Germany against Russia, he might well have been tempted to see whether he could not again come to terms with Hitler, much more difficult though this might have proved than in 1939. My answer even today to those who argue that we should have given greater encouragement to the German Resistance is that the arguments against doing so were compelling.

8 | Poland and Other Allies in Exile

1940–44

The success of Hitler's blitzkrieg in the West left the UK alone among the Allies unoccupied and also at war with Mussolini's Italy in the Mediterranean. One of our tasks in the Central Department, of which I became the Deputy Head later in 1940 and the Head early in 1943, was that of settling in the UK the Heads of State and the Governments of our Western allies, the Netherlands and Luxemburg (a third, Norway, was the responsibility of the Northern Department), eventually the Government but not the King of the Belgians, and the Head of State, the Government and the important armed forces of Poland, the former Head of State and Government of pre-Munich Czechoslovakia, and last but by no means least, General de Gaulle and his Free French. His chief initial contribution was to provide through his broadcasts a rallying centre for the then small number of French at home opposed to the Vichy regime of Pétain and Laval. The Free French also had some military forces and some minor French colonies under their authority.

The Free French problem was so obviously a very special one that it required its own Department. But I remained personally in contact with Free French affairs for a year or two as interpreter between the Prime Minister and General de Gaulle at some of their major and usually difficult meetings. It has often been suggested that General de Gaulle and Churchill disliked each other. It is true that Churchill described de Gaulle's Cross of Lorraine as one of the greatest crosses he had to bear. It is also true that General de Gaulle resented his dependence upon Churchill and what he called the English. But there was nevertheless great respect between them. I saw this for myself at one of their most stormy meetings after the Free French had seized the islands of St Pierre and Micquelon in the St Lawrence Estuary, while Churchill was in Quebec conferring with Roosevelt and Mackenzie King, unable to defend his protégé against Cordell Hull's wrath. On Churchill's return to London he summoned de Gaulle and subjected him to a torrent of indignation, some of which I tried in vain to bowdlerize in my translation. His anger related to its manner and timing rather than to the operation itself. De Gaulle, with great dignity, made little attempt to excuse or even to explain matters, and took his leave politely. As the door closed behind him, Churchill, whose fury until that moment had been unabated, turned round to say with obviously sincere admiration, 'That was very well done. I couldn't have done it better myself.'

It was I think on a later occasion that Churchill told de Gaulle that if he had to choose between the Continent and the Atlantic, his choice would be the Atlantic (de Gaulle's phrase was 'le grand large'). De Gaulle never forgot this, and it was at the root of his conviction that the British, whose overseas achievements he much admired, would never be appropriate members of the European Community. Like Hitler, he thought we should leave Europe to him. On the other hand, de Gaulle accepted without serious protest the military necessity of immobilizing the French battleships at Oran, whereas he seemed prepared to go to any lengths in opposing what he regarded as British designs on Syria and the Lebanon, even though the British representative there was his old friend, General Spears, who had flown him to London and was a great Francophile. I was not involved with de Gaulle during his last months in London nor after his move to North Africa in 1943. My next contacts with him were after his return to power in France in 1958, when I was Ambassador to NATO, then still in Paris.

The other Western Allies had no such problems and no such personality, with the exception of Paul-Henri Spaak, who developed his great qualities as a European and Atlanticist during those London years, trying in vain to persuade Eden to contemplate British leadership of a Western European Community after the war. Norwegian and Dutch shipping, and the Dutch and Belgian colonial empires, brought additional strength to the British war effort. Shipping, the Dutch East Indies and the Congo were not, however, handled in the Central Department.

The affairs of the Czechs, for whom we had not gone to war in 1938, and those of Poland, for whom we had a year later, were a different matter and took much of our time. The Czechs, represented in London by old friends in Beneš and Masaryk, were much handicapped by the fact that we no longer recognized Czechoslovakia as a country. After Munich it had been divided into the Protectorate of Bohemia and the independent State of Slovakia; and the Munich agreement, with all its imperfections, had become part of international law, raising for example the problem of the legal status of three and a half million Sudetens, formerly Czech nationals, who had become German subjects. For some time the Czechs, who had few assets, only a small brigade re-formed in the UK and a weak resistance movement at home, had to accept, very reluctantly, the status of a National Committee, like the Free French. Beneš and Masaryk, however, had many friends in London, and before too long, assisted also by their good relations with Moscow after Soviet entry into the war, achieved the full position of an Allied Government in Exile.

The Polish Government and armed forces absorbed most attention, more especially after Hitler attacked the Soviet Union in 1941, when we were faced with what eventually proved the impossible problem of reconciling two enemies of long standing, each of whom had become in different ways most important allies. Our first task, successfully achieved, was to transfer from France to Britain the Polish Government, many Polish political leaders and above all the bulk of the Polish armed forces. The Poles and the British, unlike the Poles and their previous hosts, the French, knew very little about each other. Their Ambassador told me that his Ministry for Foreign Affairs had been amazed when his choice for a first posting had been London and not Paris or Rome. But collectively and individually the Poles made themselves at home here to a remarkable degree and very quickly. It was above all the valuable contribution of the Polish air squadrons in the Battle of Britain, in such contrast to our own inability to help Poland at the outbreak of the war, which ensured British respect and understanding. In some ways the Poles settled down almost too well. One of their air squadrons aroused great jealousies in the Czech and British squadrons, with whom they shared an air base at Exeter, by their successes with the local girls. In Scotland, where a Polish armoured division trained before the landings in Normandy, there was a local joke that there should be a memorial for the girls of Scotland who fell for Poland. And their Commanding Officer won all Scottish hearts in Perth in a farewell speech saying how much they had enjoyed Scotland, and that they hoped 'by the grace of God' to come to like England too. On a less romantic plane, the Poles soon ran some excellent restaurants in London, and were particularly skilled in making the best of rationing restrictions. On a more serious note, the contribution of the Polish underground in providing vital intelligence concerned, for example, with the build-up of the German V1s and V2s and with penetrating German cyphers, was a major one. The Poles had also managed to evacuate from Poland their sizeable gold reserves, which ensured them a certain feeling of independence.

The Poles had the benefit of an excellent Embassy in London under a very good Ambassador, Count Raczynski. The Polish Government in exile and other political figures who came from France were less well-known to us, and General Sikorski, their political and military leader, had played a rather controversial part in Polish politics between the wars. He had the advantage, however, of having spent many years in opposition, and his greater readiness than that of most Poles to come to terms with the Soviet Union proved very helpful after the Soviet Union had been brought into the war. Given the importance of the Polish armed forces, the combination of political and military leadership was also valuable. It certainly facilitated the growth of a good personal relationship between Sikorski and Churchill, which was of great importance for the Poles and also for those of us dealing with Polish affairs in the Foreign Office. Sikorski was also well-served behind the scenes by his special adviser, Rettinger, who made excellent use of his wide circle of acquaintances in Western capitals, as he did after the war for the European Movement. He was a brave man, undertaking a dangerous personal mission to Poland, dropping by parachute for the first time in his life to check for Sikorski on the Polish underground movement. Many distrusted him, but I never found cause to do so.

Our major diplomatic problem with the Poles throughout the war was their relations or lack of them with the Russians, who had stabbed them in the back in 1939, seized half the then territory of Poland and deported Army officers and leaders of the ethnic Polish community in large numbers to Siberia. Not unnaturally, the Poles wanted more from us than verbal condemnation and there was even pressure upon us as an ally to declare war on the Soviet Union. Our sensible refusal to do this on behalf of either the Poles or the Finns, coming on top of our inability to give any effective help against the Nazi invasion, left some Poles with the feeling that the British were not entirely reliable allies, although in our treaty of alliance we had openly refused to guarantee the integrity of Polish territory and had never concealed our doubts about Poland's eastern frontiers. The problem of Polish-Soviet relations became more acute for us after Hitler's invasion had turned the Soviet Union from an unfriendly neutral into an ally in July 1941. The Poles were unhappy over the generous and unreserved way in which Churchill pledged British support to Stalin, and it required all his and Eden's skills to bring two such bitter and traditional enemies together in the Grand Alliance. Our main argument with the Poles was that in the short term this was the only way they could get their compatriots out of Siberia and in the longer term, after a major Soviet victory in the east, get themselves back to a free Poland, compensated in the west for losses in the east. This remained a major objective of British policy throughout the war to Yalta in 1945, with many disappointments but also some successes on a difficult path. We tried to convince the Poles that an early agreement was essential, since the problem would only become more difficult when the Red Army advanced to 'liberate' Eastern Europe. When that day came I could not myself see Stalin easily abandoning the gains he had made in the Ribbentrop–Molotov Pact and to which he gave such priority in his talks with Eden in December 1941, with the Germans at the gates of Moscow.

My presence in Eden's very small party for this Moscow visit must have been due to the importance of Poland in the new Anglo-Soviet relationship. It gave me my second opportunity after the 1939 Strang mission to acquire some first-hand knowledge of Stalin and the Soviet Union, with which I was to become so closely involved for six years after the war. Apart from that of Beaverbrook, who had negotiated arms deliveries with Stalin, Eden's was the first of many senior wartime British and American meetings with Stalin and Molotov. It was the prelude to the Anglo-Soviet Treaty of Alliance and was intended to improve the then anything but brilliant war prospects of either side and to clarify our own very difficult position between two allies, Poland and the Soviet Union, in a state of war with each other. Taking a longer view, our joint prospects of eventual victory had been greatly advanced by the joint action of Japan and Germany in bringing the USA into the war as an ally, but the immediate cause was in the Pacific and the extent of US assistance in the west was still unknown.

The news of the Japanese destruction of the US fleet at Pearl Harbor, conveyed to us almost triumphantly by a midshipman from a primitive transistor radio, had come to Eden's party as a complete surprise as we left London by special train for Invergordon, where we boarded a destroyer to Scapa Flow, thence to continue by a cruiser, HMS *Kent*, sailing on a dark December night, towards the Arctic Circle around Bear Island to Murmansk. En route we were bombarded with bad tidings. What had looked like victory against Rommel in the desert battle of 'Knightsbridge' had been turned into defeat; HMS *Barham*, flagship of the Mediterranean Fleet, had been sunk; and last but not least, Japanese aircraft had sunk our two battle cruisers off the coasts of Malaya. The Soviet Ambassador, Ivan Maisky, accompanying us, had I think some difficulty in deciding whether to welcome the fact that the British as well as the Russians were suffering reverses or to recall that these setbacks affected what was now an ally.

The Captain of HMS *Kent* advised us to wear lifebelts in what was an active war zone, with enemy aircraft stationed in northern Norway, but as we put to sea, the seaman looking after me clearly thought differently and commented that these northern waters were so cold that it was better to go straight down. From Murmansk we continued our journey by rail along the frontier of Finland, still at war with the Soviet Union. As the guardian of our secret papers I had been supplied with interlarded 'inflammable leaves', to which I was to set fire if Finnish troops attacked our train. It was lucky they did not, for I discovered on experimenting with one such leaf in our Moscow hotel that it took me some twenty minutes to set it alight!

Moscow in December 1941 looked like a deserted city, and indeed over half the population had been evacuated. The food available to the people was mainly black bread and salt fish, while 'luxury' goods were restricted rather oddly to balloons and ice-cream. The National Hotel had been refurbished for us and the food served to us there was of the highest quality, lavish indeed by comparison with the wartime rationing austerity of London. The German army was still only some twenty kilometres from the centre of Moscow, although during our week there it was pushed back by Siberian reinforcements in the first successful Soviet counter-attack of the war. Eden was shown the result of this victory. Moscow had not been subjected, as London had been, to air raids, so we were surprised by an air raid warning on our arrival. Eden and the senior members of our party were shown to a luxurious air raid shelter with a well-stocked buffet in one of Moscow's magnificent underground stations, but I had been left behind in our offices at the hotel and observed that there were no enemy aircraft nor any anti-aircraft fire.

When the talks began with Stalin, he at once to our surprise raised the question of the Soviet Union's post-war frontiers and pressed Eden to guarantee British support for his ill-gotten gains in Poland and elsewhere as a result of the Ribbentrop–Molotov Pact, pressing the issue when Eden suggested that we should first concentrate upon winning the war, which at that point still seemed a distant objective. Eden finally had to explain that he had no authority to discuss this subject. Our stay in Moscow was delayed by a decision to bring the British Ambassadors from Turkey and Iran to join in discussions of the position towards the war of these countries, to which Stalin showed considerable hostility. On our last evening of the talks, and as we thought with our last rich hotel dinner finished, there came an invitation to proceed immediately to a Kremlin banquet hosted by Stalin, at which the service was provided by our familiar hotel waiters. Many speeches were made, many toasts were drunk, and finally in some state of inebriation we were treated to a Russian wrestling match in which our British champion, John Russell, a junior secretary at the Embassy, performed creditably against Stalin's champion, Marshal Voroshilov.

Our return journey to London by the same route (and not, as we had once feared, by the Trans-Siberian railway and Vladivostok!) was relatively uneventful. Eden had at once agreed to a Soviet request to take on board a Soviet trade union leader, who would be able to explain the Soviet war effort in British factories. This turned out to be a woman, and the Captain had to point out that no woman could be carried on a battleship in war conditions. The crisis was got round by Maisky offering her his second cabin, and she had a great success with the ship's crew.

One of the great benefits to me from this unusual diplomatic experience was the insight it gave me into the tremendous war effort and the great privations of the Soviet people, which helped me to maintain a more balanced view in later years of adversarial relations with Stalin's and even Khrushchev's Soviet Union.

Returning to London and to the Polish problem, our negotiating hand was strengthened by the relative confidence the Russians had placed in Sikorski, by the relative flexibility of Maisky as Soviet Ambassador in London and, after America was brought into the war in December 1941, by Soviet reliance upon American as well as British economic and military assistance. The prospect of major reinforcements from Siberia for the Polish Army obviously helped to overcome the opposition of General Sosnkowski and many Polish soldiers to any deal with the Soviet Union. So our first success came with the restoration of diplomatic relations between Poland and the Soviet Union and the early release from Soviet captivity of thousands of Polish troops who, after a long journey through Iran and the Middle East, reached Europe to become the Anders Army, which distinguished itself in Italy and Western Europe. Many Poles remained in the Soviet Union to form the Berling Army, fighting with the Russians and including in its ranks the later President of Poland, General Jaruzelski. I was told by the Poles that Stalin had entrusted to Beria and Malenkov the supervision of the Polish evacuation and that while Beria, the dreaded Secret Police Chief but a Georgian, had been helpful, Malenkov, a Russian, had been the reverse.

So the Polish-Soviet reconciliation got off to a reasonable start, although the major territorial issue between them was left in suspense. At a later and more difficult stage, the Poles were pressing the Americans and ourselves at least to insist upon the mainly Polish regional capitals of Vilna and Lvov becoming Polish enclaves in surrounding Soviet Lithuanian and Ukrainian countrysides, a concept which Stalin was never prepared even to consider. Polish hopes were not easily extinguished. In addition to their good army and air force, the Poles to our surprise built up a sizeable navy, justifying a cruiser as a flagship. We had one to spare, *The Dragon* and the Admiralty were glad to see it manned. We in the Foreign Office had to stop the transaction when we heard that the Poles intended to re-christen the ship *The Lvov*. They eventually gave way, but had the last laugh, when we were invited to a 'christening' ceremony at which they unveiled an escutcheon portraying Walt Disney's Reluctant Dragon.

During the period of Polish-Soviet reconciliation we were optimistic enough to develop a plan for a post-war Polish-Czechoslovak federation to form a strong buffer state and promote stability in Central Europe. Some even thought that a union between the more romantic Poles and the more prosaic Czechs would be as successful as we thought our own United Kingdom had proved. Not even in exile were either the Poles or the Czechs attracted by the prospect. The Czechs, seeing themselves cast for the role of junior partner and being well aware of Soviet hostility to any such scheme, had little difficulty in putting the brakes on.

The first of three major setbacks to our hopes of a better Soviet-Polish relationship came with the German discovery in 1943 of the mass graves of Polish officers at Katyn in Byelorussia. In the context of the evacuation of Polish Army personnel from Siberia there had been correspondence between the Polish Government in London and the Russians about the whereabouts of many thousands of Polish officers in Russian prisoner-of-war camps after 1939 whose letters to their families overseas had suddenly ceased in 1940. The Russians had no answer, so the Poles in London jumped to what turned out to be the correct conclusion, that they had been killed by the Russians and not, as the Russians were claiming, by the Germans. Even Sikorski, at the risk of major trouble with the Russians, had to take some action and, without consulting us, he settled for what he no doubt considered the safest course of an appeal to the Swiss Red Cross to investigate. Stalin, complaining that the Poles chose to believe their enemy Hitler rather than their ally Stalin, broke off relations with the Government in London, which were never resumed, turning instead to encourage Polish Communists under his control or in the Polish underground. Since there could not be absolute proof of Soviet guilt, although we in the Foreign Office were convinced of it, British Ministers had to content themselves with public expressions of regret rather than condemnation, which disappointed the Poles. We were anxious even then not to shut the door on some future Polish-Soviet understanding.

Any such hopes were, however, dashed in June 1943 by the death of Sikorski in an air crash at Gibraltar on his return from visiting Polish troops still in camps in the Middle East. This was the second major setback to British policy towards Poland and the Soviet Union. It has been suggested, and Hochhuth even brought the slander into one of his plays, that Churchill engineered this accident to get rid of Sikorski, although no good reason has been advanced for such action on his part. Churchill was in fact deeply shocked. He had affection as well as respect for Sikorski, apart from the fact that British policy was largely based upon him as by far the most likely Polish leader to bring the Russians and Poles together again.

A good successor as Prime Minister was found in Mikolajczyk, leader of the Polish Peasant Party, who was prepared to join with us in this attempt. But his support was strongest in Poland itself and he could not have Sikorski's authority over the Poles in exile, more particularly in the Armed Forces. Our joint task became progressively more difficult with the rapid advance of the Red Army into and through Poland. Churchill took up the Polish cause again with Stalin at the 1944 Moscow Summit, taking Mikolajczyk with him, although he had recently been disowned by the London Poles and displaced as their Prime Minister. By this time Stalin had his own puppet Government in Lublin and the Red Army was making life very difficult for the underground Home Army loyal to the London Government. If they remained underground they were regarded as hostile. If they surfaced they risked arrest.

These were the circumstances in which the third major disaster overtook Poland and undermined our policy of trying to get the Poles and the Russians together. As the Germans were retreating from Warsaw, the Polish Home Army under General Bor-Komorowski, encouraged by broadcasts from the advancing Red Army, which included units of the Berling Polish forces, came into the open and took over Warsaw. The Red Army then stopped on the other side of the Vistula, alleging that they needed time to re-form after a rapid advance, leaving the lightly-armed Poles to conduct a heroic but doomed resistance to the returning German forces. We and the Americans flew supplies to the Poles but Warsaw was the limit of the endurance of our aircraft flying from Bari, so that our casualties were high and the supplies limited. Personal appeals to Stalin from Churchill and Roosevelt to allow our planes to land and refuel at Soviet airfields near to Warsaw were refused with accusations that the Polish rising had been irresponsible and badly coordinated. After ten days or so the Poles surrendered to the Germans. It was not long before the Russians crossed the Vistula and took Warsaw themselves.

It was impossible to resist the conclusion that Stalin had encouraged the Poles to fight and then failed to support them or to allow us to support them more effectively simply to secure the destruction of those Polish forces loyal to the London Government. At all events, I am convinced that this played a major part in persuading Churchill that a victorious Stalin could not be trusted to behave as a reliable ally, still less as he and Roosevelt had once hoped, as 'a member of the Club'. It still remained our duty to try to reach some settlement with Stalin which would enable the Poles in the West to return home and share in the reconstruction of their country. Mikolajczyk was still prepared to work with us to this end, although there was no longer much hope of cooperation with a right-wing Polish Government in London opposed to any dealing with him and unacceptable to Moscow. Fortunately the Polish armed forces continued to fight as bravely as ever within the Allied armies preparing to invade Germany.

My time in the Central Department came to an end late in 1944 on my appointment as Minister in Moscow, but my close connection with

Polish affairs continued at the Yalta Conference early in 1945 and then at the Moscow Embassy, where we struggled with the Russians over the execution of the Yalta Agreements on Poland and Eastern Europe.

When I left London at the end of 1944 the outlook for the Czechoslovak Government in London under Beneš and Masaryk and the latter's able Deputy Hubert Ripka was much brighter than that of the Poles, although their contribution to the Allied cause, through no fault of their own, had been much smaller, limited as it was to a small brigade, too small to be risked on active service. One of its first recruits in France and then in Britain was Robert Maxwell, a native of Sub-Carpathian Ruthenia. Rightly sensing this, he transferred to the British Army, where he had a good war record, winning the MC and promotion to officer rank and joining in the liberation of Paris, where he met his future wife. Although the Czech resistance was nothing like so important or so active as that of the Poles, it achieved one notable success with the murder of the Nazi Gauleiter and SS leader Heydrich, although a heavy price was paid in the Lidice massacre. The Czechs, unlike the Poles, had good relations with Moscow as well as in the West, where they benefited to some extent from guilty feelings left by Munich. I added to my duties in the Central Department for some time those of Chargé d'Affaires with the Czechoslovaks in London, which helped me to add to my many Polish friendships at all levels equally valuable friendships with the smaller group of Czechs. This could not, however, be a long-term arrangement, since I had far too much other work. Fortunately, Sir Robert Bruce Lockhart, who had made many close Czech friends, including Beneš and Masaryk, as a British diplomat in Czechoslovakia after the First World War, could take my place, although he also had an important job in charge of British propaganda overseas. As he was also on terms of personal friendship with the Foreign Secretary, Anthony Eden, this provided a good solution until a full-time Ambassador, Sir Philip Nichols, was appointed, who went with the Czechoslovak Government to Prague after the war.

9 | Spain and Portugal

1940–44

I have left to the last the responsibilities of the Central Department for Spain and Portugal, which came nearest to traditional diplomacy with Governments in their own capitals. Our relations with each of them became particularly important after the fall of France. Both were dictatorships, but whereas Portugal under the civilian leadership of a Professor of Economics, Salazar, was ever mindful of the Anglo-Portuguese Alliance, Spain was under a military dictator, Franco, who owed much to the Germans and Italians for his success in the Spanish Civil War. Our allies, the French, had backed the losing side, but Marshal Pétain, who had been sent as a special Ambassador to Franco before becoming the head of the Vichy Government, had done much to restore the position and to fend off any designs which Franco, a Spanish colonial soldier from the Canaries, might have had upon the French Empire in North Africa. On our side, we had to consider the position of Gibraltar, now a vital link in British communications through the Mediterranean to the Middle East and India but surrounded by a potentially unfriendly Spain. Spain had, however, been bled white by the Civil War. She needed overseas supplies, in particular wheat, and could only get them through the Allied blockade. As against this, we needed certain minerals, in particular wolfram, essential at that time for arms production. Fortunately for us Hitler could hardly do a deal with Franco at the expense of Pétain, and Franco, a cautious Galician, was determined not to fall, as Mussolini had, into Hitler's arms. At a famous meeting in France between Franco and Hitler, Franco resisted Hitler so successfully that Hitler afterwards said that it was the most impossible meeting he could remember and he never wanted to see Franco again. Franco's capacity for resistance was indeed very great. Sir Samuel Hoare once complained that putting points to Franco was rather like putting pins in a feather bolster, and never seemed to have the slightest effect. However, had Hitler been able to offer Franco French territories in North Africa, things could have been different.

Churchill killed two birds with one stone by sending Sir Samuel Hoare as a distinguished special Ambassador to Franco, at the same time ridding his Cabinet of one of Neville Chamberlain's inner circle. It turned out to be as successful an appointment as that of Lord Halifax's move to Washington. Spain was also important for us as the only escape route through Vichy France from occupied Europe. Despite much sympathy for the Nazis in the victorious Spanish Falange, which showed itself later in the despatch of the Blue Division to join in Hitler's invasion of the Soviet Union, many of Franco's Ministers, and in particular the Foreign Minister, Colonel Begbeider, were not unhelpful, even though the escapees included Allied airmen and Allied personalities such as Spaak and Pierlot. As the war developed, increasing numbers of Frenchmen reluctant to join de Gaulle in the early days found their way over the Pyrenees via Spain to Britain. One in particular, a former diplomat at the London Embassy, was reported to have crossed by one of the most difficult mountain tracks with his Brigg umbrella, his Lock hat and his Lobb shoes.

Sir Samuel Hoare was assisted by a rising young Conservative politician, later Lord Eccles, who conducted the complicated wolfram negotiations with Spain and with Portugal, using as his trump card the system of Navy Certificates which enabled Spain to get sufficient wheat through the British blockade. We accepted that Franco should appease Hitler with smaller shipments of wolfram to Germany. Since the armed forces were in control in Spain, high-powered and friendly Service Attachés were appointed to Madrid, who played a considerable diplomatic role. One of them, the Naval Attaché, Captain Hilgarth, personally known to Churchill, played a major part later in deceiving the Germans about our landings in North Africa, to the extent of driving down to Gibraltar with a dead man at his side whose presence would have given the Germans a different idea of where we were likely to land. There was a good deal of old-fashioned cloak-and-dagger diplomacy in Spain at that time. The only contacts I ever had in my diplomatic career with Philby were not over the Soviet Union but over our wartime activities in the Spanish colonies, where our interests in, for example, dealing with German ships in Spanish harbours, were identical. Philby was not as senior a member of the Secret Service as has often been suggested. He was, in fact, rather junior to me, and my rank was only that of an Acting Counsellor. Philby had a good knowledge of Spain and a perfect cover story because, unlike the other British pro-Soviet traitors, he had been a correspondent on Franco's side throughout the Civil War.

With Portugal the situation was entirely different. Portugal was our oldest ally. Under the terms of the Anglo-Portuguese alliance dating back to the fourteenth century and often subsequently revised, we had commitments to assist Portugal if required to do so, but Portugal was not bound to join in war on our behalf except by agreement. In 1940, when we were alone against Germany and uncertain whether Pétain's French Government at Vichy might not join the Germans, we had no interest in involving Portugal in the war either at home or in her overseas territories. Portugal was like Spain a beneficiary of the Navy Certificate system allowing grain imports through the British naval blockade. Salazar's influence upon Franco was useful to us. Portugal also played her part as the last link in the escape route to Britain.

Portugal became even more important to us in 1943, when the Battle of the Atlantic was going against us. The Germans had increased their submarine campaign against the vital convoys, and had improved their tactics to such an extent that, had losses continued at the then rate of attrition, we might have had real difficulty in continuing the war. The aircraft of that period did not have sufficient range to cover the whole of the Atlantic, and there was an area in the middle where the only protection came from surface ships, which was not enough. This focused attention upon the Azores, which alone could provide air bases for the control of the central Atlantic. The question therefore arose of asking Salazar to provide facilities without, however, requiring him to join in the war against Hitler. But since Hitler might have regarded this as a hostile act, the operation was one of considerable delicacy. Although the Americans were fully involved in a joint Atlantic strategy, it was only the British who, under our alliance with Portugal, could request these facilities from the Portuguese.

HM Ambassador in Lisbon, Sir Ronald Campbell, was a very skilful diplomat. He had been Minister in Paris, where I had served under him in 1935, and Ambassador in Paris at the fall of France. He shared our confidence in the Central Department that Salazar would respond to our request if we negotiated with great discretion and solely under the Anglo-Portuguese alliance. Anthony Eden accepted this view and defended it throughout a rather difficult period of discussion, not only with the Americans but also with Churchill. The Prime Minister at times got rather romantic about the Azores, and in the midst of meetings would recite from Tennyson's poem, 'The Revenge' (an Elizabethan privateer),

> At Flores in the Azores,
> Sir Richard Grenville lay,
> And a pinnace, like a fluttered bird, came flying from far away,

and so forth, but he seemed to have overlooked that Sir Richard Grenville's *Revenge*, far from taking over the Azores, was itself sunk by a large Spanish fleet, a conclusion hardly encouraging for our particular operation.

What was more serious was that the American Chiefs of Staff and in particular General Arnold, the Head of the American Air Force, refused to believe that Dr Salazar would give us what we wanted and advocated seizing the islands by a military coup, regardless of the Anglo-Portuguese Alliance. He came near persuading the President and at times even the Prime Minister. So Eden and his Foreign Office advisers had formidable obstacles to surmount. We were allowed to try our hand, but with a sceptical Prime Minister and more than sceptical American allies breathing down our necks in what was bound to be a lengthy negotiation. Time was, however, important, because we not only needed the facilities but we then had to establish bases. Meanwhile, shipping was being sunk on an unacceptable scale.

I then had one of the two most interesting experiences of my diplomatic career, the other coming later in the Berlin Airlift. I spent seven weeks in Lisbon in July and August 1943 to support the Ambassador in his negotiations with Dr Salazar in what was intended as a highly confidential mission. Lisbon was at that time one of the two main spy centres in southern Europe, the other being Tangier. The place was stiff with every kind of agent, Allied and German, who were meeting in all the bars and hotels in town. I had with me a small military delegation of about fourteen, under Air Vice-Marshal Medhurst. But Salazar, even in more normal circumstances, insisted on doing everything himself and, in my recollection, he only referred to the elderly head of his Ministry for Foreign Affairs, Sampayo, for assistance, so there was not much scope for our disguised officers.

They had to spend much of their time, rather obviously soldiers in mufti in grey flannel trousers and blue blazers, available if and when required, in a pub opposite the front door of the British Embassy. As ill luck would have it, the Portuguese were repairing the roads around our own and the neighbouring German Embassy. The German Ambassador was not supposed to be a keen Nazi, but he obviously had keen Nazis on his staff, apart from the spies propping up bars all over Lisbon. But throughout the seven weeks they appear to have discovered nothing. At an early stage we lost our Secretary-General, Colonel Capel-Cure. We had in the Embassy a 'fixer', who knew the Portuguese police well, and after twenty-four hours discovered that he was in a Portuguese gaol. He had been having a cup of coffee in 'Black Horse' square near the Tagus; somebody came along who he thought was trying to sell him filthy postcards, so he pushed him away; but the man turned out to be a member of the secret police, asking him to show his papers, with the result that he was locked in jail. When this matter came before Salazar – as everything in Portugal did – he was deeply embarrassed at this evidence of a police state. Our officers were later able to talk with their Portuguese opposite numbers, and in particular with a first-class soldier, then Colonel, later General Pina, and Chief of the Portuguese General Staff, who was as helpful as possible with Salazar keeping the strings in his own hands.

Salazar led an extremely simple life for an all-powerful dictator. He lived in a relatively modest flat, looked after by an old housekeeper with no other visible staff. That is where the Ambassador and I had our talks with him, all alone: he never had anybody there, not even to keep a record.

By the summer of 1943, the tide of the war was turning. American troops were crossing the Atlantic, and the landings in North Africa had taken place. I think Franco had decided that Hitler was not going to win and had enough on his hands without taking on the Iberian Peninsula as well. Our negotiations with Salazar proceeded smoothly, but since they had to be conducted with Salazar himself and he was running every detail of Government in Portugal at the same time, they were not speedy, which meant that the Americans and the Prime Minister occasionally became impatient. It was during one of these bouts of impatience that I first got to know George Kennan. The Americans, who today have a large Embassy in Lisbon, then had a small Legation with a small diplomatic staff. The Minister, Bert Fish, whom I had known in Cairo, died during our talks, and a young

Secretary, George Kennan, who had left Berlin with the Embassy staff when Hitler declared war on America in December 1941, had stayed in Lisbon and was now in charge of the Legation. He was kept fully informed and agreed with our approach, and was ready to help, if necessary, with Salazar. But at this point he received high-level instructions to take a line which he was convinced would be unhelpful. Junior though he then was, he queried these instructions and pressed to come back to Washington to explain his concern directly to the President, also the Commander-in-Chief and as such advised by his Chiefs of Staff. The State Department would do nothing more than arrange his meeting with the President, and warned him that it might have bad results for him personally. He still went ahead, and persuaded the President to accept our line of action rather than that of the American Chiefs of Staff. This was for me an excellent prelude to our later close cooperation in Moscow at the end of the war.

We finished negotiations successfully in August and, since it would take time to set up the air defences of Lisbon, it was agreed that the whole matter should remain secret – as, indeed, to my surprise, it did – until Churchill made an announcement in the House of Commons in October. He then amazed the House by saying he had an important announcement to make arising out of the alliance signed by His Majesty King Edward III with King Fernando and Queen Eleanor of Portugal in the year 1373. By this time Churchill had got a different historic view of our activities and was no longer quoting from Tennyson's poem, '*The Revenge*'.

When the news of the Azores agreement came out in October, the Foreign Office wanted to make much of this success story, and since the Ambassador was not in London, the publicity centred on me. In those days I rode a bicycle because, living in the centre of London, I had no case for a petrol allowance. So the newspapers were filled with photographs of 'the bicycling diplomat Mr Frank Roberts' and to my wife's horror many journalists reached our flat in Cornwall Gardens to photograph her cooking the evening meal.

In the event, everything passed off as we had hoped it would. Salazar had explained matters to Franco, and there was no adverse reaction from him. Hitler was too occupied elsewhere to do anything about it. Our real problem therefore lay with our American allies. But we were able to assure them that, having achieved this solution under the Anglo-Portuguese Alliance, there would be little difficulty in persuading Salazar to accept American aircraft as well as a combined base in the Azores, which is exactly what happened. For many decades since then and even today, the Azores base has been of great importance to the American Air Force, although no longer of interest to us, and has been used regularly in many crises.

While Spain and Portugal continued to be very important to us diplomatically, once the Allied armies, having cleared the Axis forces from North Africa, were moving forward in Italy, and above all after the 1944 landings in Normandy, the Iberian Peninsula ceased to play such a key part in wartime diplomacy. But Salazar's attitude throughout the war was one of great statesmanship and helpful to our war effort. And we might have had a more difficult passage than we did with Franco. It had been a pleasurable as well as instructive experience to get so close a view of such an unusual dictator as Dr Salazar. Although his authority in Portugal was absolute and this undoubtedly held back Portuguese development as a modern state, he had none of the outward trappings of a successful dictator and retained the appearance and the manner of the quiet Coimbra professor, whose achievement had been the reform of Portuguese finances and the maintenance of political stability, particularly important under the increasing pressures of the war upon Portugal. He proved a wise, responsible and reliable ally who deserved the tributes paid to him by Churchill and Eden.

10 | Yalta

1945

At the end of 1944, in the middle of the unpleasant V2 Blitz which succeeded that of the V1s which had been mastered, we flew to Cairo for a holiday with my wife's family, which I was to break to attend the Yalta Conference preparatory to taking up my post as Minister in Moscow. I was not sent there in any way as a Russian expert, and indeed I knew no Russian, but mainly, I suppose, because I had been dealing with Germany and with Poland, which were likely to be two of the major problems affecting our relations with the Soviet Union at the end of and after the war.

Cairo was a wonderful change from wartime London. The war was far away from Egypt. I was surprised to find how social life had developed since we had left in 1937. Moslem as well as Coptic ladies attended dinners of considerable opulence. There were already many stories about the excesses of King Farouk, who had so nearly lost his throne when the Germans were approaching Cairo in 1943, and our High Commissioner had had to read the riot act to him.

In the middle of this Cairo leave came the Yalta Summit, preceded by a meeting in Malta between Churchill and Roosevelt. Stalin's refusal to move far from the Soviet Union, despite Roosevelt's obvious ill health, dictated the choice of what Churchill described as the most inconvenient possible site, only recently liberated from German occupation. Churchill's final agreement came in a telegram to Roosevelt: 'So let it be Yalta. We'll first meet in Malta. Let none of us falter.'

I flew to Malta from Cairo on a military plane to meet the British delegation which should have arrived from London in two aircraft.

One of them, unfortunately, with several of my colleagues on board, crashed with all killed just on reaching Malta. A very minor part of the disaster which affected us was that we had certain of our lighter effects for Moscow on this plane, including the draft of a book which my wife was then writing and which would, I am sure, have been more readable than the one which I am now writing, but which she never had the heart to begin again. Our spirits were also dampened by Roosevelt's appearance as a very sick man indeed. He had not originally wanted a joint meeting with the British before the tripartite Summit, and the very fact that he had been more or less forced into it no doubt made him all the more determined, at Yalta, to play up to Stalin and to play down the special relationship with Churchill, which was, I think, unfortunate.

We moved on by air to Simferopol, the airport of the Crimea, and proceeded by car about one hundred miles through the mountains to Yalta. We were amazed to find that the Russians, who were desperately fighting the closing battles of the war, had lined the route at short intervals with military police, male and female, who could surely have been better employed elsewhere. Whether this was for security or a typical Russian gesture, we may never know. Destruction by the Germans on leaving the Crimea had left few houses available for the conference, and the delegates were scattered over a wide area. Roosevelt was given the Tsar's old summer palace at Livadia, where the meetings also took place. Stalin's house I never saw. Churchill was placed some twenty miles away, in the Vorontsov villa, built for a Russian Ambassador to London in the early nineteenth century, with an avenue of lions leading down to the sea. There was only room there for Churchill and Eden and a few senior people. The rest of us were a further twenty miles or so away in a building which had obviously been hastily restored and whose main asset was a sauna, which only our Royal Marines had time to use. They were intrigued to find elderly ladies using the birch twigs on them. Our base and communications centre was yet further away, beyond Balaclava on a British ship in the harbour of Sebastopol. Yalta's claim to be a rather unusual international conference was further emphasized by the complete absence of the press and of opportunities for the participants to meet each other except at the official meetings or, in the case of the senior people, at the dinners they gave one another. Although, therefore, Gromyko was present, I do not remember meeting him socially. I did, however, attend a large number of the meetings at Livadia because the Polish question, for which I was at Yalta, took up a great deal of time.

Yalta has often been misrepresented as a sort of final peace conference like Versailles after the First World War. It has also been argued that the West were at a disadvantage because of the illness of Roosevelt, who had been put in the chair by Stalin. It has further been argued that the West abandoned Eastern Europe to Stalin. None of these things are in fact true. Yalta was one of a series of summit meetings, the first having been at Teheran in 1943, and the third at Potsdam in July 1945, interspersed with a visit from Churchill without the Americans to Moscow in 1944 and several meetings between Foreign Ministers. Roosevelt, although certainly a sick man, handled the conference exactly as he had intended, and got out of it what he had come to get. As regards Eastern Europe, the conference took place when the Red Army was already in occupation of almost all of Eastern Europe and was in fact advancing into Germany from Poland. There was therefore no question of the West giving the Soviet Union what the Red Army had already taken.

There were four main issues for decision at Yalta. All of the participants were interested in reaching agreement on how the war against Germany should be finished and what should happen afterwards. Here there were few problems. The European Advisory Commission (the US, USSR and Great Britain) had already laid down the general arrangements for occupation, and these were approved. The German success in the Ardennes had been brought to a halt, and it was only a matter of time before the war was brought to an end, with the very important undecided question of how far west the Russians and how far east the Allies would get before Germany capitulated under the agreed policy of unconditional surrender. The Russians did raise what became the very controversial issue of reparations, but this was left to be settled later at Potsdam.

Stalin's main priority at Yalta was to get Allied agreement to what amounted to Soviet control of Eastern Europe. Roosevelt's two priorities were quite different, although very important and understandable. The first, looking to the post-war world, was to ensure that the United Nations, which was to be set up shortly at the San Francisco Conference, would not suffer from the major weakness of the League of Nations, and would from the start have as members the two major powers, the United States and the Soviet Union. In the light of hindsight, I cannot understand why Roosevelt should have thought that Stalin might be reluctant to join in this exercise, but he was, admittedly, making some impossible conditions, one of which was that all fifteen Soviet Republics should be separate members of the United Nations. He eventually settled for the Ukraine and Byelorussia in addition to the Soviet Union itself. Roosevelt's second priority was to ensure Russian entry into the war against Japan after the war in Europe. Here again, it could be argued in the light of hindsight that this was unnecessary, since the two atom bombs on Hiroshima and Nagasaki ended that war without Soviet assistance. But at that time nobody knew whether the atom bomb would really work, and there were very few of them. It was generally expected, after the great expense in human lives in capturing island after island in the Pacific, that an actual landing in Japan might well have cost the Americans hundreds of thousands in casualties. In fact, Stalin was very ready to enter the war against Japan in the closing stages and to pick up many advantages for the Soviet Union in a secret protocol, some of them at the expense of China, an ally of the United States, which was not consulted.

Churchill was also concerned with the future United Nations; perhaps a little less so with the arrangements for ending the war in the Far East; and of course very closely with the arrangements concerning Germany. While Churchill did not have the same close interest in Eastern Europe as Stalin, Britain had gone to war for Poland, and Churchill attached great importance, however difficult the circumstances, to reaching an acceptable Polish settlement. For the rest of Eastern Europe he was no doubt guided by the notorious bit of paper he had given Stalin at Moscow in 1944, dividing Soviet and Western interests in each country in varying proportions.

In wartime, armies carry more weight than diplomats, and although at Yalta we did obtain two satisfactory documents – one, the declaration on liberated Europe enshrining the principles of democracy and free elections, and the other, the special arrangements to be made for free elections and for a coalition Government in Poland – the fact remains that from 1939, at the time of our negotiations with Stalin which were brought to an end by the Ribbentrop–Molotov Pact, Stalin had always intended to get back under Russian control the states of Eastern Europe which had since Versailles formed the Western cordon Sanitair against Russia, and to bring back within the boundaries of the Soviet Union those territories which had been part of the Tsarist Empire. He had got this from Hitler; lost it when Hitler invaded Russia; but made it once again a priority in his talks with Anthony Eden in Moscow in December 1941. It was therefore clear that with the Red Army in occupation of the whole of Eastern Europe and in particular of the whole of Poland we were faced with great difficulties in achieving anything satisfactory for the London Poles, more especially since the Polish Government in exile had thrown out Mikolajczyk the Prime Minister most acceptable to us and the Russians, and were at that time conducting what we considered a very negative and non-possumus policy.

Churchill had to take the lead in fighting the Polish case. It has been argued, with some justification, that Roosevelt did not give him as strong support as he could have done. Eastern Europe was not his priority. A cynic might also add that he had already won his re-election, and did not need the Pittsburg Polish vote for the time being. But, however this might be, the only weapon available even to Roosevelt at that time would have been the threat of denying Stalin economic assistance for Russian recovery after the war. In the light of Stalin's subsequent behaviour in turning down offers of continued American assistance and refusing to join in the European Recovery Programme, it seems unlikely that this would have weighed heavily in the balance against territorial gains. At that time Russia was regarded as a gallant ally which had suffered great losses in the common cause, and it would have been very difficult for either the American or the British Government to make such a threat, and quite impossible to make the threat which has sometimes been mentioned by Polish exiles of using the atom bomb as a means of pressure. Any British Government which had suggested such a thing would not have remained long in office in the prevailing state of public opinion over our gallant Soviet allies.

Churchill was therefore left with a rather weak hand to play. He did, indeed, achieve the promise of free elections in Poland, sceptical though we were at the time about Soviet execution of such a commitment. He also got Soviet agreement that Mikolajczyk and other representative Poles in the West should return and join the new Polish Government. On paper, the solution was not too bad. The declaration on liberated Europe was equally acceptable, incorporating democratic principles, but again we were sceptical of Stalin's inter-pretations of such concepts as 'democracy' and 'free elections'. But diplomacy is a matter of documents, and war is a matter of where armies end up. Looking back on Yalta, the only alternative course open to Churchill and Roosevelt would have been to refuse to sign any agreement on Poland and Eastern Europe, on the assumption that

Stalin was going to carry out policies there regardless of Western interests or those of the local inhabitants. I cannot see that this would have done much good. It certainly would not have enabled Mikolajczyk to return to Poland. He himself told me that he was grateful to us for having made this possible, and there were indeed relatively free elections in Poland with good results for Mikolajczyk and his Peasant Party – elections which the Soviet and Polish Communists took care would not be repeated, while they built up a separate 'stooge' Peasant Party. But there were many other major issues at stake in addition to Eastern Europe, three of them under discussion at Yalta, which required Stalin's cooperation. It was therefore inconceivable that Churchill and Roosevelt could have refused their signatures on documents which were, diplomatically speaking, acceptable.

One other important issue was settled at Yalta. The occupation of Germany as it had been planned was to be left to the Soviet Union, the United States and the United Kingdom. Churchill, already disturbed about the prospect of a post-war Europe in which the Soviet Union would be potentially the most powerful country, confronting a weakened Britain, was, however, so shocked by Roosevelt's statement to Stalin that American troops would be withdrawn within two years that he was determined to bring France back into the picture with a similar occupation role in Germany. He had against him Roosevelt, who had always disliked de Gaulle and favoured Pétain, and Stalin, who had never forgiven the French for crumpling up before the Germans in 1940 and so enabling Hitler to invade Russia a year later. It was only Churchill's strong pressure that finally persuaded them to give way on France. I do not, however, recall General de Gaulle, who was always condemning Yalta as a disaster because France was not there, ever recording any gratitude to Britain for this very important result of the Yalta conference.

The main protagonists left Yalta for the most part well pleased with what had happened. Churchill, indeed, showed this pleasure with rather more enthusiasm than wisdom in a statement in the House of Commons, recording his confidence in Stalin and his reliance upon Stalin carrying out his commitments. I think Churchill regretted this statement almost as soon as Neville Chamberlain regretted showing the cheering crowds at Number 10 the piece of paper signed with Hitler at Munich in 1938. But there is no reason to regard Yalta as having decided the fate of the world and above all that of Eastern Europe. That was the work of the Red Army, although I do not imagine I would ever persuade my Polish friends to regard it in that light.

11 | Moscow: Transition from War to Peace

1945–7

The 'captains and the kings' went their several ways from Yalta, Churchill and Eden by sea to Athens and thence to Cairo. I returned on an American transport plane to Cairo to pick up my wife. Our journey to Moscow was in some ways more eventful. The route even at that time, which was only a few months before the end of the war, which I would have had to follow in any case had I gone direct from London, was via Teheran and from there by Soviet aircraft. We were put up by our long-suffering Ambassador, Sir Reader Bullard, who had to act as host to all the British going to Moscow. He was an acknowledged expert on Middle Eastern affairs. He told me the first night that everything depended on the weather, and he might have the pleasure of our company for a few days, a week or even longer. I cheerfully said that I hoped this would give us the opportunity to see Isfahan, Persepolis and Shiraz, since Persia was the only major Middle Eastern Islamic country which my wife and I did not know. His reply was that on the contrary we had to be ready at six o'clock every morning in Teheran in case the Soviet plane should take off.

We and he were rather lucky; we only had three days' delay, which gave us time to see something of Teheran itself, a less exciting city than those I have just mentioned. It emerged that there had been relatively few flights for some time, and the diplomatic mail had piled up to the extent of over fifty large diplomatic bags, for which I had to be responsible with the help of one courier. We got them loaded fairly easily with the Embassy's assistance, and set out for Baku. This was our first experience of a Soviet wartime Dakota, a most reliable plane but with the petrol tank running down the middle and the Russians quite happily sitting on it smoking cigarettes. There were bucket seats, and no nonsense about seat belts or anything of that kind. These planes, on which we later travelled frequently in the Soviet Union, had the great advantage that you could talk to other people on board and get to know Russians far better than you could do in Moscow itself or could have done in a plane with a modern seating pattern. They were luckily retained even on the Berlin route for several years, although they might well have been replaced by more modern Ilyushins, because the Russian occupation forces in Berlin found it much easier to send loot including grand pianos back to Moscow in bucket-seat Dakotas than in Ilyushins with normal seating.

We landed in Baku in the evening, with the problem of our fifty diplomatic bags. We had to be responsible for getting them off the plane and then for taking them up to our hotel bedrooms which were on the top floor at the very end of the corridor. We just about managed this before the restaurant closed for dinner, and were then faced with the horrible thought that we had to get up especially early to get them all down again for the plane leaving at six am. It is the only time in my life that I have been a diplomatic courier, and the experience left me with even greater sympathy for the profession. We just made it before the bus left for the airport.

We then flew in good weather over the snowy expanses of southern Russia, and reaching Stalingrad, we began to come down. My wife and I thought this was a kind gesture on the part of our pilot to show us something of ruined Stalingrad and the famous battlefields. Not at all. Word had come through that the weather had deteriorated in Moscow and that we would have to spend the night – and maybe several nights – at the airport of Stalingrad. There had been little time to restore conditions since the general destruction. There was only one small hut on the airport for passengers benighted as we were, with one room for the ladies and one for the gentlemen, beds next to each other as in a hospital ward, and the loos what looked like a kilometre away over the snowy wastes. As my wife set out on this journey, she turned round to me and said, 'Frank, whatever happens in our married life, I hope you will always remember this.'

We were, however, very fortunate, as we only had to spend one night in these Spartan conditions and got to Moscow successfully the next day. We inherited the ground-floor flat in a late eighteenth- or early nineteenth-century house in one of the old quarters of Moscow. It was a pleasant but relatively small flat, luckily under the charge of two excellent Volga-German servants. They obviously came from well-to-do farming families who had been exiled by Stalin from the Volga region to Siberia during the war. One, Emma, was a tall and very ladylike parlourmaid, and the other, Amalia, the best cook we have ever had, although we were also lucky elsewhere, in our diplomatic career.

No sooner had we entered the flat, and I had just sat down, than the telephone rang. My wife picked it up. There was a female voice at the other end, asking in less than perfect English if she could speak to Mr Roberts. My wife explained that this was Mrs Roberts. 'No, no, my instructions are to speak to Mr Roberts.' So I took the phone, and it was fairly clear that the strategy of the NKVD had gone a bit wrong, because the instructions had been to establish an early contact with me without the intervention of Mrs Roberts. I never met the lady, but it showed the relative (but not 100%) efficiency of the NKVD, aided no doubt by the militia-men who stood constant guard on our door.

Shortly after our arrival we had to give a small dinner party, and Emma asked whether I could let her know who the guests were. I suppose I must have looked surprised, for she added that it was much better for her to know in advance than to have to find out for herself, since she must report in any case. We had no Russian guests at that early stage, so when I had finished the list her immediate comment was 'The Lord be thanked. There are no Russians.' She explained that my predecessor, Herr Balfour, constantly invited Russians. All that happened was that she nearly always had to change the seating when they failed to turn up.

Living conditions in Moscow were very difficult in those last months of the war, but there were peasant black markets where Amalia used to find good food at prices which would have been very difficult for Russians but luckily we benefited from a favourable pound-rouble exchange. The diplomatic corps and foreign journalists, who were treated similarly, also benefited from a special diplomatic shop. Caviar from the diplomatic shop and steaks from the black market ensured we certainly lived much better in austere wartime Moscow than we had lived in austere wartime London, but this would most certainly not have been the case for the average inhabitant of Moscow. I had hoped to have a few quiet weeks in which to begin learning Russian, which I had had no time to do in London, but this proved an idle hope. I did, of course, take Russian lessons, as did my wife. In the end we made between us about a quarter of a Russian speaker, my eighth being rather dull political and *Pravda* Russian and my wife's the far more useful and pleasant household Russian and Russian poetry which she much enjoyed.

The major issue facing the British Embassy when I arrived was the follow-through to the Yalta agreements on Poland and Eastern Europe. For Poland, a commission consisting of the Soviet Foreign Minister, Molotov, and the American and British Ambassadors, was set up. As I had been dealing with Poland throughout the war, I was the chief adviser to our Ambassador. We also had to deal with setting up what were presented as tripartite administrations in the other Eastern European countries, Roumania, Bulgaria and Hungary, of which I knew much less. The main issue was setting up the new Coalition Government in Poland. We on our side wanted to know who were the Lublin Poles who were always presented to us as the legitimate Government of Poland. The Russians were very reluctant to accept any of the candidates put forward by the Americans or ourselves as democratic Polish leaders from the West. We were not insisting upon the Polish Government in London, which had refused to have anything to do with the Yalta settlement and would in any case have been unacceptable to Moscow. But we were determined to get Mikolajczyk back to Poland, and there were other less famous names on our list.

It emerged before long that the Polish underground, which was still loyal to the Polish Government in London, had been persuaded against their better instincts to obey instructions to come out of hiding and announce themselves to the Red Army then moving through Poland. This was, on the face of it, a not unreasonable Soviet request. But as so often in Polish-Soviet relations, what would have been reasonable elsewhere was anything but reasonable when dealing with Russians in Poland. No sooner had the leaders of the Polish underground, who had taken over from General Bor-Komorowski after the disasters in Warsaw the previous year, declared themselves than they were arrested and brought to Moscow for a Soviet show trial in the Hall of Columns. When we and the Americans strongly protested, the Russians maintained that they had been guilty of acts of hostility against the Red Army, a claim which could not be put to the test. We felt that we had gone back to the starting point.

We had meeting after meeting with Molotov usually, since Stalin set the tone, late at night. As we sat in the Kremlin wrangling over the Polish question and making little progress, the Red Army was still advancing and frequently there was some big success, always greated by a great artillery salute and illuminations. Molotov, who had a wry sense of humour, used to comment that it was a good thing that the soldiers were doing so much better than we were. Finally, we did succeed in persuading Molotov to put us in contact with the Lublin Poles and they came to the British Embassy. There were five leaders, four of whom (Bierut, the President, Osubka Morawsky, the Prime Minister, Rola Zymirski, the Minister of Defence, and Spichalski) had been brought into Poland with the Red Army. The fifth member of the delegation turned out to be quite a different character, Gomulka, later Prime Minister of Poland, who had been with the Communist underground in Poland throughout the war and was not 'Moscow-trained'. The others were the relics of the Polish Communists and Socialists, many of whom had been shot by Stalin in 1937. They were only too ready to tread the path laid down by him.

As a junior member of our team, I was put with an interpreter to look after Gomulka, with whom I had rather an amusing conversation. He made it clear that he had little in common with the other four and was, unlike them, a patriotic Pole. In the course of conversation I referred to the attempts made in London during the war to bring the Poles and the Czechs together. Gomulka was surprised by this, and asked me why. I suggested it might have led to a solution of the vexed question of Teschen, claimed by both countries. I received the reply that there was no problem, since Teschen was Polish. I said that this time I was surprised to hear Gomulka talking just like Colonel Beck, the pre-war Foreign Minister. 'Oh,' said Gomulka, 'I must begin to think more highly of Colonel Beck than I have hitherto.' After this, I was not surprised a few years later when Gomulka was put in prison as a Polish nationalist. He did, however, when brought out of prison and later made Prime Minister in 1956, learn to toe the Russian line. But the others certainly did not strike us as very promising material for a free Polish Government to be recognized by the West.

The Russians were also holding up progress in San Francisco on setting up the United Nations. So Truman, who had inherited Roosevelt's policies and personnel, decided to break the deadlock by sending to Moscow Harry Hopkins, who had already played a major role in Soviet-American and also in American-British relations. By a mixture of carrot and stick – although it had to be mainly carrot, I imagine – Hopkins did persuade Stalin that something must be done, and agreement was reached before the end of the war enabling

Mikolajczyk and the other Western candidates to return to Poland as members of the new coalition Government, which was then recognized by all three Governments, we having to withdraw recognition from the exiled Polish Government still in London, with resulting but not insuperable complications in our relationship with the Polish Army still fighting in the field.

Similar difficulties were taking place in the other Eastern European countries. In each of them there was a tripartite commission of control, but the British and American members had less and less say in what was done. Things came to a head first in Roumania, where Vyshinski, the deputy Foreign Minister, was the Russian representative. Roumania had a relatively good record, insofar as a *coup d'état* had been organized with the support of the King to take Roumania out of its German alliance. There were at first few Communists in Roumania, and another coup had to be organized by Vyshinski to ensure Communist control. This was clearly unwelcome to London and Washington, and the British and American Ambassadors in Moscow were sent down to Bucharest to see if they could improve matters and incidentally safeguard British property interests, but they returned empty-handed.

Bulgaria, being a traditionally pro-Russian country, was left more latitude for a little bit longer. Indeed, when I passed through Sofia later in 1946, Petkov, the head of the Agrarian Party, was still able to meet me at lunch and talk to my mind much too freely for his own good – it was not very long before he too was arrested and shot. In Hungary, which was much nearer to the main fronts where fighting was still going on, the Russian control became absolute earlier, despite Churchill's agreement with Stalin on 50%–50% Eastern and Western interest. It therefore became very clear in these last months of the war that Stalin intended to control Eastern Europe completely and in his own way. Since Communists were rather rare in those countries, many of them having been killed by Stalin himself before the war, this control had to be exercised at first by coalition governments which superficially could have been made to appear acceptable to the West. But the Communists, however few, always held the key positions, for example in charge of the police and of justice, in which they could ensure control of the internal situation. For a year or two there were, however, some hopes in the West that these coalition governments might develop in a non-Communist direction, provided always that they remained, as the saying then went, 'friendly to Moscow'.

Another major issue that we were following from Moscow was the advance of our armies into Germany, and there was, of course, discussion of the various issues such as reparations touched on at Yalta and eventually settled at Potsdam. The Western advance in Italy was gaining ground, and seemed to cause intense suspicion in Moscow. This came to a head when the time came for the Italian surrender, naturally arranged by the Americans and the British, but which provoked Stalin to send a vicious and much-resented protest to Churchill. Churchill had pocketed his strong anti-Communist convictions when Hitler invaded Russia, and as the war went on he and Roosevelt, who had no more than the normal American anti-Communist background, began to find Stalin, although often extremely difficult, a man with whom, in the modern phrase, they could do business. They even developed some affection or at least regard for the Soviet leader, to whom they referred as 'Uncle Joe' and the strange concept that if they treated Uncle Joe 'like a member of their club' he might eventually behave as such. But by the end of the war Churchill, well before Roosevelt, was beginning to see that Uncle Joe had no intention of being a member of any Western club dominated by the Americans, least of all a 'country member', more especially since he had his own Communist or Cominform club which he could run in his own way with decreasing consultation with his wartime allies.

It was at this point, during the last weeks of the war, that Mrs Churchill came to Russia on the invitation of the Russian Red Cross, for whom she had raised a lot of money in Britain, used very well by many hospitals across the length and breadth of the Soviet Union. I was for much of her visit in charge of the Embassy, with my Ambassador Sir Archibald Clark Kerr attending the San Francisco Conference with his American colleague Averell Harriman. By this time I had developed a close relationship, begun in Lisbon in 1943, with my American opposite number, George Kennan. Mrs Churchill had a very successful tour round the Soviet Union and arrived back in Moscow just as the war was coming to an end.

We gave a lunch party at the Embassy with Mrs Churchill to celebrate the end of the war, the guests including the Kennans, the French Ambassador, General Catroux and his wife, a remarkable couple who had joined General de Gaulle at an early stage, and the former French Prime Minister, M. Herriot, who had been picked up by the Russians in a prison in eastern Germany. It was a moving occasion. Mrs Churchill felt that we should also have a thanksgiving service at the Embassy. I said that we had no Embassy chaplain, and that normally speaking either I or someone from the American or Commonwealth Missions took a Sunday service. She had just heard that the Dean of Canterbury, Dr Hewlett Johnson, known as the 'Red Dean', had arrived in Leningrad, and suggested that I might get him to Moscow for the service. I rang up the Red Dean, who was very pro-Soviet and always telling the world how well religion was treated by the Russian Communists. His first reaction was revealing. He said that the very last thing he had expected to receive was such a request in the Soviet Union. However, he was a man of great dignity, and rose to the occasion.

We also hosted a party in the Embassy with the Americans and the French and all the Commonwealth representatives to celebrate the end of the war, at which Mrs Churchill made a charming speech and there was a stirring message from the Prime Minister which did not reflect his growing distrust of Stalin. Behind the scenes things were not going well. The Russians were organizing a gala performance at the Bolshoi Theatre in Mrs Churchill's honour. The day before this great event a telegram came from Churchill for Mrs Churchill, who was staying at a Soviet guest house, saying that she was on no account to get mixed up in Soviet celebrations in her honour: 'Uncle Joe' was, he explained, behaving badly. When I handed the telegram to Mrs Churchill, we could not discuss it because of Soviet listening devices. Her immediate reaction, to my great relief, was to suggest that telegrams were surely sometimes delayed and that perhaps this one might have arrived *after* the gala performance. We agreed on this but I thought it my duty to ask how this was to be explained to the Prime Minister. She replied that she would remind Winston of Nelson putting up his telescope to his blind eye at the Battle of Copenhagen.

Relations between Churchill and Stalin had reached a serious state. One of the most urgent issues was to reach agreement on the date when the war was to end. The Germans were surrendering to the British and Americans in the west but continuing to fight hard against the Russians in the east. So George Kennan and I had no success in persuading the Russians that 8 May would be appropriate for joint Allied signature of the armistice with German military representatives in Reims. While we were still awaiting a Soviet reply, the Diplomatic Corps were invited to a gala performance at the Bolshoi that evening. We assumed this was to celebrate the end of the war, only to find, to

85

our amazement, that we were to celebrate the centenary of the birth of Popov, the 'inventor' of radio. During the interval George Kennan and I went to our host, Vyshinski, and said that, quite apart from the question whether Marconi had not been the inventor of radio, we had to leave to celebrate the end of the war at the nearby American Embassy. We later discovered that Marshal Zhukov had received belated instructions to go to Reims, pending another ceremony at Soviet Headquarters near Berlin.

The Russians later held a victory parade on Red Square. There were delegations from all the 'liberated' countries and we, the diplomats, stood with them at the foot of the Lenin Memorial, on which, as usual, the leaders were all standing. I found myself next to a Czechoslovak friend who had been in London during the war and who was now in the Government in Prague. When the band was blaring or the guns were firing he whispered to me, 'Why didn't Western troops come to Prague first?' I hardly satisfied him with my reply that Eisenhower's plan to end the war quickly did not provide for General Patton to divert his armoured columns to Prague.

Our direct concern in Moscow was with the Middle East, where the future of Iran was particularly important. We and the Russians had occupied most of Iran during the war, and it was important that not only we but also the Russians should leave. They were in no hurry to do so, since they were in occupation of a rich prize in Iranian Azerbaijan, so close to their own republic of Azerbaijan. They finally left in 1946 as the unlikely result of talks conducted in Moscow by the elderly and ailing Iranian Prime Minister, Qawan es Sultanieh. He remained most of the time in bed, where he received George Kennan and myself separately, indicating that we had nothing to worry about, since he was confident of success. To our great surprise his confidence was justified.

There were problems also with Turkey, since among Stalin's war aims was the return of Kars and Ardahan, which had been fought over during the Turkish-Russian wars of the nineteenth century. Far more important were the Dardanelles, where the Russians wanted to achieve their long-standing ambition of free movement for their own battleships from Black Sea bases. Stalin was not yet ready to intervene in the Arab world. Later on, when Ernest Bevin came to Moscow for the Four-Power conference in March 1947, Stalin left him with the clear impression at a long meeting that he was not even then working for the departure of the British, since he realized that he could not take

The author bicycling to the Foreign Office.

The author with his wife Celeste (Cella) in their Kensington flat.

News of the World cartoon showing the author returning from Lisbon (on a bicycle) with the Azores *Pact*.

Mrs (later Lady) Churchill outside a Kremlin church during her visit to the Soviet Union. The author behind on her left, Maisky (former Soviet Ambassador in London) on her right.

Ernest Bevin signing the Brussels Treaty.

The author with General Robertson, British Military Governor in Germany, leaving Northolt to represent the UK in Moscow negotiations.

The author in Moscow with his colleagues, the US Ambassador, General Bedell-Smith and the French Ambassador, M. Chataigneau.

Illingworth—London *Daily Mail*

"KREMLIN AUGUST FAIR"
No more minuets.

Time cartoon with Molotov pushing the author and his two colleagues into Stalin's 'Cavern of Mystery'.

The author with the Indian Prime Minister Jawaharlal Nehru at a Government House reception.

The author with Marshal Tito at one of the latter's hunting lodges.

The author (UK Permanent Representative at NATO) with the US President General Eisenhower: Robert Macnamara (Defence Secretary) behind and Randolph Burgess (US Permanent Representative) on the President's left.

The author with Harold Macmillan (Prime Minister), Sir Patrick Dean, Selwyn Lloyd (Foreign Secretary) and John Foster Dulles (US Secretary of State).

The author with Paul Henri Spaak (Secretary General) and Selwyn Lloyd.

The author with Selwyn Lloyd in Spain.

The author with Ted Heath (then Lord Privy Seal) and the Supreme Allied Commander of Europe, General Norstad, and Sir Evelyn Shuckburgh (on right).

our place and did not want to see the Americans even more strongly entrenched than they already were, more especially in Saudi Arabia. It was, however, thought desirable in London to warn the newly independent Arab States against probable Soviet infiltration tactics. While I was on leave in Cairo in the early winter months of 1946–47 I was instructed to make myself available for private talks on the Soviet scene with the heads of Government in Beirut, Damascus, Amman and Baghdad. They listened to me with great courtesy and I think interest, and I hope were at least encouraged to pursue realistic policies in their new relationship with the Soviet Union.

Moving into the Mediterranean, the main issue between us and the Russians was Greece. Under the notorious bit of paper handed to Stalin by Churchill at the Moscow Conference of 1944, Greece was to be within the Western sphere of interest. But there were strong Communist forces who had played a big part in the Resistance, poised to take over from what was at that time a rather weaker and disjointed group of anti-Communists, some Royalists and some not. The result was a bitter civil war in which Churchill committed British forces on the ground to prevent a Communist takeover in Athens. Stalin was careful not to oppose us openly. But the Yugoslavs, at that time playing a rather independent but anti-Western hand under Tito, did his work for him, as also did the Communist Albanians. Stalin could claim that he had stuck to the letter of his understanding with Churchill, although an important development for the future was his acceptance of large numbers of young Greek children to be educated and brought up as good Communists in the Soviet Union. Further down the Mediterranean, Stalin had put forward a claim (not, I think, a very serious one) for a direct share in the control of the former Italian colony of Tripolitania and also for a share in the international government of Tangier.

More important even than these quarrels, actual or potential, in the Middle East was the position in Germany and Austria, where the victorious Allies were taking over their different occupation zones and where, after Western forces had withdrawn from east of the Elbe, a central authority was set up in Berlin. Final agreement on occupation arrangements had been reached at the last Summit at Potsdam, during which Churchill was rejected by the British electorate and his place taken by Attlee and Bevin. The Russians were amazed and indeed put out by this, since they had clearly thought they would have an easier task with the British public at that time in criticizing a right-wing

Conservative Government than in dealing with what they could represent as Social Democratic traitors to the workers' cause. Although this may not have been widely realized in 1945, the Russians did indeed find themselves faced, in Attlee and above all in Bevin, with very experienced and influential members of Churchill's Coalition Government, fully in the picture on foreign affairs. In Bevin, the outstanding Trade Union leader in Britain for many decades, who had in his youth been tempted by Communism and had read Karl Marx from cover to cover during his remarkable process of self-education, they met a more formidable adversary than Churchill himself might have proved. The new American President, Truman, had been given few opportunities to master international affairs when Vice-President. At first he and his Secretary of State, Jimmy Byrnes, followed in Roosevelt's footsteps with a policy of accommodation with the Russians, before Truman revealed his own great qualities and strength of purpose.

These changes were to the Soviet advantage for the time being. By the time of Potsdam, Churchill had decided that cooperation with the Russians after the war would be extremely difficult, if not impossible. He had not yet reached the entirely negative assessment which later came out in 1946 in his Fulton speech but, as his exchanges with Mrs Churchill in Moscow had shown, he was anything but ready to give Stalin the benefit of any doubts. The Labour leaders, on the other hand, represented a party which, on the whole, was moved by the heroic deeds of the Russians during the war and by the general principle of Left speaking to Left, and Bevin himself wished to give every opportunity for post-war cooperation at least on the same level as our difficult wartime cooperation. So after Potsdam US and UK policies in Germany were similar and based on cooperation, however difficult, with the Soviet Union. This did not create insuperable problems in our first tasks of de-Nazification and de-militarization. But since procedures differed in each zone, the Russians introduced Communist concepts in the east while the British and the Americans introduced their different concepts of democracy in the west. As Stalin told the dissident Yugoslav leader, Milovan Djilas, the winners in a modern war were bound to introduce their social systems into conquered countries.

The special Russian pressure was for reparations, which had been discussed at Yalta and then again at Potsdam. From their own zone the Russians took everything they fancied, but the main German industrial strength was in the British zone, in the Ruhr and on the Rhine. We accepted that Soviet claims were in principle legitimate and to that extent we were prepared to help. But in return we expected Soviet cooperation in restoring the German economy to provide at least a minimal acceptable living standard. A tripartite commission, of which Sir Walter Monckton was the British head, was set up, which worked in Moscow in the autumn of 1945, with results that were never accepted as entirely satisfactory by the Russians, which hampered our immediate task of restoring the German economy, but in the long run contributed to the modernization of German industry. I recall a visit to Salzgitter in 1952 when I saw the same British firm dismantling one furnace under the continuing reparations programme and replacing it with the newest model by its side.

12 | Moscow: The Internal Scene 1945–7

In Moscow one of our main tasks at the Embassy was to assess probable Soviet behaviour after victory in the Great Patriotic War. The Soviet Union had suffered enormously, with millions of dead and with most of the western Soviet Union up to the Urals occupied and devastated by the German invasion and their own scorched earth policy. It seemed to most people probable that Stalin would want to get American assistance for the recovery of the Soviet Union on similar lines to that which he had got from the Americans and ourselves during the war. But it soon emerged that this was not his plan. The American Ambassador told me that he had been amazed at a recent meeting when Stalin had in effect turned down what amounted to an offer of continued UNRRA aid. In the light of hindsight, it is clear that Stalin did not wish to have any part, even as a beneficiary, in a recovery programme under American leadership. This became even clearer later on when the Soviet Union was offered but refused participation in the Marshall Plan.

There were other signs of reluctance to be involved in joint action. George Kennan and I used to have a monthly lunch with the then *Times* correspondent in Moscow, Ralph Parker, who later came out in his true colours as the Communist *Daily Worker* correspondent. He informed us in April, just before the end of the war, that the 'agitators' (lecturers) in the Soviet factories had been taking the line that it had been purely fortuitous that the Russians had fought the war with the Americans and British as allies against the Germans and the Italians, and it might equally well have been the other way; and that the British and the Americans should no longer be regarded as allies but as

90

capitalist adversaries. Stalin's behaviour over the next months bore out the correctness of this information.

We also found that Soviet propaganda was strongly anti-Western. Soviet prisoners of war, of whom there were very many coming back from German camps, were regarded not as heroes but as dangerously infected citizens who had to be put into camps if not worse before they could be released into Soviet life and incidentally tell their Soviet friends how much better conditions were in the West. This unfortunately was not clear enough to Western leaders when they had agreed at Yalta to the repatriation of Soviet prisoners of war, who, alas, also in practice included many White Russians who had been caught up in the very confused conditions in Central Europe at the end of the war.

In some ways, Stalin seemed anxious to continue with his position as a modern Russian Tsar who had relied upon the great Russian people, to whom he gave most of the credit, for the winning of the war. He had rehabilitated to a considerable extent the Orthodox Church. As a former seminarist in Georgia, he had realized its importance throughout the Middle East where he wished to spread Russian influence. The Russian Patriarch, Alexei, who had been a page at the court of the last Tsar, had been a prisoner digging on the Don Canal some months before the end of the war, when he was tapped on the shoulder by a guard and told he had to meet Stalin in Moscow. He was more than surprised to be appointed Patriarch and told that Stalin now wished to work with the Orthodox Church, more especially with the Orthodox Churches of the Middle and Near East.

The victorious Soviet marshals in the early days after the war were treated as very favoured citizens. They had the usual privileges, special shops, front seats in the theatres and in addition, sable on their greatcoats, with similar privileges for their wives. But it soon became clear that they were meant to toe the line. The leading and most independent of them, Marshal Zhukov, disappeared from view, and it was not until a year or more later that it emerged that he had been demoted to command the local garrison at Odessa.

Behind all this Stalin was determined, with the war over and patriotic devotion no longer the main requirement, to re-establish ideological purity, as he conceived it, under the strict control of the Communist Party inside and also, insofar as his power reached, outside the Soviet Union. This was fairly easy for him in the Eastern European countries occupied by the Red Army, but was also a possible goal in countries such as France or Italy where there were strong

Communist parties. The Communist International had been wound up to remove Western fears at the beginning of the war, but it was now replaced by the Communist Information Centre, or Cominform, under the leadership of Zhdanov, who was one of Stalin's tougher Politburo colleagues from Leningrad. The propaganda put out by the Cominform, welcomed by people like the Italian Communist leader Togliatti, was anything but reassuring from the Western point of view. The then British Empire was an obvious target. What the Russians described as 'national liberation movements' had already started in the Indian sub-continent and were obviously going to spread throughout the British colonies in Africa, which had been relatively untouched by the war, and in the Far East, where the Japanese takeover had much impaired British prestige.

At the British Embassy we had close working relations with the Soviet authorities: there were so many problems arising out of the war and the post-war settlement that we were in more or less constant though not always easy contact. Since many of these problems also concerned the United States, the working relationship between the two Embassies and, to a lesser extent, the French Embassy, also became very close. I was very lucky in my American opposite number, George Kennan, who was a great expert on the Russian scene, which I had not been. On the other hand, having served throughout the war in a fairly important position in the Foreign Office, I was in closer contact with my own Government at home than he was with his. So each had something to offer the other. We were also constantly meeting socially in the small but interesting Moscow diplomatic world.

There were a great many visitors from many professions coming to Moscow at that time, and there was none of the feeling that diplomats had later on in the Cold War of being entirely restricted to each other's company. The diplomats sent to Moscow at that time, even from the smaller countries, and the journalists, with whom the diplomats shared most facilities and worked closely together, were usually of high quality. The result was that there was a constant exchange of information between diplomats and journalists, and it was rarely a waste of time to converse with colleagues, including those in the Communist missions in Moscow, many of whom found themselves as much in a strange world as the Western diplomats. One of the Polish Communists once told me that it was like being on the moon!

Clearly, with the Soviet Union now playing such a major role in world affairs, it was important that a diplomatic mission to Moscow should have a rather more solid knowledge of what was going on in the Soviet Union than had hitherto been possible with rather small staffs. Exchanging information with correspondents and fellow diplomats was valuable but not enough. What I and my colleagues in the British Embassy found was that a thorough study of the Soviet press – not merely *Pravda* and *Izvestia*, but all the technical journals as well – was an excellent way of finding out what was really going on in the Soviet Union and also what were the long-term intentions of the Soviet leaders, since it was in this way that they gave a lead to their own people, which clearly they could not hide from others studying the media. We therefore set up in the British Embassy, and this was done on an even bigger scale in the American Embassy, a special section to read and report on the Soviet press which turned out to be invaluable. In London they must sometimes have got rather bored with all this information, but without it we should never have been able to follow what was going on and what were the long-term intentions of the Soviet Government. It was not, of course, possible to follow their immediate tactical moves since, unlike diplomats in more normal capitals, we were not constantly meeting Soviet politicians, each of them happy to tell us what they thought was going on. But maybe we were saved from many mistakes by not being able to pay too much attention to the last person we happened to have met.

I was lucky in having on the staff with me an excellent and very sensible expert on the Soviet scene in George Bolsover, later head of the London School of Slavonic Studies, and some bright younger diplomats, in particular Edward Tomkins and Adam Watson. We also had the advantage that during the war we had run a magazine called *The British Ally*, which was very successful in the Soviet Union. Second-hand copies used to sell at about fifty times the original price. At our press section in Moscow, which was open to Soviet citizens brave enough to enter the door, the one journal we had to chain was *Vogue*. Even at this time my wife was invited to a dress show in Moscow, and it was clear that the models, both female and male, were not yet used to the catwalk. When my wife was asked her opinion, she replied that it was all rather more serious than in the West, to which Mrs Molotov, who was running the show, replied that it was indeed very serious, because the dresses chosen would be worn by several million Soviet women. This is a far cry from Moscow today, when the

Soviet dress sense has much improved without having yet reached the sophistication of the West.

We naturally needed a number of people other than professional diplomats for the editorial staff of *The British Ally*. They had close connections with Soviet journalists and indeed with Soviet citizens with whom diplomats would not normally have come into contact. Another advantage we had in those days was that our junior staff, such as the messengers and porters, some of whom had come to Moscow because of their special interest in the Soviet scene, even perhaps because of leanings towards the Left if not towards Communism, also had their own contacts, sometimes at a surprisingly high level. One of these was a clever Cockney called Eldridge, who afterwards served on the Ambassadors' door at the Foreign Office for many years. In the rather difficult conditions in Moscow at the end of the war, relationships had been established between many of the foreigners in Moscow and Soviet girls, who after the war tended to get into trouble for having got so involved. One day Eldridge came to me and asked if I could assist him to get his trousers back. I asked him what on earth he meant. He replied that his girlfriend had been picked up by the police. He had left a suit in her room, and he wanted me to send an official note to reclaim it. When I told him I would do no such thing, he ended the conversation rather portentously, saying that if I could not help him, he would have to help himself. A few weeks later the Embassy received a third-person note from the Ministry of Foreign Affairs asking us to see that junior members of the British Embassy staff did not approach senior members of the Soviet Administration. Recalling our conversation, I asked Eldridge what he had been up to. He replied that he had written to Beria – and he was glad to say that he had got his trousers back.

Apart from privileges with concert, ballet and theatre tickets, the Diplomatic Corps had to arrange its own entertainment. There was a dance band provided by the American Embassy in which the otherwise rather serious-minded George Kennan played the double bass. They called themselves The Kremlin Crows. The American Embassy received a similar third-person note saying that, while the Soviet authorities did not wish to interfere with the legitimate relaxations of the diplomatic corps, they would be glad if care could be exercised over the names given to dance bands. From then on the American band called itself The Plucked Crows.

Slightly more seriously, we had an interesting experience in my family circle. Stalin had signed a treaty with the Poles and, as a Georgian without the usual Russian prejudices against the Poles, was anxious to set up institutes in each country. The one in Warsaw was started with around a thousand students learning Russian, and they were kept at it. The one in Moscow, whose Director used to call on my wife, was also started with a thousand Russian students, but before long it had sunk to well below a hundred.

All details were important in Moscow. It was useful to go round the shops to see what was on sale and what was not and for whom. Bookshops were extremely interesting; the Russians were keen readers, and many books were sold out on the very day of publication. This usually happened with the Russian classics, but fortunately the Russians did produce an enormous number of books, many of them foreign works in translation. We also travelled around Russia as much as we could. In those days there was no ban on foreign travel. It was difficult to get around, because most of the places one wanted to go to had suffered badly during the war. Hotels were being rebuilt with great difficulty. There was so much travel with returning soldiers and families coming together that it was hard to get seats on planes or trains. I do not therefore think that it was Soviet ill-will which made this kind of travel such a problem for diplomats. On the bucket-seat Dakotas and on the trains, and in the towns we visited far from Moscow, one had open conversations with Soviet citizens which one would never have had with the more cautious inhabitants of Moscow.

One such visit was to Kiev. Recalling Stalin's successful insistence on the Ukrainian and White Russian Republics being independent members of the United Nations, I decided as Chargé d'Affaires, tongue in cheek, to visit Kiev with one of my colleagues, Edward Tomkins, ostensibly to enquire into establishing relations with the supposedly independent Ukrainian Republic. When we arrived at Kiev, the Intourist guide at once offered us a visit to places destroyed by the Germans and seats at the ballet, but we said, no, we had come down on official business and wished first to call on the Ukrainian Foreign Minister. This was quite unexpected: nobody seemed to know who the Foreign Minister was or where he was to be found. I knew, because he was a rather famous old Soviet Communist called Manuilski. Plainly, we could hardly be told that there was no such person or that we could not call at the Ministry of Foreign Affairs. We were kept waiting a day or two, and then taken to one of the better buildings in Kiev which had survived bombardment, on which a brand new brass plate had been put with the words 'The Ministry of Foreign Affairs of the Ukraine'. At this point the Soviet arrangements went astray, because when we were received by the chief of protocol of the Ukrainian Foreign Ministry I recognized him as a Soviet diplomat I had last met a week before in an entirely different capacity in Moscow. The two days' wait had presumably been necessary to get him to Kiev. Having established our point, we turned to the Intourist programme.

It was important to see how much the Soviet Union had suffered and what was being done to get things going again. These visits, usually with my wife but sometimes with members of the Embassy staff, gave us a better picture of the Soviet Union than we had in Moscow, or even Leningrad, which had also suffered greatly, but which was even then well on the way to restoration. It was clear how ready ordinary Russians in contrast to the Establishment were to talk – and on the whole, how well-disposed they were towards their former wartime allies, despite all the propaganda.

13 | Diplomatic Life in Moscow: Arts, Science and Sport

1945–7

There were so many other aspects of life in Russia apart from politics, each of them with a bearing on the political scene. First, and perhaps most important, was the whole world of writing, the theatre and the arts. Stalin himself took a keen interest in these matters and after the war appointed Zhdanov as his cultural supremo to lay down what was acceptable and what was not.

Stalin's personal influence showed itself in strange ways, sometimes even beneficent. There was a famous Russian historian from Tsarist times, Evgenie Tarle, who came into his own during the war, when Stalin was encouraging Russian patriotism. He wrote what was considered to be the best biography of the Tsar Nicholas I, who defended Russia against Britain and France in the Crimean War. His first volume, very much approved by Stalin, appeared towards the end of the Great Patriotic War in an edition of some two million. His second volume was written after the war when the emphasis was again upon ideology and less upon wartime patriotism. It was condemned by Zhdanov and his Cultural Committee, and poor Tarle was no doubt preparing to end his days in Siberia. One night, the phone rang – for Stalin to tell him how pleased he was with the second volume. Tarle had the presence of mind to ask Stalin to pass this on to Zhdanov, whereupon the condemnation was reversed.

Rather less happily, while we were all awaiting the first post-war production of *Boris Goudonov*, Stalin took a keen interest in which of the two versions of this great opera was to be produced. He went frequently to the Bolshoi Theatre, always in a box with the curtains half-closed so that the audience could not actually see him although they knew that he was there. The version chosen on this occasion was the second, which ends with the Russian masses complaining bitterly about their fate under the authoritarian Boris. This was too near the bone for Stalin, and *Boris Goudonov* was taken off the programme, to reappear some months later with the first ending at the death of the Tsar without the popular discontent.

Even the musicians suffered. There was a play produced two or three years ago at the Old Vic in London which reflected pretty accurately what happened at a conference of Soviet musicians summoned by Zhdanov after our departure, in, I think, 1948. Zhdanov's object was to condemn the more independent musicians, like Shostakovitch and Prokoviev, for not producing the kind of Socialist music which could be at once appreciated by good honest Soviet workers. During the conference, Prokoviev and Shostakovitch were summoned to the Kremlin, as usual after midnight, wondering what their fate was to be. In fact, they got away pretty lightly, with Stalin explaining to them the kind of music he liked, Georgian folk music, and making it fairly clear that what he did not like was the kind of music which Shostakovitch was then producing. Shostakovitch was an unworldly person, who found it difficult to hold his own in discussions with Stalin, whereas Prokoviev was much more a man of the world who had lived for a long time in Paris and had married a Spanish wife before returning to Russia some time before the war. He managed to handle the situation better, benefiting also from the fact that he was writing operas on themes such as *War and Peace*, which suited Stalin's general political ideas. But Shostakovitch's career was set back a long way and he was indeed in deep trouble for many years, at least until the death of Stalin in 1953.

The ballet, opera, concerts and the theatre were among the main attractions of life in Moscow for diplomats at that time. In the immediate post-war period, Russian translations of Somerset Maugham and Oscar Wilde were particularly popular, not only because of the wit of the authors but because they had to be produced with a lot of Edwardian splendour, with evening dresses and white ties, which appealed to Muscovites then going through a very austere period. At the better-known classical theatres like the Arts Theatre, famous for Chekhov plays, and the Maly, which produced every kind of classic, the main difficulty was that the actors and actresses were engaged for life and acquired a sort of right to their parts, so that you would find Desdemonas and Ophelias continuing to play these parts well into their sixties and even seventies.

At the Arts Theatre, Chekhov had to be produced exactly as Stanislavsky had laid down, and if you had an actor doing a different gesture from the one that was expected, this was at once frowned upon. So there was a lack of excitement in these productions. Now and again some new play on what might be considered a delicate political theme would be produced, and at once there was a tremendous run on the tickets.

It was a great period for Russian ballerinas – Ulanova, Semeonova, Lepeshinskya and Plessitzkaya were the great names – and the standard of the dancing was very high. But the ballets were nearly all the old classics or on Soviet ideological themes, and anything new and modern was deeply frowned upon. This was noticed in London later when the Bolshoi came on their first visit after the war. Ulanova, then nearing her fifties, explained that the Russians had been through a period of interest in new ballets and had decided that it was better to return to the classics.

There was great excitement in Moscow when, as happened during our time in Moscow then and later when I returned as Ambassador, we had visits from the Royal Shakespeare Company and from Laurence Olivier and Vivien Leigh, then playing at the National Theatre at the Old Vic. There were also exciting visits from other countries, and in this respect Russia was wide open to influences from the outside world.

We saw some approved Russian writers, living in the writers' colony at Peredelkino. One of the most attractive was Marshak, who combined the advantages of writing good children's stories with being a translator into Russian of Robert Burns, a writer approved in Russia as a rebel against the then Scottish Establishment. I have always wondered how he found appropriate Russian translations for such very special Scottish verses. We heard of writers like Pasternak, but not of Solzhenitsyn, who was then in a labour camp. Pasternak was then reduced to making remarkable translations of Shakespeare because these could not be the object of ideological criticism.

Painting, which had before and during the Revolution reached such heights, was the worst sufferer under Stalin, the only pictures approved being those of Soviet Realism. Happy workers in factories or in the fields vied with Stalin himself embracing young children for official commissions, while behind the scenes were many young Soviet artists who, remarkably in contact with artists in the rest of the world, produced much the same kind of painting or sculpture as they did, remaining, however, dependent upon a few Soviet individual patrons and foreigners for their livelihood. Icons were approved as part of Russian history. Indeed, one of the old monasteries was later restored to become a centre for the restoration of icons. It always amazed me how many had survived the Civil War and the War itself and the strong attacks on religion in the earlier days of the Revolution.

We in the Diplomatic Corps were eagerly awaiting the re-opening of the museums closed during the war. The Russians were known to have taken to Russia all the pictures of the famous Dresden collection, and for some time it was their plan to open a museum in Moscow with these pictures, which would only have repeated what Napoleon had done with the pictures he had picked up in Germany and Italy. But when the Russians had to encourage their own Communists in East Germany and later on to create the German Democratic Republic, it became politically wiser to return the pictures to Dresden.

The pictures we were most wanting to see were the outstanding French Impressionists collected in the nineteenth century by two remarkable Russians, Schuikin and Morozov. They were the sons of Russian merchants with lots of money who went to Paris in the very early days of the great French Impressionists and picked up their best pictures for a song. During my brief visit to Russia in 1939 I visited the family house of Morozov, turned into a picture gallery with Morozov himself on the door. These pictures had been divided between Moscow and Leningrad but they took some time to reappear. At a dinner for British fellow-travellers, one of our journalists, Alexander Werth, asked the then Minister for the Arts, who had the rather surprising name of Romanov, when these pictures would be on show again, to be told that this would never happen, since such decadent art must not be allowed to spoil the taste of the Soviet population. Encouraged by the vodka and brandy, Alexander Werth then suggested that they could be sold profitably to the West, only to receive the reply from Mr Romanov that, while the Soviet Union could not protect the whole world, they would not themselves contribute to the spread of decadent art; and the pictures would remain in the cellars. Fortunately, good sense eventually prevailed and they were on show by the end of the Forties. But it was very much later – indeed, not until the Eighties – that the Russians were beginning to show the pictures of their own great artists of the early twentieth century, such as Kandinsky, Chagall and Malevitch.

100

We in the British Embassy were very fortunate in that Isaiah Berlin came to Moscow just after the war for a few months. He still spoke good Russian; he still had some relatives around; and being a man of great enterprise and looking anything but a foreign diplomat, he managed to establish closer contacts in the Russian artistic and writing world than diplomats could normally hope to do. He wrote a fascinating memorandum on the subject. We in the Embassy were glad to find that his conclusions on the whole supported what we had been reporting from our more superficial studies. Commenting on the Soviet Government's attitude to the arts in general, he wrote that they were like a rather minor public school wanting to win all matches against everybody else, deeply concerned and feeling hard done by when their efforts were not successful or not appreciated.

The Soviet authorities made some efforts to keep diplomats happy. There was a Mr Alexandrov, whose official position was the artistic director of Burobin, the department which looked after the practical requirements of foreign Embassies. He had good taste and a deep French culture. He used to give parties for selected diplomats, amongst whom we were lucky enough to be numbered, when he would put on the best Soviet films and introduce us to the best Soviet cinema people or, alternatively, produce some new film of Cocteau and generally suggest that Russia was artistically rather more abreast of the times than would appear from reading the Soviet papers. We met Eisenstein there and saw his final film on Ivan the Terrible. Stalin had much approved the earlier film, seeing in it certain resemblances to his own rule in the way Ivan managed to expand the Russian state, to behave ruthlessly towards the decadent Russian boyars and, above all, to build up the Oprichniki, who were, in terms of the sixteenth century, pretty close to the NKVD in their effective ruthlessness. But he was not happy with the sequel and it was never produced. This disturbed Eisenstein professionally and even more for the doubts it cast upon his own future.

We were also invited to see what the Russians did well, which was looking after their young children. They used to invite thousands of children to such places as the Hall of Columns in Moscow, where they were treated to what would elsewhere have been Christmas or Easter parties, given at the same time of year. There was a school with which the Embassy had been connected during the war, to which we were invited on special occasions. This, I think, was in many ways the best side of Soviet culture, although it was sad to think that all these charming children, who were on the whole well-educated, were also being taught Marxism-Leninism with all its anti-foreign connotations.

Much attention was also given by the Soviet leaders to the natural sciences, in many branches of which Russia had a good record. We were very lucky at the Embassy because the Australians had just opened an Embassy in Moscow, with a rather unusual Chargé d'Affaires, the distinguished scientist Eric Ashby, now Lord Ashby, and Vice-Chancellor of Cambridge some years ago. We ourselves had, in Brenda Tripp, a representative of the British Council without any pretensions to being a great scientist herself but expert at organizing scientific contacts. Between them they opened doors into the Soviet Academy of Sciences and its many daughter institutes.

They built up a particularly close connection with a Polish Nobel Prize-winner, a biologist called Parnas. He had been picked up by the Russians when they 'liberated' Lvov, and brought to Russia. He was given a suite in one of the Moscow hotels and a dacha in the country. He once told us that whilst he could not complain in any way of his treatment he found it very irritating that anything he wanted he could only obtain by writing directly to Molotov, then Foreign Minister. What he then needed were bedroom slippers, and he found it hard to bring himself, in the middle of the war, to ask Mr Molotov for them. More seriously, Parnas told us that the Russians would be good at aspects of science which, in military terms, required a field marshal and one or two generals and then a large number of ordinary troops, but much less good in fields which required a smaller but more expert band of colonels and brigadiers. Nuclear science fell into the first category, and his own discipline of biology into the second.

Where we might have expected good contacts but were disappointed was in the case of the great physicist, Kapitza. He had been one of the most promising young Cambridge physicists under Rutherford in my time at Trinity. He had gone to Russia in the early Thirties to see his old home, but the Russians would not let him return to Cambridge. It ended up rather oddly with Trinity having to send him his laboratory equipment so that he could continue his studies in Russia. Perhaps because of the potential difficulties of his position, he went out of his way not to have contact with the British Embassy, even during our wartime alliance. He got into trouble with Stalin at the end of the war, when the Russian troops were discovering all kinds of scientific establishments in Germany and other parts of Western Europe about which Kapitza had never told them.

We also heard a certain amount about German space and rocket scientists, who had been picked up by the Russians. They were supposed to be concentrated in a rather fine old house with big grounds outside Moscow but nobody knew where it was. My wife and I used to have our own 'walks in the woods' on Sundays. On one of these walks we went through a gate which was normally closed into a park, and heard people talking German. When we asked them who they were, they were happy to tell us, and we found that we had discovered this great centre. On another 'walk in the woods' we found ourselves in the garden of the Patriarch's dacha and were asked to stay to tea. In these ways even diplomats sometimes evaded the tight NKVD controls.

Sport was an important feature of Soviet life. At football, the Russians were already becoming quite good, their top teams being the various Dynamo teams, above all in Moscow or Kiev. These were run by the NKVD, the players, although technically amateurs, having positions in the NKVD which allowed them to concentrate on football. Some time after the end of the war we received an urgent request from the Ministry for Foreign Affairs for visas for a Dynamo football team with several 'camp-followers' oddly described as 'tennis trainers' to play football in England. As this was the beginning of summer, we were a little surprised and asked London for guidance. Nobody could think of any such invitation until the President of the Football League, Stanley Rouse, suddenly remembered that just after the war he had told his Russian opposite number in the course of general conversation that he hoped that one day a Soviet team would come to England. This was construed into the invitation which the Russians were now taking up.

It was a most inconvenient moment, outside the normal football season, but it was decided – in my view, wrongly – to have the Russians along. Our teams were out of training. The Russians did rather well, and were naturally pleased to have defeated or drawn with well-known English teams like Chelsea, so much so that they produced a successful musical in Moscow called *The Eleven Unknowns*. It was quite amusing, complete with an English beauty instructed to seduce the best Russian player on the night before the match. The whole affair was a warning that it does not always pay to fit in with last-minute Soviet proposals.

I and my American colleague did our best to persuade the Russians that they should do something about golf. We were not, in the end, successful. Golf was regarded as an individualist capitalist sport. I did break the ice when I explained that in St Andrews, the home of the game, every citizen including the very poorest, was welcome on the golf links, for what was even then the very small sum of sixpence. We also suggested that it would be a suitable sport for some of the Russian Generals, who appeared rather portly on parade in Red Square. We made enough progress for the Chief of Protocol to tell me that the Politburo had expressed some interest, and to ask me to have the rules of golf translated into Russian for submission to them. I did not think this would help matters much. Whatever interest the Politburo may have shown soon dwindled.

While I never thought of cricket as a suitable game for the Soviet Union, one cricket match took place in Moscow in the summer of 1945 between the British Embassy under my captaincy and the British Military Mission, which rated a column report in the *New York Times* – more, I think, than that paper has ever accorded to far more prestigious Test Matches. We played on a football ground with a right of way running across the pitch used at intervals by elderly Russian 'baboushkas' returning from market. Between these crossings I made the top score of thirty-two runs, compiled entirely in singles. This left me with a bad knee and unable for some days to join in the dancing which was a welcome feature of Moscow diplomatic entertaining. I had, however, achieved in US publicity terms more than the greatest international cricketers of our time!

A major aspect of life in Moscow was dealing with visitors, who always came to Moscow with strong prejudices, fairly evenly divided in the days after the war between those who felt that our great Russian allies could do no wrong and others who felt exactly the reverse. The first trade union delegation was from the Iron and Steel Federation, who took a sensible view of the Russian scene – quite friendly, but by no means bowled over by what they saw. They sent me their report, which reflected this attitude. But such was Soviet sensitivity that a brief critical comment on the Moscow Metro system over-shadowed everything else in the report when I discussed it with the head of the Soviet trade unions, Kuznetsov, later Head of State.

One of our more colourful visitors was a British jazz singer called Gerry Scott. In those days jazz was very much frowned upon in Russia, and I cannot think why she was allowed in. She filled the halls and was a great success. She was modest with it all and told me that the Russians ought to have had Ella Fitzgerald, who was so much better. She had a German manager, and they decided to get married. For the only time in my diplomatic career I exercised what is a diplomatic responsibility, if required, of performing an official wedding, which they wanted in addition to the rather more colourful ceremony they had at the Moscow Palace of Marriages.

Like many people who came to work in the Soviet Union, she was worried about what to do with her rouble fees, and ended up buying air tickets on a big scale to cover her world travels. The same problem disturbed another and more distinguished British visitor, J. B. Priestley, who came with his then wife and as a left-wing friend of the Soviet Union. He claimed to have large royalties in a blocked Soviet bank account as the 'most read foreign author' in the Soviet Union. Since he was the guest of the Russians everything was paid for, but as a good Yorkshireman he was indignant that he could not use his own roubles.

It was through another visitor, not quite a Communist, Mr Pritt MP, that my wife got into the Kremlin Hospital, because his wife fell ill and was given the best treatment. As my wife had also seen the inside of normal Soviet hospitals, visiting our own Embassy patients and at one point our cook, who suddenly had to be operated on for appendicitis, she realized what a vast improvement there was in the Kremlin Hospital, which was first-class by any standards. In the Embassy we took the view that if our people got ill it was better that they should either have a simple illness, when they could be sent back to England, or a very complicated one, which would ensure treatment in the Kremlin Hospital. Treatment in-between was rugged, as one or two of our Embassy wives, who in my view rather rashly decided to have children in Soviet hospitals, discovered.

To turn to more official visits, we had in addition to Field Marshal Montgomery and the Commander-in-Chief of the Mediterranean Fleet, whose visits are covered in a later chapter, a successful naval visit to Leningrad itself by Admiral Fraser, then Commander of the Home Fleet.

Another interesting visitor was Harold Wilson, then a very young President of the Board of Trade. There was a tendency after the war for politicians to come to Moscow with the idea that they alone knew how to negotiate with the Russians, and I was rather worried at the prospect of so young and inexperienced a British Minister negotiating about animal feed-stuffs with Mikoyan, who was the most experienced 'carpet-dealer' in the business. But I need not have worried. At the end of the first session Mikoyan indicated that, since each side knew the other's position, there was no point in wasting time and a deal could be struck at once on Soviet terms! Harold Wilson, without even consulting his own staff or myself as Chargé d'Affaires, at once replied that in that case they had indeed been wasting their time; he hoped his aeroplane was still at the airport so that he could leave in the morning. Mikoyan rapidly climbed down. After several days of this, during which Mikoyan repeated his tactics, Harold Wilson was able to return to Moscow at the end of 1947 to sign an agreement more or less on the terms he had wanted.

This was the beginning of Harold Wilson's prolonged interest in the Soviet Union. In office he was often looking for special trade deals with the Russians; out of office he became connected with a British timber firm trading in the Soviet Union; after his final resignation he became President of the Anglo-Soviet Association and again paid visits to the Soviet Union, but of course without the possibility of seeing his old friend Mikoyan, who had disappeared long before.

Although we made no progress on major matters we did at least sign a peace treaty with Bulgaria. Britain was still in a period of austerity, and the documents with which I was supplied were in a papier-mâché folder, with no Morocco leather or gilt. Nor had we yet brought our diplomatic uniforms up to date, while the Russians were then putting all their diplomats into brand-new uniforms. I was received by Vyshinski in his splendid uniform as Deputy Foreign Minister; I still had my old Third Secretary's uniform with gold braid only on the cuffs. Vyshinski accused me of being improperly dressed in a Third Secretary's uniform although I was a Minister. He was even more scathing about our austerity documents. The Soviet documents were in magnificent vellum with plenty of gilt, beautifully printed on excellent paper. This was a typical example of the Soviet sense of relative values at that time, when living conditions even in Moscow were very difficult indeed.

14 | The Kennan Long Telegram and the Roberts Long Despatches

1946

The really serious problem facing George Kennan and myself in the absence of our Ambassadors for such long periods was how to bring home to our Governments the difficulties, and at times the impossibility, of working with Stalin's Soviet Union. I did not want to give the impression that we should not try to get on with our former wartime ally if we possibly could, nor that the Soviet Union was just another totalitarian state like Hitler's Germany, although often its treatment even of its own nationals was even worse. At the same time, I did want to bring home that the only way to have any acceptable working relationship was on a basis of real understanding and tough realism.

George Kennan's task was, I think, more difficult than mine, because until Byrnes's Stuttgart speech in the autumn of 1946 the Rooseveltian approach was still in favour, and the main task of American diplomacy was to work with Stalin's Soviet Union, however difficult. In the United Kingdom we had never gone so far down this road, although Bevin certainly wanted to give a policy of continued cooperation every chance. Indeed, early in the spring of 1946, when a new Ambassador, Sir Maurice Peterson, came to Moscow, he arrived with Bevin's proposal for a new peacetime treaty of fifty years with the Soviet Union to replace our wartime alliance. I was very sceptical about this, and indeed Stalin showed no interest in it whatsoever, which was perhaps just as well because otherwise we would have been misled.

By February 1946 we had so peppered our home Departments with bits and pieces of information and warnings of all kinds that first George Kennan and then I myself were asked to put down on paper our considered views on relations with the Soviet Union. George Kennan was asked first, and produced what is now well-known as 'The Long Telegram', which formed the basis for his subsequent article signed X in *Foreign Affairs*, on both of which American policy towards the Soviet Union was based. I doubt if any diplomatic document has had a greater effect than Kennan's Long Telegram. With his deep knowledge of Russian history and Soviet ideology, he explained why the Soviet state could not be treated like any other country, hostile or friendly, and why it should be regarded as an adversary with long-term ambitions which were inconsistent with Western democracy, but also as a country with which, if approached with strength and realism, one could hope to live in peace in a way which had proved impossible with Hitler's Germany.

George showed me his Long Telegram and allowed me to send a summary back to London. London then asked me for my own views. With the help of our own experts, particularly George Bolsover, Adam Watson and Edward Tomkins, we produced a series of three despatches which were together rather longer than the Long Telegram. When I left the Soviet Union in 1947 I was given the unusual honour for a mere Chargé d'Affaires of a command from King George VI to visit His Majesty for a talk about Russia. His Majesty charmingly opened the conversation with 'You wrote very interesting – but very *long* – despatches from Russia,' to which I had to plead guilty.

The conclusions reached by George Kennan and myself were very close, as indeed they were bound to be; we were living in the same place, studying and reacting to the same policies of the same person, Stalin, and we were in constant consultation with each other. Recently there has been some interest among British historians in what has sometimes been called my Long Telegram, and some of them were surprised that the two were so similar. I should have been surprised if they had been different in essentials. Mine did, of course, differ in the sense that the British and American positions were different and that I was writing not only about the position in the Soviet Union, as George Kennan had been, but also about Soviet policy towards the British Empire and what our policy should be in handling this unusual and difficult situation. I was looking at it from the point of view of a declining power, or at best one hoping to recover its former position, vulnerable to Soviet propaganda and potentially to Soviet diplomatic action in years ahead when we would be dismantling the British

Empire and turning it into a Commonwealth – problems with which the Americans were not faced.

We were both, however, agreed that what was needed was a long-term approach to the Soviet Union and not just reacting in the traditional Anglo-Saxon way to situations as they arose. Like Kennan, I advocated a planning staff in London, not just for the Foreign Office, still less only for the Northern Department, which would keep constantly under review Soviet activities worldwide. In the American case, this affected the building up of the Planning Staff, and George Kennan returned to Washington to head it. In my own case, it resulted in the setting up of a Russia Committee under the future Lord Gladwyn, which reported to the Foreign Office and which I found working well when I returned as Private Secretary to the Foreign Secretary at the end of 1947 and became one of its members.

We both agreed that, provided we took a realistic view, and provided that we understood that the policies, at all events of Stalin's Soviet Union, were bound to be adversarial, there was no reason why we should come to war with each other, and equally, there was a possibility even of cooperation on issues where our interests did not diverge. I was writing to a Foreign Office which had many of these considerations already in mind, although at times it seemed to me too inclined to take a black or white approach, and to ignore the many more possible shades of grey in between. Unlike George Kennan, I took into account our historical relationship with Russia, always ideologically hostile, often involving conflicts of interest worldwide, but rarely leading to war (the exceptions being the Crimean War and Intervention after the First World War), and resulting in cooperation and alliance in major world conflicts against Napoleon, the Kaiser and Hitler.

There were, of course, some differences between the Embassy and London. We in Moscow, whilst perhaps even more shocked by Stalin's behaviour, of which we had firsthand evidence, particularly when he began again to execute his people or to send them to concentration camps, were at the same time more ready to emphasize the possibility of continued cooperation in certain limited fields. Back in London there was a tendency in some circles to rule out any kind of cooperation with the kind of country which they thought we had so accurately described. But the differences were slight, and my own despatches were well received in London and certainly did me no harm in my future career. They must have contributed to Mr Bevin's invitation to return to London as his Principal Private Secretary. It is gratifying that historians have been studying them and finding out that it was not only George Kennan who was sending such warnings and recommendations from Moscow.

Looking back, I suppose that this was the most important thing that I was able to do in a long Foreign Office career. Diplomats in Moscow have very little chance of influencing Soviet Government behaviour, but they do have more opportunities than in most other posts of influencing their own Government's policies; and this is an equally important part of diplomacy, although it can be more difficult and even dangerous. I was fortunate in having an outstanding Foreign Secretary, Ernest Bevin, who understood Marxism-Leninism, who was a realist and, whilst by no means agreeing with everything I wrote, was ready to take in the message and to act upon it. Luckily, also, he had the authority in the then Labour Government to get his policies approved. As so often in foreign affairs, policies were not changed overnight. They usually change only gradually, with both ends of the equation – the policy-makers at home and the advisers overseas – thinking on rather similar lines, so that a door already ajar can then be opened, as indeed happened in this case, with our policies towards the Soviet Union finally adjusting to what I would consider more realistic if, alas, more adversarial policies towards the end of 1946, but flexible enough to react to changes for the better in the Soviet Union under Khrushchev and Brezhnev, in their earlier years, and above all more recently under Gorbachev. I hope that George Kennan and I made some contribution in 1946 to a relatively consistent Western policy of realism, strength and firmness, coupled with understanding and readiness for East-West discussion and negotiation which, pursued for nearly half a century, has led to the rejection of Communist regimes throughout Central and Eastern Europe, to German unification and to major changes within the Soviet Union itself.

15 | Official Contacts

We saw a lot of the Russians, including, from time to time, Stalin himself. As Chargé d'Affaires of one of the three great victorious powers I was treated very well by the Russians and could see Molotov or Vyshinski whenever I needed to. But I never at that time did business directly with Stalin, who reserved himself for prime ministers, foreign ministers, VIP visitors and important correspondents when he wished to make public announcements. For Molotov I acquired a grudging respect. He was, of course, 'Mr Nyet', and nobody could be more exasperating in repeating the same negative position during a long negotiation. But once the word had come from Stalin to conclude and reach agreement, no one was more efficient and quick in reaching a solution.

For his Deputy Mr Vyshinski I acquired a complete contempt, I am sorry to say. Unlike Molotov, he had not been an early Bolshevik but a Menshevik, a position which he was always trying to live down. He was of Polish origins, and had come to fame in the Thirties as the prosecutor in the many show-trials in which Stalin got rid of the majority of the Central Committee and of his Politburo colleagues. There are lawyers now in the Soviet Union, with one of whom, Vaksberg, I have been in touch, who have written books to show how Vyshinski twisted Soviet law in order to force Stalin's victims into confession. Vyshinski was clever, with no kind of moral inhibitions. But he was a toady as well as a bully. I was delighted to note in an otherwise very bland autobiography in which he had little ill to say about anyone that Gromyko let himself go about his former chief, Vyshinski, to the extent of saying that he remembered once, when

Beria rang Vyshinski on the telephone, Vyshinski's immediate attitude was that of a dog cringing before its master. I saw Vyshinski in a similar cringing attitude towards Stalin on one occasion.

At one of my meetings with Vyshinski, when the flagship of the Mediterranean Fleet, HMS *Liverpool*, was to pay a visit to Sebastopol, which until then had been an entirely closed port having been very much battered during the war, I had to insist on my Naval Attaché and also myself being given facilities to fly down to Sebastopol to meet the Commander-in-Chief. Vyshinski produced every kind of excuse to prevent this, until finally I had to take it upon myself, with no authority whatever, to say that in that case I was going to telegraph at once to the Commander-in-Chief, who at that time was approaching the Dardanelles, to tell him that he was not wanted in the Soviet Union and that he should turn back to the Mediterranean. Within a very short time there were places on aeroplanes to Sebastopol, and there would be somewhere for the Naval Attaché to stay there. I was going later, and would be staying in HMS *Liverpool*.

In 1947 at a Buckingham Palace reception during the last of the then series of Four-Power meetings, as I had just come back from Russia, I was asked to see that Princess Margaret, who was then very young, met some of the Russians. When I asked HRH whom she wished to meet, rather to my surprise she opted for Vyshinski. So I brought a very flattered Vyshinski to her. I introduced him, correctly, as the Vice-Minister for Foreign Affairs, but he had realized why the Princess wanted to talk to him and said in his fluent French, 'And please add, the well-known prosecutor in the trials of the Thirties.' Princess Margaret played him like a fish. I got rather worried at one time, but he was so flattered that it came out all right.

Although I never then did business with Stalin, I did have one rather startling passage with him at a banquet for the two Foreign Ministers, Bevin and Byrnes, towards the end of 1945. It was one of the typical Kremlin banquets of those days, with far too much to drink. It went on into the small hours, followed by a cinema show with more drink. At about three in the morning everybody was staggering out. There were twelve British and twelve American guests, and the Soviet 'establishment'. I was the least important British guest, and Dr Conant was also number twelve among the Americans, so we were alone when all our seniors had departed. Stalin was interested in Dr Conant, who had been involved in nuclear affairs, and talked to him for some time. When he left, I was alone. Somebody obviously whispered to Stalin,

'This is the British Minister, Mr Roberts,' whereupon Stalin said, 'I know you. You are our enemy,' which to me, all alone in the Kremlin, was a bit of a shock. While I was thinking what to say, he added, 'And what's more, you are a member of the British intelligence service.' Having done my best in my rather poor Russian to reassure him that I was neither of these things, I left the room wondering whether I had better not ask for transfer to London by the next plane. Thinking it over when more sober in the morning, I realized that Stalin had in mind that I had been fighting the Polish battle frequently during the war against what he regarded as Russian interests; and I was told by a Russian friend that he could not have paid me a higher compliment than 'promoting' me to the British intelligence service. What is, however, interesting in an otherwise silly story is that Stalin knew who was the twelfth member of the British contingent, and knew about him, too. I cannot believe that even Mrs Thatcher would have taken the trouble to recall the biography of the twelfth member of a Soviet delegation in similar circumstances at Number 10 Downing Street. This is the kind of detail one always had to have in mind when negotiating with the Russians. The top man handling the negotiations had always mastered his brief, and one had to master one's own to a degree that would not be thought necessary anywhere in the Western world.

Another notable Kremlin banquet which I recall was when Field Marshal Montgomery finally visited the Soviet Union. This was in 1947, after the Cold War had descended and when relations were anything but good. I was in charge of the Embassy when a telegram came from the Field Marshal saying that he was now able, in the interval before taking up his new post as Chief of General Staff, to accept Marshal Zhukov's invitation, which he had been given in Berlin at the end of the war, to visit Russia, and would like to come the following week.

By this time Marshal Zhukov had disappeared and might not even be alive. I was not sure whether with the Cold War already started the Russians would want to see a British Field Marshal. Once again, I had to speak to Vyshinski, who pointed out that Marshal Zhukov was not available but added that his successor, Marshal Koniev, would be delighted to receive Field Marshal Montgomery, whom they were obviously very curious to see in Moscow. The Field Marshal arrived, wearing his famous sheepskin jacket, and in the course of two or three days was shown all the appropriate Soviet military establishments. At the Artillery Academy they were showing him the artillery formations drawn up for the crossing of the Don. Having explained that there were so many guns to the kilometre, they got no response from the Field Marshal. Three times this was repeated, whereupon he said, 'I understood you the first time. Only, I had more guns to the mile at Alamein, so why should I be impressed by this?'

Marshal Koniev gave him a gala evening at the Bolshoi, in a box with many of the leading Russian Marshals in which I was the only civilian. By this time, most subjects of conversation had been exhausted, and in the interval Monty turned round to his hosts and said, through the interpreter, 'Have you read my St Andrew's Day lecture?' which the Russians had not heard of. They expressed polite interest and asked what it was all about. 'Military leadership,' said Monty. More polite interest was expressed. 'I had this lecture reprinted and distributed round the officers of the British Army, captains and above. You could not do better, Marshal, than to have this translated into Russian and distributed round the officers in your army. But standards in education, I am told, being rather different, I think in your case perhaps colonels and above would do.' At this point I looked for the door. I saw the Russian Marshals looking at each other, deciding whether they should be deeply offended or whether it was just what they had been told about the Field Marshal's rather unusual approach. Luckily they opted for the second alternative.

The next night we accompanied Monty to a Kremlin banquet hosted by Stalin. The Russians are good hosts, and although they then normally started their banquets late and went on well into the night, on this occasion, to meet Monty's known preferences, we started about an hour or two earlier than usual and everything was served with such speed that our Service Attachés, who had never been at a Kremlin banquet before and were sitting at the end of the table, hardly had time to eat at all. The dinner was all over in about an hour and a half, whereupon Monty informed Marshal Stalin that he had had a very good evening but would like to go to bed early, since he had to fly back the next morning, and made to take his leave. This was too quick for the Russian hospitality, because Stalin insisted on his waiting a few minutes longer in order that a Russian Field Marshal's greatcoat with fur lining should be duly presented. I recall with amazement that we were out of the Kremlin by about ten o'clock that evening. Monty was taking me home on his flight the next morning, and wore his Russian greatcoat as he was saying goodbye and getting on the plane. As the door shut Monty looked round at me and said, 'Nice coat they've given me. And this fur, now. What would it be?' I said, 'Well, I think it's usually sable.' 'Sable?' he said. 'Are you sure it's sable?' I said, 'Not absolutely, but I'm pretty sure.' 'How would I get to know?' I said, 'Well, Field Marshal, when you get home you might ask one of your lady friends.' 'Would she know?' asked Monty, to my surprise.

The Four-Power Conference in Moscow, which lasted seven weeks in March and April 1947, was a more serious occasion. By this time we and the Americans had decided that we had to build up our two zones together in order to restore the German economy, which involved moving towards a West German administration. The British Government had also decided that they could no longer bear the expense of supporting Greece and Turkey in the eastern Mediterranean and were trying to hand over these responsibilities to the Americans in what became known later as the Truman Doctrine, which was the first US step towards NATO in the acceptance of lasting foreign commitments. General Marshall had become the American Secretary of State, and although they were temperamentally and in their backgrounds very different, he and Ernie Bevin worked well together. The main task was to discover whether it was still possible to find some basis for working with the Russians, particularly in Germany but also in other parts of the world. The French had come to Moscow still hoping to reach some agreement on their own with the Russians which would enable the Saar or the Ruhr or both to be kept under French or Allied control. It was, in fact, in Moscow that Stalin finally refused to consider any Franco-Soviet deal. Bideault concluded that France should join the French zone together with the Anglo-American bi-zone to form what was before long to become the Federal Republic.

It was during one of our meetings that the news came that Truman had announced the Truman Doctrine. I gave Bevin this information, which he greeted with much relief. It was also during this conference that I met John Foster Dulles for the first time. Although it was a Democratic administration, he had been invited as a Republican, but there was really nothing for him to do. The American Ambassador, General Bedell Smith, had asked my wife, who by that time was rather expert on the museums and the commission shops selling antiques, to look after Mr Dulles and take him round, which she was very happy to do. John Foster Dulles has not usually had a good press in Britain, and he certainly did not get on well with Anthony Eden as Foreign Secretary, although the faults lay on both sides. But he never forgot these small kindnesses, and when I went to Washington in 1953 as a senior British official with Lord Salisbury, who was replacing a sick Anthony Eden, John Foster Dulles, now Secretary of State, invited me alone to a charming small family dinner, at which he displayed an unexpectedly happy side to his character.

It was a long seven weeks in Moscow, and members of the British and the French and the American delegations got to know each other well. We were constantly giving lunch and dinner parties throughout the whole of the seven weeks, and were grateful for our admirable Volga-German servants. The British, for once, were delighted to spend a long time in Moscow, because this was the coldest winter in Britain since the war, and Moscow was at least better heated than London. As I had been in charge of the Embassy for such a long period since 1945, the British delegation tended to come to me for advice, and Bevin asked me to return to the Foreign Office in the autumn as his Principal Private Secretary.

For those of us who had been in Moscow during and since the war and who already had our contacts, the existence by the end of 1946 of a much colder climate in social and official intercourse, which led on to the Cold War after the Berlin crisis of 1948–49, was not so obvious as it was to new arrivals. By the beginning of 1947 life was becoming dangerous as well as difficult for the Russians. There were strange stories which one could never quite confirm. Anti-Semitism was rife, and the manager of the very distinguished Jewish theatre in Moscow, Mikhoels, disappeared and was afterwards reported to have been killed in a motor accident in Belorussia organized, as was later discovered, by the NKVD.

In the British Embassy we noticed the change first in the attitude towards our monthly paper, *The British Ally*, and in the contacts which its editorial staff had with their Russian opposite numbers. Our practice during and after the war was to invite Soviet editors to an annual dinner. At one such dinner my wife found herself next to Borodin, the editor of the *Moscow Evening News*, then by no means the important Glasnost paper which it has become but purely an English-language paper for the benefit of the Diplomatic Corps. He had been the main Soviet agent in China in the Twenties and early Thirties, during the period when Chiang Kai-shek was taking over power and working with the Communists. There had come, however, the troubles in Shanghai, about which Malraux wrote a remarkable book, in which Chiang Kai-shek turned on his Communist allies and arrested or killed many of them. The survivors emerged much later to make the Long March under Mao. Borodin had been closely involved in all these events, which had not advanced his career with Stalin. He was lucky to be still alive and editing the *Moscow Evening News*. He chanced his luck further by telling my wife that the only thing in which the Soviet Union was ahead of other countries was its Security Police and that Soviet champagne was made on the principle of the bicycle pump. Not surprisingly, he disappeared in Stalin's next purges.

In 1946 we still published *The British Ally*, but relations had distinctly cooled. We never took the initiative in breaking off any kind of relationship, and so we sent out invitations for the usual autumn dinner. As we had expected, nearly every one of our earlier editorial contacts had previous engagements, and only people who were involved in the actual printing of the paper had permission to accept. We were, however, surprised to find two editors who turned up and were extremely ill at ease to discover themselves almost alone. We found that the previous year they had not been invited, so obviously the warnings not to come had not gone to them.

But worse things were happening to the Russians. A famous victim at that time was Molotov's wife, who had her own career and had been, among other things, the Commissar for cosmetics production. Molotov had not been able to save her (or even to try to save her) at the Politburo meeting when Stalin condemned her to exile in Siberia. Later on, just before Stalin's death, Molotov himself, who had been a most loyal supporter, was himself in great danger. I always had a warm spot for Mrs Molotov. When we had to host a lunch for Mrs Churchill with Mrs Molotov as the main guest, I hardly knew any Russian, having only been in Russia for a few weeks, and wondered how I was going to talk to her. Towards the beginning of the lunch Mrs Molotov, who spoke good German, turned to me and said, 'I don't think we can yet talk German, but perhaps we could talk Austrian.'

There were two people with whom I dealt closely in the Ministry for Foreign Affairs, one at working level and another at Under-Secretary level. At working level, the head of the department was a rather nice man called Yerofeev, who tried to be as helpful as he could. In the immediate post-war period there was a Parliamentary Question in London asking for statistics on the losses of the different Allies during the war, which it was very much to the advantage of the Russians to have answered correctly. But I could not get the statistics. When I pressed Yerofeev for the third time, insisting that it would be to their advantage to give them to me, he lost his temper and said, 'You know as well as I do that we haven't got such accurate statistics. But I come from Leningrad, and both my parents, my brothers and sisters all died there. So you can decide whether our figure of twenty million dead is exaggerated or not.' These were things to remember when, as so often, we became critical or despondent about our Soviet hosts.

Yerofeev's chief, Novikov, was a rather bear-like Russian of some importance in the Party, with whom I used to discuss one of the most vexed questions of those days, which seems a very odd one today – that of the 'Soviet wives'. During the war we had a military mission in Moscow with time on its hands. Many of the other ranks and one or two of the officers got entangled with Russian girls and in some cases married them. There were also one or two such marriages outside the military mission. After the war, when the military mission came to an end, the husbands wanted to take their Soviet wives back with them but they were not allowed to go. This caused a great deal of trouble, and the popular British press had a field day, for once to the discredit of the Soviet Union.

One day I argued with Novikov that to let the girls out could not harm the Soviet Union, and that it would be so easy to avoid such a small but important human case damaging our overall relations. Novikov replied that he understood that in England we thought that progress over little things helped to improve the climate for bigger issues, but in Russia, until the major issues were settled, it was thought a waste of time to bother about smaller things. I discovered, however, that this question of the wives went back much further than the Soviet period. I picked up a book about the fifteenth-century Russian Tsar, Ivan the Third. There was a passage in which a claimant to the Danish throne had got into trouble at home, taken refuge in Russia, and married the daughter of the Russian Tsar. Things improved for him and he returned to Denmark as King. He then asked the Tsar to arrange for his wife to join him as the Queen of Denmark. The Tsarist historian wrote that the King of Denmark received the appropriate reply, that Russia did not send daughters of her soil to live in slavery abroad. There was an additional Soviet argument that their nationals, who had been educated in the Soviet Union, should stay at home for the benefit of their own country.

I did, however, succeed in one case. Harold Elvin, one of the junior staff, had fallen in love with one of the young dancers in the Bolshoi, a very good dancer and a very nice girl. After a lot of trouble we managed to get her out. As Violetta Elvin, she became one of the Royal Ballet's major stars in the late Forties. Unfortunately for an otherwise romantic story, the marriage broke up, and she eventually married an Italian and has lived happily with him ever since. Sir Archibald Clark Kerr did better, in numbers at least. Stalin asked him at his farewell dinner (an unusual honour) to suggest a present to take away. He replied that he had become a Moslem and wanted four wives. It was left to me after his departure to sort this out in an unpleasant bazaar haggle with Dekanozov, the NKVD Deputy Foreign Minister, although we had both been at the Stalin dinner. I knew the Russians had special reasons for not letting out one of the four, and eventually had to settle for three after Dekanozov had tried to insist on only two.

When we finally left Russia in October 1947, the relationship between our two countries had obviously cooled very considerably, but we were still engaged in many matters of mutual concern. We were still working together to some extent in Germany, where the break did not come until the early summer of 1948. Russian policies throughout Eastern Europe had, however, toughened. On our return to Moscow from leave in the summer of 1947, we took the first Orient Express then running via Prague. In Prague my wife and I called on Jan Masaryk in the Hradschin Palace. He had just returned from an official visit to Norway, and was so gloomy that, regardless of what were no doubt microphones around us, my wife asked him why he had not stayed in Norway, to receive the reply that one could be an exile once in one's life, but he could not be an exile twice.

Only a few months later his body was thrown out of a window very near to where we had been talking to him. It may have been suicide, but in my view was more likely to have been murder. This was followed early in 1948 by the Communist coup in Prague against a Czechoslovak Government which had been neutral between East and West and, if anything, leant more towards Moscow than either to London or Paris. But that was no longer enough for Stalin. An ice age had descended upon Europe, in Churchill's words, now divided by an Iron Curtain.

16 | Bevin's Private Secretary

1947–9

It was during the Four-Power conference in Moscow in the spring of 1947 that Bevin's doctor, Dr McCall, informed my wife that Mr Bevin had it in mind to invite me to be his Principal Private Secretary in the autumn. This is a 'plum' appointment in the Foreign Service, all the more attractive under such a great and unusual personality as Bevin. My predecessor Bob Dixon and two successors, Roddie Barclay and Nico Henderson, have written very well about the Private Secretary's office and their personal contacts with Bevin, but I think that in the case of so great a man I should add my own assessment.

The post of Principal Private Secretary is obviously one of the most interesting in the Foreign Office but also perhaps the most delicate. Being close to the Foreign Secretary all the time, and seeing so much of him on both official and non-official occasions, particularly the latter, when Ministers 'unwind' from the day's tensions and open their minds, there is always a temptation to point him in a particular direction; but one has to remember that the Private Secretary is not there to make policy but rather to ensure that the policy recommended by the Foreign Office is properly presented to the Foreign Secretary, and also that the Foreign Secretary's views are properly known in the Foreign Office, as well, of course, as ensuring liaison with the Prime Minister and other senior Ministers. In fact, one is basically a link and should not try to be a privileged policy-maker. I was always particularly careful not to volunteer any suggestions on the Middle East, where Bevin had problems enough without being faced with potential attacks on his having a Private Secretary with a Lebanese-Egyptian wife.

120

However, a Private Secretary in his master's confidence cannot fail to have some influence. I often found myself thinking of the time my old Paris chief, Lord Tyrrell, had spent before the First World War as Private Secretary to Edward Grey, working closely with the Permanent Under-Secretary, Eyre Crowe.

By the time I joined Bevin at the end of 1947, he was well established as Foreign Secretary. In his life of Bevin, Lord Bullock has divided his periods at the Foreign Office into what he calls a period of frustration in 1945–46, a period of achievement from 1947 to 1949, and a period of ill-health and disappointment in 1950–51. I was lucky enough to be with him in the period of achievement although, frankly, having seen a certain amount of Bevin's activities from Moscow in the earlier period, I did not myself see it as a period of frustration.

Bevin had decided that his own and the American attempts to work with the Soviet Union had been condemned to failure by the autumn of 1946, and that our policy must be based upon bringing the Americans back into Europe; building up France and Western Europe; and protecting what he always called 'the Rim', in effect the rest of the world comprising most of the British Empire surrounding China, shortly to become a Communist ally of the Soviet Union, and the Soviet Union itself. Bevin himself had obvious priorities in Germany and the Middle East, but this did not lessen his interest in the rest of the world. It was he who decided that Britain should be represented in Peking after the Communist takeover, before any other major Western power. It was he who sent Malcolm MacDonald as Commissioner General to South-East Asia to pull together all the threads in a complicated scene there. He was extremely interested in developments connected with Indian and Pakistani independence. He promoted the Colombo Plan for economic cooperation in South-East Asia.

Bevin was described by Michael Howard in a Chatham House lecture on the holders of the office of Foreign Secretary in the last two centuries as either the greatest or with only Palmerston as an equal. Many of those who worked with him in the Foreign Office certainly regarded him, as I did myself, as the greatest of the modern Foreign Secretaries. He was a man of vision, and not only a Foreign Secretary reacting to the many crises developing throughout the world. As long ago as 1926, when addressing a trade union conference, he had warned his audience that a united Europe was needed to withstand future competition from such rivals as the United States or the Soviet Union. He had what the Foreign Office wants most of all in a Foreign

Secretary – the ability to make up his own mind after listening to advice and to get his policy through the Cabinet and, what is alas much less usual, the capacity of getting on well with his Prime Minister, Attlee, who had the highest respect for Ernie Bevin, although they did not always agree, as, for example, on the Middle East. Attlee summed up what was a relationship of complete mutual confidence in the words, 'If you had a very good dog, you didn't bark yourself, and I have a very good dog in Ernest Bevin.' Bevin on his side was always loyal to Attlee. He dismissed with massive contempt feelers from some colleagues in the Cabinet to put him in Attlee's place as Prime Minister. On several occasions when relatively minor decisions had to be taken, Bevin would say, 'Get me Clem on the line,' and I would say, 'But are you sure you need to worry the Prime Minister with this? I'm sure he'd leave it to you.' He would always conclude, 'No, no, get me Clem. I value his judgement and then, you never know, things may turn out wrong. Better have him on board from the beginning.' This was typical of Ernie's common sense.

He tended to be dismissive of party intellectuals and more especially of Dick Crossman, to whom he often referred as 'that double Crossman'. And one of his less attractive qualities, suspicion that rivals were waiting to stab him in the back, often centred on Nye Bevan and Herbert Morrison.

He had initially been regarded as a strange choice for Foreign Secretary. Indeed, he himself had wanted to be Chancellor of the Exchequer, since he was very interested in economics, but it was decided at the last moment – and some say the King himself had a hand in this – that a really strong man was required at the Foreign Office in those days of major post-war negotiations, so that a much weaker Britain could hold its own with the two super-powers with whom we were still regarded as forming the Big Three. What people forgot was that Ernie had spent a lifetime in trade union negotiation, which had provided him with very good training for international negotiation. He was equally good at negotiating with allies on whom we depended, represented by people who came from different social backgrounds, like the United States, or with allies in Europe who depended on us, or with adversaries like the Russians. He was already, when I joined him, highly regarded in Europe and the United States. Although certainly not highly regarded in the Soviet Union, he was regarded as an adversary of considerable weight.

He had many other qualifications for the post. One was his interest in economic affairs, since diplomacy was getting much more tied up with economics: indeed, the first of his great successes was the Marshall Plan and its development into the European Recovery Programme. He had had invaluable experience in Churchill's small War Cabinet, when his influence had extended far beyond his particular job as Minister of Labour. It was then that he and Eden established very close working relations, which sometimes resulted in Bevin rather than Eden persuading Churchill to accept policies put forward by Eden. This stood Bevin in good stead after the war, when he was always strongly supported by Eden, as I know very well since I was often the intermediary between them.

Bevin had also great international experience in the trade union movement. He knew America very well. He had the memory of an elephant, and could recall his displeasure with German Socialists for not stopping the Kaiser starting the First World War, as he saw it; and he had also supported the dock strikes after the First World War which were intended to prevent the Poles from invading the Soviet Union.

He had, above all, robust and practical common sense. When King George VI once asked him where and how he had acquired his knowledge and judgement, his reply was, 'In the hedgerows of experience, Sir.' Although entirely self-educated, he had read a great deal. He was the only Minister I met who had read Karl Marx from cover to cover, to the extent of quoting him back at Molotov, often to the latter's extreme irritation. He had also been interested in Buddhism and comparative religion, and recalled this when he visited Ceylon in the early Fifties, towards the end of his career.

He had himself been tempted by Communism in his early years. When I asked him what had changed his mind, he said rather typically that it was at a big trade union rally on Blackheath: he was between two other equally portly trade unionists, singing the Internationale, and when they came to the line, 'Starvelings of the world, unite,' he said, 'This isn't right, and from then on I changed my mind.' He also had a simple explanation for his skill, which was rare at the time, in negotiating with the Russians. It went back, he said, to his time as a very young man organizing dock labour in Bristol. In those days he would go aboard each of the ships for an individual negotiation. The captains got to know him and would say, 'Come down, Ernie, and have a drink, and we'll talk it over.' There was an occasional Russian ship that came in, and he discovered that with the Russians you did your negotiating first and you had your drink afterwards. 'And that,' he said, 'has stood me in very good stead.' Indeed, many of our troubles with the Russians at the end of the war lay in people adopting the other method of negotiation.

It was a delight to work with him because, apart from being obviously a great man, he was a very human figure. He took immense trouble with all his staff. The Foreign Service had become his trade union, and he would worry as much about the problems of a wife of a junior vice-consul whom he had met on some foreign trip or of a messenger as he would about an ambassador. The result was that he was adored in the Foreign Service and when the time finally came for him to retire the whole Service contributed to a bust which stands in the Foreign Office, subscriptions being limited to sixpence, and every single person of whatever rank contributed.

What tends to be forgotten today is that Bevin was really doing two big jobs as Foreign Secretary. In addition to the normal worldwide problems he was also in a sense the Prime Minister of the British zone of Germany, which was the major industrial zone of some twenty million inhabitants, for whose government he was responsible. There was a Department of State as big as the Foreign Office itself running Germany at that time under him. He had a great sense of responsibility and gave great attention to all the aspects of running that part of Germany, and indeed it was as he got immersed in the problem of producing some kind of acceptable living conditions for the population that his original anti-German feelings became modified. Fortunately he had an outstanding High Commissioner in Germany at that time in General Robertson, for whose opinions Bevin had the highest respect, and who in Germany proved the perfect partner for his more exuberant American colleague, General Clay. Adenauer later shared Bevin's high respect for Robertson. By the time I arrived we were committed to establishing the bi-zone with the Americans and proceeding towards setting up the Federal Republic of Germany in the west. This involved many complicated economic questions in which the French and the Benelux countries were highly interested, such as the future of the Ruhr and of the Saar, from which the Russians soon found themselves excluded.

Bevin's other main problem was the Middle East and in particular Palestine. He had an overall approach set out in a document headed 'Peasants, not Pashas', which was designed for very different regimes from those with which he actually had to deal. He worked hard to get treaties with Egypt and also with Iraq which would bring to an end their de facto 'Protectorate' status. With Iraq he actually succeeded with the Treaty of Portsmouth, signed on HMS *Victory* but almost immediately repudiated in Baghdad. With Egypt success had to await Anthony Eden in 1954.

Palestine was his most difficult problem. Bevin has often been accused of being anti-Jewish, which is quite untrue. He had many Jewish friends, and he felt so bitterly over these accusations that in my time he refused even to go to the United States, where he was the victim of Zionist demonstrations. He was certainly anti-Zionist, in the sense that he saw British interests in the area as much wider than Palestine, and felt strongly that the Arabs should not be ignored. He started with his customary self-confidence and said he would eat his hat if he failed to find a solution. But he had to work against the Americans, with whom on everything else he was so closely united. He was very bitter indeed when a possible solution was torpedoed in the UN by President Truman himself. By the time I joined Bevin he was in a mood of frustration, and in 1948 threw in his hand and returned responsibility to the United Nations. He was, however, by no means the only Western statesman who has tried but failed to settle the Jewish-Arab problem.

His major achievement was to bring America back into Europe through the Marshall plan and the Atlantic Alliance. In contrast to Middle Eastern affairs, I was very closely involved in all this, and in the summer of 1948 I was sent back to Moscow as his personal representative in the negotiations with Stalin on the Berlin blockade and airlift. This arose because Sir Maurice Peterson, who had been my second Ambassador in Moscow had come home with a heart condition and could not be flown back to Moscow. So it fell to me to work with the American Ambassador, General Bedell Smith, who was an old friend, and the new French Ambassador, Yves Chataigneau, on this question, which I will deal with separately. It was a great responsibility, because although Bevin was as convinced as I was that the Russians did not want war, the situation might have got out of hand. It was a joy to be negotiating in Moscow under a chief who knew exactly what he wanted; and although he was quick to react if he felt something was going wrong, he was loyalty itself to his representatives in the field.

This meant that I was in Moscow for some seven weeks in the summer, and when the negotiations finally broke down in Moscow they were resumed in the Security Council of the United Nations, then meeting in Paris. So I then had to go out to Paris for another month or so, with the result that I was away from my main job as Private Secretary for many months. This led to much publicity as I was very junior for this particular responsibility, and Bevin, I think, thought – wrongly – that I might not want to return to the less glamorous backstage role of Private Secretary.

At that time he was very interested in Indian independence, just being achieved. He had wanted our relations with the newly independent countries of the Indian sub-continent – India, Pakistan and Sri Lanka – to come directly under the Foreign Office, as indeed they did in the fullness of time. But the Commonwealth Relations Office was set up in an expansion of the old Dominions Office. Bevin was determined to have his finger in the Indian pie, which Nehru himself also wanted. It was arranged between them while I was in Paris that I should go in the spring of 1949 as Deputy High Commissioner to Delhi on secondment to the Commonwealth Relations Service. When I was told of this in Paris I was rather indignant as I very much wanted to come back to my post in London, but plainly I would not have been a very acceptable Private Secretary meeting the Foreign Secretary at all times as the man who refused to go to Delhi.

The economic build-up through the Marshall Plan and the European Recovery Programme had been completed before I joined Bevin, and he was then seeking to fill the security vacuum. The Treaty of Dunkirk with France had been signed in 1947 shortly before I arrived on the scene. The sequel was discussed at a meeting in London in November 1947 between Bevin and Marshall and during the Four-Power meeting with Molotov, which proved the last in the immediate post-war series. Bevin pointed out to Marshall that the Western European countries needed reassurance on defence if they were to have the confidence needed to make effective use of Marshall aid. Britain could not provide it alone; France and Italy were not yet strong enough; and indeed the only sizeable armies on the Continent other than the Russian army were those of the Swedes, the Swiss and the Yugoslavs. Therefore, the Americans must come back and join us.

Marshall pointed out that this would be a complete revolution in an American policy hitherto based upon isolation with no treaty commitments in peacetime: he would need all the help he could get to ensure the approval of Congress. It was therefore left that Bevin would build up all he could in Western Europe and then turn to Marshall to show that this was not enough. It was against this background that the

Brussels Treaty between Britain, France and Benelux was negotiated in the early summer of 1948. A military headquarters under Field Marshal Montgomery was set up at Fontainebleau. It was too early to bring Italy as a former enemy state into this combination, but Bevin could then turn to Marshall and the negotiations for an Atlantic Alliance could begin.

At the meetings in Brussels at the signing of the Treaty I was privileged to be the only official with the five Ministers because Bevin alone needed a translator. It was heartwarming to see what a high regard they all had for him. It was remarkable how people from entirely different social backgrounds appreciated him: this applied to the whole of the Diplomatic Corps in London. The only exception, I recall, was poor Count Sforza, who was Foreign Minister of Italy. Bevin always referred to him as 'that man Stortzer' and for some reason had no confidence in him whatsoever. Luckily, Italy was not yet ready for the new set-up.

One event which made the negotiations for the Atlantic Alliance much easier was the Communist takeover in Prague early in 1948. This persuaded a country like Norway, for example, to come in on the negotiations. Then, the Berlin blockade and the eventual success of the airlift were very important in, first of all, showing the danger, and secondly, proving that it could and would be met. I was away in Moscow or in Paris during much of the period during which these negotiations took place in Washington, and it was just about the time of the signature of the Atlantic Treaty in April 1949 that I set out for a very different world in India.

This was really the culminating point of Bevin's career as Foreign Secretary. He had played a major and often the decisive part in achievements of such importance as the European Economic Recovery Programme, the establishment of West Germany as an essential part of a democratic Western Europe, and the Atlantic Alliance; and through the Berlin airlift, which was started on his personal initiative, a stop had been put to any Russian plans for seeping further forwards into Western Europe and a new relationship established between West Germany and its Western occupying powers.

It is remarkable that all this was achieved by a man who had been told by his doctors shortly before the war that he only had a year to live, which he had decided to spend travelling around the Commonwealth. He was brought back as a supposedly dying man into the wartime Government of Churchill to become a great Minister of

Labour, but he did have great trouble with what he called his 'ticker', or his heart. He kept going very largely through his 'pellets' and the devotion and skill of Dr McCall. He had a near shave when he made his great speech in January 1948 which developed the whole concept of Western Union and of bringing the United States back into Europe. The House of Commons then met in the House of Lords, and it was a long walk from Bevin's office in the House of Commons to the House of Lords. Half-way, he had one of his attacks, and we wondered whether we would ever get him to the House. With the aid of his pellets, and more or less carrying him, a very heavy load, we got him into the Chamber and he made this, the greatest speech of his career. He had immense courage and determination; but he did also partly contribute to his troubles through his zest for life. He enjoyed all the good things in life, and wanted his guests to enjoy them too. In those days we were still rationed, and even official parties were only allowed three courses, of which bread was one, and therefore never served. I remember Ernie saying to me sadly, 'My 'eart goes out to those poor foreign Ambassadors, putting out their 'ands for the roll that isn't there.'

Bevin, despite his great humanity and good fellowship, never got used to political life. His whole background was in the trade union movement and he had not brooked much opposition. He was not eloquent in the usual parliamentary sense, but his speeches, however ungrammatical, put his message across very clearly and to great effect. He never felt at home in the House of Commons, which he had only joined late in life. While I was with him, Labour had a very big majority and he was not subjected to three-line Whips. Sometimes weeks would pass without Ernie having been to the House. Having persuaded him to go there, if only to see and be seen, I often found that he had played truant and had slipped off instead to the Trade Union Congress building, then in Smith Square, where he was much more at home.

We had a special arrangement with the Hansard editors. Normally no changes can be made to a speech in the House, but Ernie's speeches were really so ungrammatical that we were given special permission to tidy them up, providing we did not change the sense. Ernie accepted all this as perfectly normal and natural. There was an occasion when, a new drafter having prepared an important speech for him, we gathered in the morning to discuss it. Ernie began by most politely thanking the new drafter but adding that there was only one thing wrong with the draft. 'It's just not me. You won't mind, I hope, if I take it away and de-grammaticize it?'

It was before my time that Ernie and Eden had come together on what became known as the Eden–Bevin Reforms of the Diplomatic Service. They amounted to bringing the diplomatic, consular and commercial-diplomatic services all together in one Service; doing away with what were considered rather elitist requirements such as insistence upon knowledge of German and French at a high level before joining the Service, which it was thought helped richer candidates who had the time and money to go round Europe; and generally producing a Service which was more suited to the conditions of 1945. They both shared in this, and it is hard to say which of them had the greater influence upon these reforms.

Bevin was determined that the Foreign Office should do some economic thinking itself. This view was very much disapproved by the Treasury and the Board of Trade, and I do not think that anybody in those departments was at all happy about Ernie's approach. He did, however, have a Deputy Under-Secretary seconded from one of the economic departments, Sir Edward Hall-Patch, to assist him in taking a view himself on the economic aspects of foreign policy, which were becoming more and more important. Indeed, he himself said that the one thing he needed for a successful foreign policy was greater coal exports. This was a statement to which he attached as much importance as to his other very pregnant statement when he was asked what his foreign policy was and replied that it was that anybody could go to Victoria Station, get on a train, and go anywhere he wanted without a passport, as indeed had been the case before the First World War. I'm afraid we are still a long way from that. Indeed, it has recently become very difficult to get a passport at all within a reasonable period of time. I can't help thinking Ernie would have done something about that.

I think I can best show the greatness of Bevin by quoting Dean Acheson's tribute to him: 'To work with him inevitably evoked deep affection, respect and trust. His indomitable courage, simplicity and directness, his love of his country and his understanding of the grandeur of its contribution to the cause of human liberty, his humanity and knowledge of the struggles and aspirations of his fellow men, his own warm affectionate good humour, made him both loved and trusted.' Would that there had been a similar relationship later between Anthony Eden and John Foster Dulles at the time of Suez.

His own Prime Minister Attlee paid tribute to his great loyalty, his great administrative ability, to the breadth of his knowledge, to his great skill in negotiation, and to his power of inspiring affection in all those who worked with him. But at the same time Attlee mentioned his faults: his egotism, his impatience of opposition, and some prejudices. But, Attlee concluded, these were outweighed by immense moral and physical courage, by a great sense of humour, by his compassion and his conviction that international as well as national politics should be conducted with concern for the lives of ordinary men and women. He was a great patriot, and I recall him once saying to me, 'I should like to see the day when my people [by which he meant trade union members] will feel the same sense of responsibility for this country as you have in the Foreign Office.' He was a great Englishman, warts and all, worthy to stand comparison in his own day with Churchill or in the past with such figures as Oliver Cromwell or Palmerston. He saw big, and achieved great things, despite the relative weakness of post-war Britain, and no one made a greater contribution to European economic reconstruction, Atlantic security and the revival of a democratic Germany as a major component in European and Atlantic organizations. It is one of my greatest prides and joys to have worked so closely with him as well as with Churchill.

17 | The Berlin Airlift
1948–9

Although it was in our view the Russian failure to carry out their commitments made at Yalta and Potsdam which had made continued attempts at quadrilateral cooperation in Germany impossible and which, above all, had blocked the effective restoration of the German economy, the Russians themselves watched with obvious concern and probably some indignation what they considered the Western refusal to be guided by Potsdam, coupled with the build-up of the Anglo-American bi-zone and Western plans for the Ruhr. What worried them most of all was the building up in Western Germany of a post-war German administration, as the obvious precursor of a West German state. They were also worried because they saw any possibility of a Russian voice in the control of the German economy in the Ruhr and the Saar disappearing, and by a conference held in London early in 1948 between the British, the French and the Benelux countries, for the first time without a Soviet representative. Their concern increased with Erhard's currency reforms pointing the way to an economic recovery in Western Germany which could not be parallelled in East Germany.

What brought all these concerns to a head, however, was the question of what was to be done in Berlin itself with this new and successful West German Deutschmark. There was no Wall in Berlin then, and communications were easy throughout the whole city: a Deutschmark from the west could get very easily to the east. So plainly it was only common sense to try and reach some sort of agreement. We had realized this, and said that we were certainly not going to introduce the West German currency into Berlin except in agreement with the Russians. But Stalin had determined to give us a clear warning at a spot where he had geographical advantage on his side.

The first step came with the well-publicized exit from the Allied Control Commission in Berlin of the Soviet Commander-in-Chief, but it was not clear whether he would come back or not. Then, one by one, a series of measures followed: interference, first, with the Allied train communications with Berlin; secondly, with the barge traffic on the canals; and finally, and most obvious of all, with the road and rail traffic over the Elbe on the pretext that the bridge there needed repairs. By June it was clear that, although the word had never been used, there was in effect a Soviet surface blockade of Berlin. The only remaining communications were by air. This was not quite as surprising as it seems, because there had never been any written agreement in 1945 on surface communications, although there had to be written agreements on the air corridors and cooperation between the four countries on air control from a joint office in Berlin. The Russians, as always, were careful to observe the letter of written agreements, and did not interfere with the air agreements at any time.

It is odd, looking back, that it was the American military who had in 1945 turned down suggestions from American and British diplomats that there should be written agreements on surface traffic on the grounds that this would limit our rights which should be to use all and any surface communication. It proved to be a great mistake. The problem was how to handle the situation. First of all – and this was the smaller part of the problem – the Allied forces in Berlin had to be supplied. Then came the two million Berliners in the Western sector, who were already living in austere conditions but who still had to be fed and, above all, heated, with the factories still operating and providing employment. Coal had to be got in to keep the power stations going.

The first reaction of the Americans in Germany, General Clay and his diplomatic adviser Mr Murphy, was that we should drive a military convoy through. We in London, and for that matter the Americans in Washington, were unhappy about this. The first military convoy might perhaps get through, but it could be stopped coming back again merely by putting a tree-trunk across the road. A key principle in the complex inter-allied relationship in Germany was that neither side wanted to fire first; and in this case it would have had to be the West, and who knew what would happen then? Secondly, such convoys might be able to supply the Allied forces in Berlin, but they would clearly be inadequate for the two million West Berliners.

It was Ernest Bevin who first insisted that the answer must be an airlift. At first, and not surprisingly, the Americans were very much against this. They had worldwide responsibilities; aircraft were very much needed in the Far East; and they were by no means convinced that they could bring enough aircraft to Europe to make the airlift a success. At this stage a senior General in the American Air Force, came to explain these difficulties to Bevin. Ernie listened politely, and when the General had finished, said, 'General, you surprise and disappoint me. I never thought I would hear an American General explain that his Air Force can't do what the Royal Air Force is going to do.' I took the General out of the room, and he said, 'I suppose we've got to do it?' I said, 'That was the message.' Of course, there were many other negotiations after that, but this was the kind of influence which Ernie Bevin was so well able to bring to bear. An airlift would put the onus upon the Russians to breach existing agreements and perhaps even to open fire, neither of which they would normally want to do.

So the airlift began in mid-summer. In recent years it has often been described, even in Germany, as an American airlift. Apart from Bevin's personal influence, the airlift started with one-third of the aircraft British, and that remained roughly the case throughout. It is true that the British planes were for the most part rather smaller than the American and therefore that the proportion of the goods carried in British aircraft fell below one-third, but on the other hand we did carry some of the most unpleasant loads, in particular coal and also oil, which went better in our Dakotas and Sutherland flying boats. The airfields from which the airlift was conducted with full American support were in the British zone, which again increased our part in the operation. There is an air memorial at the Tempelhof airfield in Berlin with the names of those who died during the airlift. The British dead are two or three more than the American dead, some thirty-seven to thirty-four. The French were not yet able to contribute to the airlift but the new and bigger airfield at Tegel, in use at the end of the airlift, was in their zone. It was an extraordinary operation on the British side, not entirely done by the Royal Air Force. All kinds of private operators were brought in, with all kinds of aircraft, for example, old Sutherlands landing on the Berlin lakes. Altogether, it was a remarkable feat, but without the immense American effort it could never have been successful.

The next question was, should one negotiate with the Russians? The Americans were very much in favour. They felt it was important for German and world public opinion, since things might go wrong and it was going to be a very difficult time for the Berlin population, to show that we had tried everything. Bevin was at first against negotiation. He thought it would be a sign of weakness. But he gave way to the Americans, who in my view were right. The position of the West Berlin population was crucial. They had no particular reason at that time to think well of the Allied occupiers, or vice versa. We were fortunately the lesser evil compared with the Soviet occupation forces, who had not lived down Soviet pillage and raping in the last months of the war nor their even harsher occupation. This was very important because the Russians did offer the West Berliners ration cards if they would come over and collect them in the East. Fortunately, Berlin had a great Mayor, Reuter, who had once been a Communist, had taken refuge in Turkey from Hitler, and come back to Berlin as a good Social Democrat. His son is now the head of Daimler-Benz in Germany and one of the few leading German industrialists with a Socialist party-card. At an early stage in the airlift he and his CDU colleague, Frau Schroeder, called on the Western Commandants with the vitally important message that they need not worry about the attitude of the Berlin population, who were fully behind the airlift, however unpleasant living conditions might become. This was decisive. Without the Berlin population on our side, the airlift could not have succeeded.

We were lucky also in a relatively mild winter. RAF friends working at the bases in West Germany have told me that otherwise they could probably not have got the aircraft turned round in time. I saw something of this for myself on my way to Moscow, flying into our airfield at Gatow with General Robertson: we landed with another plane just taxi-ing off the airstrip ahead and another already coming in to land behind us. It was a great technical achievement at that time.

It was decided that negotiations would be conducted with Stalin himself by the three Ambassadors in Moscow. Our Ambassador was home on sick leave, so I replaced him as Bevin's personal representative. It was a great honour and responsibility for a relatively junior official, but I had had recent experience of Stalin and the Soviet Union, and General Bedell Smith was a close friend. Bedell Smith, the American Ambassador, became our main spokesman, because the French Ambassador was very newly arrived in Moscow and in any case France at that time was unable to make much of a contribution to the airlift.

We were seven weeks in Moscow and had seven meetings with the Russians, two with Stalin himself. There was a certain amount of shadow-boxing, because what we were discussing was the withdrawal of the Soviet blockade measures against agreed agreements for introducing new currency into Berlin. But the main underlying issue was Stalin's concern over the building up of the West German administration. Although he never made this an absolute condition, two or three times during the negotiations he made it clear that this was his main concern and that what he wanted was a postponement, or ideally a withdrawal, of the arrangements which we were then negotiating for a West German administration. Although we were not prepared to give way at all on this, we did reach a point at which agreement was reached on instructions to the Commandants in Berlin to work out in detail an arrangement under which currency in Berlin would be the East German currency but controlled by a Four-Power committee. Great problems arose on the interpretation of the word 'controlled', both in English and in Russian.

The climate for negotiation was not as good in Berlin as it had been with Stalin and Molotov in the Kremlin, and the Russians were stirring up a lot of trouble with demonstrations and so on. Despite our initial hopes, it proved impossible to convert our Moscow directive into a detailed agreement, and this crisis returned to us in Moscow. We wanted to resume negotiations with Stalin. But he had no doubt decided that he was not going to get his way on his overriding requirement, and since there was no certainty of the airlift succeeding when winter came, he brought our negotiations to an end with the news that he was already on holiday at the Black Sea.

Stalin and Molotov conducted our negotiations in a businesslike way and with complete courtesy. But we had some tricky moments with them and among ourselves. Once, late at night or rather, early in the morning, Bedell Smith turned to Molotov and said, 'Neither I nor my colleagues fully understand some of these currency technicalities. Perhaps we could ask Mr Smirnov, as an expert from Berlin, to explain the details to us.' With all top Russian negotiators, indeed with all their negotiators, it was then taken for granted (and in my experience, correctly) that they understood what it was all about and did not need to refer to expert advice. Molotov when angry used to turn pea-green and stammer. His reply was the Russian equivalent of 'Well, I suppose all things are p-p-possible. It is even p-p-possible that Mr Smirnov might know something that I do not know.' Whereupon Mr Smirnov, who was six-foot-six, appeared to be shrinking below the table. We were relieved at the next meeting to find that he was still around and had not been sent off to Siberia as a stooge of the West. With Stalin,

Bedell Smith adopted what proved a good technique, based on the principle of 'We Generals together . . .' Stalin always wore his Generalissimo uniform and seemed to like being treated in this way. On the Allied team my old friendship with Bedell Smith was a great help.

While we were in Moscow Zhdanov, a potential successor to Stalin, who had been actively engaged in the restoration of ideological orthodoxy, died, and state mourning, with all theatres and restaurants closed, was decreed, covering an evening when one of my old friends among the American correspondents had invited me to dinner at the famous Georgian restaurant, the Aragvi. The Georgian security overlord, Beria, was thought to have been an enemy of Zhdanov's, and my experienced host thought it might still be worth seeing whether the Aragvi had defied the ban. The door was locked but it did not take long to secure admission, and we then spent an evening surrounded by Georgians rejoicing in the death of Zhdanov. It was in these odd ways that one could check on Moscow rumours.

After the collapse of the Moscow talks there was further discussion in the Western capitals on whether to continue negotiations with the same objective of persuading public opinion but at the risk of giving Stalin the impression that we had little faith in our airlift. The only negotiating possibility was in the Security Council of the UN, meeting in the autumn in Paris. There were legitimate doubts about the wisdom of bringing a complicated Berlin issue, reserved to the Four Powers, into the UN Security Council. But it was decided to take the risk. The President of the Security Council at that time was the Argentine Foreign Minister, a rather distinguished politician called Bramuglia. It was hard enough for us fully to understand all the Berlin technicalities, and almost impossible that he or indeed any members of the Security Council other than the Four Powers should understand them. But Bramuglia and his colleagues did a good and on the whole helpful job, avoiding putting forward impossible proposals which might have seemed attractive to public opinion and which could have been seized on by the Russians to weaken Western rights in Berlin. But no progress was made, and again it was left to the winter to decide. Fortunately, the airlift was kept going, even indeed with some improvements for the inhabitants of Berlin. They stood firm, and Stalin was defeated. For Bramuglia the result was less fortunate. He was Peron's Foreign Minister, and Evita, jealous over the great publicity he had been given in Paris, had his returning ship diverted to another dock to deprive him of a deserved public welcome. Before long he had ceased to be Foreign Minister!

There were other happier and more important results of the Berlin airlift. First and foremost, it had changed the Western role in Berlin and therefore in the Federal Republic as a whole from occupation to protection, without which we would not have built up so successfully a new relationship with Germany as a pillar of the European Community and of NATO. Secondly, it convinced other countries in Europe that Soviet pressures were dangerous and had to be resisted. And thirdly, it showed that the West was capable of resisting them diplomatically, without the risk of war, even when the geography seemed all against us. All in all, it contributed to the concluding of the Atlantic Alliance in 1949. So the Berlin airlift was a major achievement of the post-war period, and I am proud to have been associated with it. Much of the credit on the Western side should go to Bevin, and the major credit overall to the impressive efficiency of the American and British Air Forces. A less satisfactory but in the circumstances inevitable result was a further lowering of the temperature in preparation for Stalin's Cold War and the division of Germany and of Europe.

18 | Independent India

1949–51

India, even more than Egypt had been before the war, was a complete break in my diplomatic career, which otherwise was centred upon the Continent, in particular on Germany, the Soviet Union and NATO. I was sorry not to return to my work as Private Secretary to a great Foreign Secretary after the excitements of negotiating with Stalin on the Berlin airlift. But in the event, two years in India as Deputy High Commissioner gave me some insight into the new Commonwealth and the Third World, and both of us the opportunity to see a greal deal of one of the world's great civilizations and to make good friends in the Indian 'Establishment', starting with Pandit Nehru and his remarkable family.

I was also lucky enough to be again in a key country of special interest to the then Labour Government. Bevin, in spite of his European, Atlantic and Middle Eastern preoccupations, regarded the Indian sub-continent as the most important single area in what he called 'the Rim' of countries surrounding the Soviet Union and China, on whose future development towards a democratic or a Communist society so much would depend. The Prime Minister, Clement Attlee, never lost the keen interest he had taken in India since he had gone there with the Simon Commission in the Thirties. One example of this was my farewell call on him. Normally a man of very few words, he kept me for thirty minutes instead of the five I had expected, to talk with unusual freedom about India. Attlee also felt that Ernie Bevin, whose health was anything but good, was already overburdened. The combination of these two factors had led to the creation of the new Commonwealth Relations Office, whose first Secretaries of State,

Philip Noel Baker and Patrick Gordon Walker, were distinguished members of the Labour Party but not towering figures like Ernest Bevin himself. My High Commissioner, General Sir Archibald Nye, formerly Vice-Chief of the General Staff in London, with whom I had worked during the war, had the complete confidence of the Prime Minister and Foreign Secretary, and he and his wife Colleen got on well with the Nehrus. I was told that he had asked for me, and he made me most welcome.

Bevin maintained his interest in South-East Asia, especially after the outbreak of the Korean War in 1950. The Colombo Plan, bringing the countries of South-East Asia together on the model of the European OECD, was very much of his devising. He came to the inaugural meeting in Colombo in 1950. Inspired by his youthful studies of Buddhism and comparative religions, he insisted on visiting Kandy, although he had to be taken up the rather steep hill to the temple by bearers. I wrote to him from Delhi and got a letter back in which he said he had been glad to launch the Plan on the spot although it had placed a great strain on his 'ticker'. It was probably time for him to retire, but he felt there were still one or two things which he felt he was better placed than others to complete. This, I'm afraid, is the inevitable approach of any great political leader, and no doubt accounts for the fact that so few ever willingly resign. To take the story further forwards, Bevin was absent ill from the Foreign Office more and more frequently in 1950 and 1951, and finally Attlee insisted on his resignation on grounds of health. He was succeeded for the few months before Labour left office by Herbert Morrison, who had always been one of Ernie Bevin's '*bêtes noires*' and who, for all his great qualities in handling home affairs, particularly during the war, was not so well suited to foreign affairs.

One of my main qualifications for post-Independence India was that neither I nor my family had ever been to India or had anything to do with it. It was thought, probably rightly, that former Indian civil servants, despite all they had done for India, might have found it difficult to adjust to the new situation – and, even more to the point, that the new masters of India, who were even in Nehru's case anything but well-disposed towards the Indian Civil Service, whether British or Indian, would prefer to see new faces around them. There were exceptions, for example, Humphrey Trevelyan, who transferred to a brilliant career in the Foreign Office. And I was much helped by John Shattock, who stayed on partly to ease my path and through whom I made many Indian friends.

Fortunately we had the best of all introductions through Nehru's sister, Mrs Pandit, whom we had met in Moscow in 1947 and I again in 1948. In Moscow, like all diplomats setting up new missions, she had been put in a Moscow hotel, in her case the not very comfortable Metropole. She had arrived just before India's Independence Day, 15 August. My wife and I felt that the Metropole was not an appropriate setting to celebrate such a day and we sent a message asking whether she would honour us by having lunch with us with her very small staff on that day. We also had the ladies of the Embassy, on their own initiative, sewing a large Indian flag for the occasion, which was afterwards declared to be correct. We could only have twelve to lunch, and this was one of the most delightful lunch parties I recall during the whole of our stay in Moscow. It certainly brought in great and important benefits to both Cella and myself later on.

Mrs Pandit was one of the three brilliant sisters of Pandit Nehru and had a most distinguished career as Ambassador in Moscow and Peking and High Commissioner in London as well as representing India at the United Nations. She herself felt qualified to be Prime Minister of India. There was, however, considerable jealousy of the Nehru family, and she was always fobbed off after her brother's death with the idea that there could not be another Nehru as Prime Minister – hence her great indignation when her niece, who was on the face of it a much less brilliant figure in the family, became Prime Minister and she herself had to be satisfied with the dignified but by no means politically important post of Governor of Bombay.

I found myself in Moscow again in August 1948, a year after our small Independence Day lunch, and was most warmly entertained by Mrs Pandit, then in her own Embassy. We met her again in Paris later in the summer of 1948 when I was dealing with the Berlin blockade at the UN meetings there. By this time it was a more or less open secret that I was to go to India, and we had one or two very agreeable and valuable meetings which stood me in good stead. Oddly enough, since this was rather a far cry from the Indian scene, one of them I well remember was a splendid night at the then leading Paris nightclub, when my wife and I were the guests of J. R. Tata, the Parsee Indian industrialist, and Mrs Pandit. I have to admit that what I remember most clearly of that evening was the beautiful singing of 'La vie en rose' by the best French nightclub singer of the day.

I did of course spend my last few months in London as Private Secretary with Ernie Bevin, months during which the Atlantic

Alliance, his greatest achievement, was negotiated in Washington. I was duly promoted to Assistant Under-Secretary of State to make my status as Deputy High Commissioner in India more normal. We spent our leave travelling to India by sea in April 1949, once again, as on the way to Moscow in 1945, breaking the journey in Egypt. It had become very prosperous during the war and had developed an even more sophisticated social life, still graced by King Farouk but, as we now know, with the nationalist army officers under Nasser, disgusted by events in Palestine, already working against him underground. The high standard of the Cairo dinner parties contrasted with the more austere London we had just left, where rationing was only abolished after the return to power of the Conservative Government in the autumn of 1951. A matter of more serious concern was the continued and rather ostentatious presence in the centre of Cairo of uniformed British troops forming our Middle East HQ, whose departure to the Suez Canal, where they were more out of sight if not out of mind, was only negotiated by Anthony Eden in 1954.

The end of April was not the ideal time to arrive in India in those pre-air conditioning days. Although we were used to the heat of Egypt, my wife and I both wilted as, for the next three days in Bombay, we led an extremely active social life, being introduced to everybody at large cocktail parties at which Cella felt like a column of melting ice. We were staying in the vast Taj Mahal Hotel, which was comfortable, but prohibition had begun and, although Bombay was the most cosmopolitan centre in India, there were many dry days, which must have affected the receipts of the Taj Mahal Hotel. We met mainly the British, Parsee and Hindu business communities in Bombay, which had already taken over from Calcutta as the leading Indian commercial centre.

A spacious air-conditioned compartment had been reserved on the Delhi overnight express for the Deputy High Commissioner and his wife, but Thomas Cook's had for once slipped up and we found we were sharing it with a young Indian couple. He turned out to be a high-caste sub-commissioner of police from a native state in Rajputana, who was taking his new bride back with a large suite of followers in the next coach. We probably learned more about life in India in that one night than we did in most of our subsequent two years there.

It is normal in India, or was then, for conversation to begin with a polite enquiry about one's salary. My Indian sub-commissioner of police at once gave me his, and it is perhaps fortunate that I had

141

forgotten what mine was. He did, however, ask me, where were my men? Of course there were none, which must have seemed to him very peculiar since he himself had about a dozen. At every stop, and there were many, they used to invade our luxury coach to kiss the feet of the bride, which did not, however, prevent them from proceeding to skin mangoes and to throw the skins and stones all over the floor. The beds were on each side of this large and very luxurious coach, we on one side and they on the other. As the night wore on, there were demands from the berth opposite, 'Bowanji! Bowanji!' Bowanji came down and did his duty, and then climbed up again. My wife was very interested in all this, and I kept on discouraging her from taking too close an interest. I was amazed to see the next morning how sprightly the police sub-commissioner still was.

The Indian Government had naturally retained all the properties of its predecessor, the British Raj. The High Commissioner's residence was in a pleasant but not imposing villa at that time. The offices were in a rather unattractive modern building in which the Deputy High Commissioner was also housed in a large flat without a garden. All this changed a decade or so later with the building of the Diplomatic Quarter on what had been the famous 'Ridge'. If I had not already known my chief from wartime days I might have misunderstood one of his first remarks, which was that he and I should not be too much together as our job was to get around India and explain the new position as widely as possible, not so much to the Indians as to the British.

Delhi had only just recovered, and not completely, from the terrible bloodletting in the Punjab which had accompanied Partition. Gandhi had been murdered only a few months earlier, fortunately not by a Moslem. Nehru himself often got out of his car to stop crowds who were murdering each other; he had a very good record as regards inter-communal relations. There were large numbers of Sikhs in Delhi and also Hindus who had fled from what is now Pakistan, and at the same time a large number of Moslems had remained behind (we had a Moslem 'bearer' or servant), so there was plenty of tension still in the air. The Sikhs were a great boon to Delhi as they were hard-working and tended to take on the mechanical jobs. We found as we travelled through India that the atmosphere in the north, which had been torn apart by Partition and the subsequent killings, which had run into millions, was very different from the south, which had been entirely unaffected although there were many millions of Moslems there.

Relations were very warm between British and Indians in those early years after Independence. This came not only from the Nehru family with their close links with the British but from far more traditional Hindus such as the Home Minister and Number Two in India, Sardar Patel, who was a sort of Indian Ernie Bevin, with great power but also loyalty to Nehru. It was he who took on the major task of bringing the native states into the new Republic of India. It was he rather than Nehru who gave confidence to the Indian Civil Service, and thereby ensured that old standards were maintained, at least in the centre.

Our major tasks at the High Commission were twofold. The first was to do all we could to ease the very difficult relationship between India and Pakistan. The second, and of course this took up more of our time, was to explain to the British community throughout India the changes that had taken place and to see that they made the most of the new opportunities instead of regretting the past. The first of these problems centred very largely on the question of Kashmir. It had been agreed at Independence that India should follow the same principles as had been applied in Germany at the time of the Reformation i.e. that the states would basically follow the religion of their rulers. But this principle was not universally applied. The most obvious case was that of Hyderabad, the largest of all the native states with a population of over twenty million, in the centre of India, where the ruler was a Moslem. India could not, however, stomach the idea of an independent Moslem state, still less a part of Pakistan, in the middle of India. So the Nizam was eased out and Hyderabad came under Indian military rule, the Governor being the most brilliant Indian soldier of his time, General Chaudhuri, of whom I shall have more to say later. The other difficult case was that of Kashmir, where the principle had been followed and the Hindu Maharajah, who had a majority Hindu population only in his less important neighbouring state of Jammu, ruled over a large Moslem majority, which would have much preferred to join Pakistan and was not won round when under the government of a pro-India Moslem, Sheikh Abdullah. Nehru was himself a Kashmiri, who could not accept the idea of his home state's future being decided on grounds of religion. The issue was made more difficult by the bad blood and ill-feeling at the top which had accompanied Partition. Mountbatten had hoped to be invited to become the Governor General of each of the two successor states. Since, however, he was so obviously a close friend of Nehru's, Jinna in

Pakistan would not hear of this. Personal relations were better but not good under Jinna's successors, Liaquat Ali Khan and his widow the Begum.

My own working relations in Delhi were mainly with the senior Indian civil servants and Generals. Within these circles there were then better prospects than at any time since for achieving agreement over Kashmir and other things. The Army had divided, but friendships had not been broken. We found a good example of this on a visit to Kashmir in 1950. There was still a state of war between India and Pakistan in Kashmir, and there were in fact Indian and Pakistani troops drawn up against each other in trenches some fifty miles from Srinagar. The Indian Brigadier had been a friend of ours in Delhi, and since there had been no fighting for some time, he invited us to visit him. Rather surprisingly, since Indian soldiers were very punctilious in such matters, we found he was not ready to receive us at the stated hour of four pm. A quarter of an hour later he came in, very apologetic, and said, 'I must explain, and I think you'll understand.' We certainly did when he told us that three times a week, on Tuesdays, Thursdays and Saturdays (and we were there on one of these days), he had an arrangement to have a conversation for about a quarter of an hour with his Pakistani opposite number some few hundred yards away, for which they had rigged up a special telephone line, and he did not want to risk any possibly dangerous misunderstanding by missing the appointment. As the years went by, these personal contacts disappeared, and a Kashmir settlement remains as far off as ever.

The top civil servants on both sides had worked closely together and wanted to find some solution. The difficulties lay much more at the top and, to a considerable extent, with Pandit Nehru. His family came originally from Kashmir. They were very distinguished Brahmins who had moved to Allahabad in the United Provinces where there was a strong mixture of Moslems and Hindus. Nehru had no strong confessional views himself; he was, in fact, in European terms, a modern agnostic or even atheist and did his best to diminish confessional troubles in India. He felt equally strongly that the future of what he still regarded as his country, Kashmir, should not be decided on old-fashioned confessional lines. Since Kashmir had become part of India, it should remain there and not be handed over to Pakistan purely on religious grounds. He had always opposed the partition of India, which he regarded as a very retrograde step imposed on an unwilling India by Jinna; and I imagine he also held us responsible on what I think was the mistaken conviction that we had always wanted to divide and rule in India. It was certainly not part of our policy in 1949. Many efforts were made to bring the two sides together with the help of outsiders, in particular a very distinguished Australian High Court judge, Sir Owen Dixon, but these always came to grief at the top.

The second of our main problems was that of the British in India. This was an important, although not the only, reason for the frequent trips the High Commissioner and I paid around the country. When later I was in Germany, another country with a federal structure, I travelled a great deal, as in India. In a vast sub-continent where there was little in common between Delhi, Calcutta, Madras and Bombay, it was even more essential. When we were visiting a school in Madras we discovered that, although a law had been passed at the centre in Delhi that within fifteen years Hindi should replace English as the official language, there was no intention of ever including Hindi in the curriculum. Although Bombay had become the main commercial centre of India, Calcutta remained important. It soon became clear that British business circles in India were in many ways better placed under the new independent Government than they had been before. The relations between business and British officialdom, which had been extremely close in the days of the old East India Company, had become rather distant in the last decades of the Raj. The British officials rather looked down on what were described as 'Box-wallahs', rather forgetting the circumstances in which we had first gone to India. Although Congress had depended greatly on the financial support of important Indian businessmen such as G. E. Birla, in whose house Gandhi always stayed in Delhi, the new Indian leaders, especially Pandit Nehru himself, did not have a higher opinion of them than the former British officials had had for their own business communities. The one exception was the Parsee community, centred in Bombay, and in particular the Tata family, who ran a whole range of modern businesses in India, from steel mills to the national airline. Multinational British businesses, such as Unilever, Shell and ICI, found themselves in a special category with the Tatas.

On our travels we found ourselves in Government bungalows, where I was confused with the former and often junior British administrative officers in the Indian Civil Service many of whom also had the title of Commissioner – they had solved all kinds of problems within a wide area with a million inhabitants and for them I was a poor substitute. Or in the palaces of Maharajahs, at that time struggling to defend their financial and other interests against the Congress rulers in Delhi. In Benares the young Maharajah, recently at Oxford and hosting a tea party for us but neither eating nor drinking with us, explained to my wife that he was regarded locally as a god and could not eat with others, even with his wife, although he could sleep with her 'for the needs of procreation'.

The absorption of the native states by the new Republic of India was a remarkable feat. It was done under the responsibility of Sardar Patel by an outstanding Indian civil servant, V. P. Menon, who had worked closely with Mountbatten and previous Viceroys. There were over six hundred such states, ranging from big states with many millions of inhabitants such as Hyderabad, Kashmir or, the most modern of them all, far more modern than India itself, Mysore, to tiny states with only a few thousand inhabitants in Rajastan, still living in the Middle Ages. The total population of these states was at that time well over a hundred million. 'V.P.' once complained to me that he had not enough officials to do this gigantic job and it turned out that he had only 180 and wanted only 50 more!

Another major problem was India's decision on Commonwealth membership. Could this be reconciled with Nehru sharing leadership of the non-committed nations, with Tito, Sukarno and, rather later, Nasser? But, despite their prison records, the Congress leaders had been brought up with a strong British culture, and once they had achieved independence they did not want to break their links with Britain. The solution of India having its own President but accepting the Queen as Head of the Commonwealth came from a very unlikely source, Krishna Menon, the Indian High Commissioner in London. Krishna Menon had been very left-wing and was distrusted by all my friends in the Indian Army and Civil Service, but he was one of Pandit Nehru's favourites. My wife asked him what he had been before he became High Commissioner. Looking back to his past as a left-wing member of an English urban council, he replied that he had been an agitator and had enjoyed that much more. My own view is that, despite all the problems we may have about cricket and rugby and South Africa and so much else, we and other member countries would be the poorer without this loose grouping of fifty nations whose leaders speak English and share a common cultural background. So we owe a debt of gratitude to Krishna Menon. Among other things, the Commonwealth has provided its members with a network of bilateral relations which might otherwise have been purely centrifugal to the hub of the wheel in the UK, imposing many burdens upon that hub. Canada and later Australia played a helpful role in the early days, which we should not forget when we sometimes find them joining the 'new' Commonwealth countries and isolating us.

India inherited from the Raj special relations as a protecting power, almost a governing power, in countries such as Nepal, Sikkim and Bhutan, and also had a special relationship with Burma, which was then in a state of very considerable unrest and had unfortunately decided against continuing membership of the Commonwealth. The new Indian Government, with so many of the same ICS officials, found it much more natural than some of the Congress leaders might have done on their own to continue the old protecting relationship and indeed almost to extend it.

Apart from Pakistan, one of the main problems concerned Nepal, the home of the Gurkhas. It was still under the rule, not of the King but of the Ranas, the 'Mayors of the Palace', and there was no inclination to welcome the substitution of Indian for British influence even though this alone enabled Gurkha recruitment to hold up. We retained some Gurkha Regiments for use overseas and especially in Hong Kong and Brunei. After considerable initial difficulties with India, we did eventually reach a satisfactory agreement to keep our own British recruiting HQ near to Darjeeling and allowing transit rights through India. The Government of India were naturally determined to take over the dominant role in Katmandu from the British. This meant substituting for the Ranas the King with a semblance of democracy achieved with the aid of popular demonstrations subsidized from the Indian Embassy and from Bihar.

The Deputy Under-Secretary in charge of Asian affairs in the Foreign Office, Sir Esler Denning, was breaking his journey home from the Far East in India, and it was decided that he and I should go to Katmandu. I was then visiting the planters in South India out of the range of telephones. Rather appropriately, given the then primitive communications between India and Nepal, a runner had to find me. Rather few people, I imagine, have gone to Katmandu via Cochin! We flew from Patna in the North Indian plain in a very small plane normally used for crop control, coming in to land at the new airfield in Katmandu over a precipice. I noticed a large crowd coming, as I thought, to greet us. They had in fact been paid to demonstrate against us. Such was their mercenary enthusiasm that only the strength and martial appearance of our Ambassador's Sikh guard prevented our plane from being pushed back over the precipice. We lunched with the Indian Ambassador the next day, but thought it better not to raise the subject. It was not, alas, a tourist visit to Nepal, and we could not spend much time visiting anything but the capital. There was clearly nothing to be done about the *coup d'état*, although perhaps our presence there did promote a settlement nearer to a compromise than would otherwise have been the case. It was in the nature of things that there should be a more democratic government in Nepal and that despite Nepal's opening up of friendly relations with China, Indian influence should be dominant in Katmandu.

In the days of the British Raj, China was weak and our concern had been almost entirely with the north-west frontier with Afghanistan and with Russia beyond. The north-eastern frontier had been neglected except for occasional expeditions to Lhasa in Tibet. But during the war, communication with Chiang Kai-shek's China had been through Burma, Assam and small native states, and ICS officials such as my friend V. P. Menon felt that with the probable increasing importance of China – whether a democratic China or a Communist China was not yet clear – India should pay more attention than it had hitherto done to that part of the world. This I also had in mind when I was visiting the British tea planters in Darjeeling, the oil wells in Assam or the battlefields against the Japanese at Imphal and Kohima. Indian officials in Delhi were extremely helpful, and we enjoyed much more than normal hospitality in Sikkim, Tripura and Imphal. The Indian Government had trouble from the Naga tribesmen, and V. P. Menon's fears about the Chinese were realized within a decade or so. Before, during and after the Korean War, Nehru had illusions about the relationship between the two Asian giants, illusions for which the Indian Army paid dearly in the early Sixties under a weak Chief of Staff and a most unlikely War Minister in Krishna Menon. Having given the Indians a lesson, the Chinese withdrew, and my old friend, General Chaudhuri, was brought back successfully to restore the efficiency and morale of the Indian Army.

Against this new background it was of much more than tourist interest to call on the Maharajah of Bhutan, whose country remained closed, in Kalimpong, to spend Christmas in Gangtok in Sikkim with a remarkable Indian couple, the Dayals, he a distinguished ICS officer, she a tennis champion and expert in Indian dancing. We called on the old Maharajah, who painted admirable landscapes of his state from photos brought to him without his ever leaving the Palace. We climbed to the frontier of Tibet on the Lhasa road and were entertained in Kalimpong, most improbably, by the Pretender to the Greek throne and his wife, Princess Irene. I thought I had indeed acted on the advice given to me in London by Lord Waverly, a former Governor of Bengal, on no account to miss Sikkim and Bhutan, of which I had not then heard. For good measure we added the Ledo supply road to China during the war until it became overgrown, at a point where an elephant stood guard – and Imphal and Kohima, where India was saved from Japanese invasion. On our way back we were the guests in Dakka of the Governor of East Pakistan, Sir Firoz Khan, and his very sophisticated Austrian wife.

It would have been foolish to neglect, for the newer problems of the North-East, Pakistan and Afghanistan, where Kipling's 'Great Game' involving underground activities along the North-West frontier was still played in Peshawar at a time when Afghanistan was looking to India for support. Changing our Hindu driver for a Moslem, we drove through Pakistan and over the Khyber Pass to Kabul, visiting en route Amritsar, the Sikh Holy City, and Rawalpindi, where General Gracey was still Commander of the Pakistan forces. Our journey to Kabul was uneventful, the worst hazard being to pass camels and other caravans in some narrow gorges over the Kabul River. We stayed in our enormous Embassy, where our Ambassador laid on an impressive dinner party for us, for some thirty people, comprising the whole of the then Government of Afghanistan, every one of whom was a member of the royal family, with the exception of the Ambassador to Delhi – and he had married a Princess, who was present. Visiting the Kabul Museum with its wonderful Indian ivories from Asoka's time, which have survived the centuries because of the dry climate, was more dangerous. Our first effort, with the Ambassador leading us and the British flag flying on his car, to get into the museum, which should have been open on that day and at that time, was met by an Afghan guard with fixed bayonet, who pushed us back very rudely to the car; but this was put right later on.

While on the north-western frontier and in Pakistan we were shown the vast irrigation schemes, requiring an agreed division with India of the waters of the Indus. On leaving India I was told by Pandit Nehru that even with the help of the many dam projects of those days India would never be able to feed itself. But he was too pessimistic. One of the great achievements of India and Pakistan has been to improve their agriculture so much that, although the population has more than doubled since those days and the monsoons have not been more frequent, India and Pakistan not only feed themselves but now export grains.

Other visits took us through the length and breadth of India and from Simla to Ceylon, taking in the great mosques and forts of the North and the Hindu temples and forts of the South. But since this is not a travel guide I thought it best to concentrate on those visits which had political – or, in the case of our British residents, consular – significance.

As I had only been loaned to the Commonwealth Relations Office for two years, our Indian period came to an end in the spring of 1951. Although I had nothing to do with India or Asia in my subsequent career, I found it a very valuable experience to have been in India at that time, to have seen something of the new Commonwealth through one of its leading members, and also something of the problems of the Third World, again through the eyes of a most important but extremely complex member of the Third World, since fifty million Indians were highly sophisticated members of the technological Western world, with the other 600 million leading a simple life in conditions which resembled those of the Middle Ages.

Looking back on it all, I think that I was most impressed by the high standards of the senior Indian officials and Army officers with whom I had to deal, and of course by the good fortune of having a direct relationship with Pandit Nehru and his family. Incidentally, although we saw a great deal of his daughter, Indira Gandhi, who acted as his hostess, we would never have suspected at that time that she would afterwards become Prime Minister of India. Pandit Nehru himself often irritated his friends in the West but I always felt that India and the world were fortunate in having a man with such modern ideas in India at that time, since it might not have been so difficult for other leaders to have taken India back to play a more traditional role. Unfortunately he regarded the Americans as brash and uncivilized to a degree which deprived them of any advantage they might have expected from their earlier support for Indian independence. He was no Communist, but his own and later Indira's keen interest in Soviet developments, which resembled that of many British left-wingers, disturbed the American Ambassador, Loy Henderson, a Soviet specialist. The Americans of those days had little sympathy for an India which, by wanting to conduct an independent and non-aligned policy, always appeared to them to be leaning towards the Soviet Union. But there was never any danger of India being taken down the Communist road; and although there were Communist parties in India – indeed, they achieved power in important provinces like Bengal and in the South – there was never any question at all of a Communist takeover, nor, I imagine, would there be today.

Comparing India with the Middle East, of which I had more experience, I found one of the most interesting things was the way Indians of the kind we met were so often dual personalities. They had not merely acquired a Western, and in particular a British, culture and education, but had mastered it; and top Indian civil servants were certainly as good as and in many cases better than our own. Gandhi even in his dhoti had a perfect English background. Above all, the Governor General of our time, who succeeded Mountbatten when he retired on Indian independence, Rajagopalachari, always in a Gandhian dhoti, was one of the best educated and most delightful 'Westerners' you could possibly have met, in addition, of course, to his great Indian culture. It was he who, as Governor of Bengal just before Independence, had been consulted by the president of the British Club in Bengal on whether they should not change their rules, because at that time Indians could not be members or even guests. Rajaji, as he was known, said, 'Well, don't change too much, because we have our clubs too, and if you open your clubs too much to the Indians I may be expected to open our clubs to the Europeans, and I would find that much more difficult. So let me suggest that you just allow Indians to go as guests. It's very normal and natural that you should want to be on your own in your club, just as we do, too.' He was a wise man, and a delightful one, and we were privileged to see him from time to time. But there was something incongruous seeing him in Lutyens' magnificent palace on official occasions in his dhoti, surrounded by the magnificently uniformed Lancers of the presidential guard; and he himself used to smile at all this.

The Foreign Secretary, who was the Number Two man at the Indian Foreign Office, K. P. S. Menon, was a brilliant writer in English and yet remained also a complete Indian. We had invited him to a dinner party a long way ahead, and he had refused on the grounds that he would then be in the South marrying his daughter. The day before our dinner party I ran into him in Delhi and said, 'Oh, but I thought you were in the South?' He said, well, no, things had changed, but he did not quite like to explain why. But it turned out that the astrologers whom the grandparents had consulted rather late in the day had decided that the chosen day was inauspicious, and it had to be changed.

India has left very many memories, but one on which I should like to end came at the very beginning of my time in Delhi, when I was sent to the Loksabha, the Indian Parliament, for the final debate on India remaining in the Commonwealth. It was a foregone conclusion that the answer would be yes. But as I arrived, there was a former member of the Indian Civil Service opposing membership of the Commonwealth in beautiful English. To make his point near the end, he turned to Hindi and even had some quotations from Sanskrit. From all round the Loksabha there came, 'Please speak in English. We do not understand you.' I doubt if any similar debate ended on quite that note in any other formerly dependent country.

19 | Free Germany Joins the West

1951–4

I came back to London in the summer of 1951 as Deputy Under-Secretary of State responsible for German affairs. The negotiation of the Bonn Agreements, under which Adenauer's Federal Republic became to all intents and purposes independent, subject only to the retention of Allied rights in Berlin and in regard to All-German questions, had almost been completed. But the accompanying negotiations for West German rearmament within the proposed European Defence Community were far from completion. My German responsibilities involved me also in the affairs of the Atlantic Alliance and of the European Communities and in negotiation with the Soviet Union, and I suppose led to my becoming Permanent Representative on the Council of the Brussels Treaty Organization in London. There was also an administrative function in completing the dismantling of the occupation administrative machinery and returning German affairs into the normal Foreign Office channels. These developments flowed naturally from the Berlin blockade and airlift, except for German rearmament, for which the Korean War was responsible. I felt I was picking up the threads again from my days with Ernie Bevin two and a half years before.

Lord Henderson, the wise and friendly Minister in charge of German affairs under Herbert Morrison, provided a link with those days, but not for long. Within a short time the Conservatives were back with Churchill and Eden, under whom I had served throughout most of the war. It was like old times, although they had to adjust themselves, not without some difficulty, to the new machinery of multinational diplomacy in the then relatively young European and

153

Atlantic organizations. One fixed star in the new constellation was Dr Adenauer, whose casting vote had brought the first post-war German Government to Bonn, widely regarded as a 'provisorium' pending return to the national capital, Berlin. On the Petersberg, high above the Rhine, the three Western High Commissioners still exercised sovereign authority, although with ever increasing discretion. One of the best examples was Eden's investigations into the activities of a group of German neo-Fascists associated with Oswald Mosley. I had myself to plough through a mass of German documentation because we no longer had younger diplomats who knew German well enough for this.

I can perhaps best illustrate the basic change in the Anglo-German relationship by referring briefly to a few of the first issues with which I had to deal. The first was the German Debt Settlement, being negotiated most skilfully by Dr Abs of the Deutsche Bank, with a British diplomat, Sir George Rendel, and the former head of Pan American Airways, Mr Pearson. This was the first of Dr Abs's many post-war contributions to his own country and to Europe. It no doubt helped to build up his considerable reputation with Dr Adenauer and his successors. Even today, some forty years later, Abs is still active. Simultaneously with this settlement the Treasury were discussing with the Foreign Office the British contribution to an all-important loan to strengthen the Deutschmark, then going through a similar crisis to those which have frequently plagued the pound in later years. I think this was the last time in post-war history that West Germany needed our financial support!

Another major issue was the sale of an important German newspaper, *Die Welt*. The British had played probably the major role in re-establishing a democratic press in Germany after the war, if only because the major press centre was in Hamburg in the British zone. *Die Welt* had been run as a British occupation regime paper with great success. There were two possible solutions. One was to establish *Die Welt* as a trust, similar to that which at that time ran the *Observer* in London. The other was to sell to a very eager buyer, Axel Springer, then building up a major press empire which caused some alarm although not because of doubts about his democratic convictions. I think the preference of many people in London would have been for the *Observer*-style trust, but Axel Springer was offering a considerable sum of money. This decided the Treasury in his favour, and all that remained for me to do was to put my signature to a document assigning *Die Welt* to Axel Springer.

A third and very difficult problem on my desk in 1951 was revision of the sentences imposed at the Nuremberg Trials upon war criminals below Hitler's own circle. These ranged from distinguished German military leaders such as General Manstein to the most appalling concentration camp guards, male and female. Fortunately for this purpose, the Minister of State then responsible for German affairs under Anthony Eden was Selwyn Lloyd, a trained lawyer, through whom I submitted our official recommendations.

Selwyn Lloyd's appointment had been unexpected. When he received a telephone call from Churchill, then choosing his first post-war Government, he assumed that he might be Solicitor General or possibly, if he were very lucky, Attorney General. When the Prime Minister said he wanted him to be Minister of State under Anthony Eden at the Foreign Office, he protested that he knew nothing about foreign affairs. 'So much the better,' said Churchill. 'Anthony knows too much.' 'But I don't like foreigners,' said Selwyn. 'Even better,' said Churchill. 'You're exactly the man I want.' So thus began a career which brought him to the post of Foreign Secretary to be faced with the Suez crisis of 1956.

Anthony Eden and Selwyn Lloyd, who had been thus imposed upon him, did not at that time get on very well. The young Parliamentary Under-Secretary, Anthony Nutting, was Eden's favourite, and indeed a personality rather in Anthony's mould. The relationship was reversed in the Suez crisis, when Tony Nutting destroyed a most promising political career on an issue of principle. Most of the major German questions with which I was concerned were, however, of such importance that I handled them direct with Anthony Eden himself and even on occasion with the Prime Minister, as in 1953 and 1954. These of course included the European Defence Community and the Bonn Agreements. These have been covered by so many historians that I shall limit myself to those episodes with which I was personally connected, with the minimum of background explanation.

The greatest change since 1949 was the revised importance of France, which had only played a minor role in the Berlin airlift. It was the French who made the greatest difficulties in the Bonn negotiations, since they found it hardest to give up old ideas of reserving special rights for themselves in the Ruhr and Rhineland, and to reconcile themselves to a strong and independent even though truncated

Germany. François Poncet, the French High Commissioner in Bonn, complained to me in 1952 that if his Government continued so blindly with their opposition to the Germans being allowed to manufacture explosives (*poudres*, or powder), the Germans would not even be able to make tooth-powder! On the other hand, it was the French under Robert Schuman who had brought Germany into the Coal and Steel Community and who, under Jean Monnet's inspiration, had been working towards what became the European Economic Community. It was no fault of theirs that outside events diverted progress by economic collaboration into a much more difficult military channel. This arose through the unexpected outbreak in 1950 of the Korean War. Fears were revived in Continental Europe of a possible Soviet advance westwards from the eastern part of Germany. It seemed at least a possibility that Stalin's Soviet Union might be tempted to repeat in Germany, the divided country of Europe, the pattern of events in Korea, the divided country of Asia.

Western Europe was beginning its economic recovery under the Marshall Plan and the European Recovery Programme, but it had already been clear to Ernie Bevin before I had left for India that the Economic Recovery Programme would be in difficulties unless the Continental European countries concerned had complete confidence in their political future. This confidence was undermined by the Korean War. It is, I think, now fairly clear that one of the main reasons which impelled Stalin to order or to allow North Korea to attack South Korea was an unfortunate speech by the American Secretary of State, Dean Acheson, giving the impression that America was not interested in maintaining a military presence in South Korea. On this analogy it seemed even more important than after the Berlin Blockade that there should be a strong American military presence in Western Europe and that Roosevelt's policy of 'taking the boys home' should be reversed.

Although the North Atlantic Alliance had been signed in 1949, by 1951 little had been done to build up strong Allied defence forces, including American troops, on the Continent. The Americans insisted that their European allies should do more to defend themselves if American troops were to be sent back to Europe, and that this must involve a German military contribution. This created great psychological problems in Western Europe, above all in France but to an almost equal degree in Germany itself. Demilitarization had been a most successful and popular part of the occupation regime. Any revival of a German army had very few supporters in the Federal Republic of Germany, and least of all in the Chancellor, Dr Adenauer, who all his life had fought for civilian control and had been a strong opponent of Prussian and to that extent military traditions. The immediate problem was, however, France, which was not yet ready, only five years after its supposed victory but in fact defeat, to see a strong German national army. Bevin in Britain had been anything but enthusiastic and in vain tried various alternatives, such as an armed police force or a strengthened frontier defence force, which, however, were clearly inadequate.

It was clear, however, that the American requirement was not unreasonable and had to be met. As so often in the post-war years, the French were the most ingenious although not always ultimately the most successful in finding a solution. The basis for what has since become the European Community had already been created in the European Coal and Steel Community Treaty, signed in 1951, consisting of France, Germany, the Benelux countries and Italy but not including Britain. With this in mind, a leading French politician, René Pleven, in consultation with Jean Monnet, had thought up in October 1950 a similar European Defence Community. It was to be so constructed that the Germans, and for that matter the other constituent countries, would not have significant national units under national control.

This idea appealed very much to the then Administration in Washington, which had put its whole weight behind the idea of a European Community. Unfortunately, it appealed much less to Churchill, who described the whole concept as a 'sludgy amalgam', and what was more important, to General de Gaulle, then sulking in his retreat at Colombey-les-deux-Eglises but still a personality of great consequence, especially in military matters. In Germany the idea was grudgingly accepted and, in the case of Dr Adenauer, possibly welcomed, since he did not want to see a German national army again.

It had been expected on the Continent that the British attitude under a Churchill Government to all such European concepts would be very different and much more promising than that of the Labour Government. These hopes were based upon Churchill's great speeches at The Hague and Zurich, when he had been a promoter and almost the father of the new European construction. But what had not been clearly realized at the time was that Churchill, genuinely enthusiastic though he was for Franco-German reconciliation and therefore for the construction of a new and more united Europe, had never regarded Britain as a member of such an organization. He was very happy to be the best man blessing France and Germany as they came to the altar and promising them every kind of assistance short of membership. But there was no question of Britain joining in, and least of all of the British Armed Forces, then still deployed worldwide, being part of any such scheme.

This came as a great disappointment to the French. They had, in my view, been prepared and even perhaps pleased to get on with the Coal and Steel Community without Britain, more especially without the then Labour Government which was set on nationalizing British coal and steel. The absence of the British Armed Forces provoked very different reactions and removed what would have been a main attraction of the new scheme. But since it was a French proposal, successive French Governments – and they changed rapidly at that time – were committed to it, and behind them was strong American support, especially from Mr Dulles himself. Rather unfortunately, as it turned out, the French insisted that the political arrangements for setting up an independent West German state should be held on ice until agreement had been reached on what had unexpectedly become the connected issue of German rearmament and, as it was then hoped, on setting up the European Defence Community.

It was clear to us in the Foreign Office that the chances of the European Defence Community were anything but bright, more especially since Britain was not to be a member. Any immediate invasion threat in Germany, which had probably never existed at all, disappeared at an early stage. There then remained the European Defence Community as what had become the key to a united Europe. Foreign Office scepticism did not disappear, more especially given de Gaulle's strong opposition from Colombey-les-deux-Eglises. But we had to be careful not to advance these sceptical ideas, since we might then be held responsible for the eventual collapse of the Defence Community concept. In these circumstances it seemed, however, essential to have some fallback plan.

Our then Ambassador and my predecessor at NATO, Christopher Steel, was an old friend from early service together in Paris. We put our heads together and produced a scheme, almost identical with that later approved in 1954. This involved expanding the Brussels Treaty of 1948 to include West Germany and Italy, at the same time bringing West Germany into NATO as a full member, with in addition a

British commitment to station troops on the Continent. But this scheme had to be kept entirely secret lest it might seem intended to undermine the Pleven Plan.

Meanwhile, the political arrangements for an independent German state had been completed, and in 1952 the three previous occupying powers assembled in Bonn for the signature of what were then called the Bonn Agreements. Johnny von Herwarth, who afterwards made a great name for himself as the first post-war Ambassador in London and who was then Chief of Protocol, felt that the rather austere surroundings of the Government buildings in Bonn were a little unsuitable for such a ceremony, and decided to bring in some fine tapestries. Luckily, he never overlooked details. The night before the ceremony he went to see what tapestries had been produced from the vast choice in Germany, and found that the subject was 'The Rape of Europa', which hardly seemed the most appropriate subject. He had them changed overnight for something more suitable.

The political side of our problem was therefore settled. From 1952 onwards, Germany was treated as an independent member of the Western camp, and Dr Adenauer as one of the leading Western leaders. Apart from his great services to Germany, he was one of the great Europeans with Jean Monnet, Paul-Henri Spaak, Robert Schuman and de Gasperi who between them created the European Community. It was during this period that I got to know and admire Adenauer. My first meeting with him was on my first official visit to Bonn, at a small lunch party at which the other Germans present were his Deputy for Foreign Affairs, Hallstein, and his other main collaborator, Herbert Blankenhorn. On our side were our High commissioner, Ivone Kirkpatrick, the Deputy High Commissioner, Jack Ward, and myself. Adenauer always liked to dissociate himself from anything Prussian. He is alleged to have said that Germany had been ruled for too long by the drinkers of Schnapps (i.e. Prussia), for a shorter period but still far too long by the drinkers of beer (i.e. Hitler from Austria), and that now at last she had a better chance with a civilized leader from the Rhineland who drank wine. He was indeed a great authority on wine. His main claim to fame had been as the Lord Mayor of Cologne for very many years, but he had also been a major political figure in the Weimar Republic as a leader of the then Catholic Centre Party. He was considered as a possible Chancellor for one of the many Governments of the Weimar period. The Nazis threw him out of Cologne, and for a time he had to take refuge in Marialaach, a monastery south of Bonn. His qualifications for high office after the war were therefore impeccable. Adenauer never weakened in his post-war conviction that Germany's future lay in a firm institutional commitment of the Federal Republic to the West, only later to be extended to the whole of Germany.

Unfortunately, he had no reason to love the British. Although he had opposed French policies in the Rhineland after the First World War, his natural affinities were with the French. England was a far-away island of which he knew extremely little. To make matters worse, there was an unhappy incident when, shortly after he had been reappointed Lord Mayor of Cologne by the British occupation authorities, a British General, later Field Marshal Templar, on an inspection visit had complained to the local Brigadier, Barraclough, that the clearing up of the bomb damage in Cologne was far behind that in other cities. On being told that this was the responsibility of the new Mayor, Adenauer, he gave the order to sack him. Adenauer was not only thrown out of office but ordered to leave Cologne, where his wife was then in hospital with a dangerous illness. It had been overlooked that since Cologne was the only major German city on the left bank of the Rhine, Adenauer's priority had been to rebuild the Rhine bridges. It was therefore with less than enthusiasm that the British Labour Government found Adenauer chosen to be the first leader of the CDU and then elected Chancellor by one vote. Adenauer did not let all this rankle too much and often joked that if he had not been thrown out of Cologne he would not have become Chancellor.

Indeed in 1951 he was presented with an opportunity to prove this, by finding a simple way out of what could at that time have been an awkward lawsuit affecting Anglo-German relations. This arose from the claim of Prince Friedrich of Prussia for the return of an eighteenth-century Hohenzollern snuff-box 'appropriated' by the Royal Irish Fusiliers at the end of the war in compensation for the 'appropriation' by German forces occupying the Channel Islands of one given to the regiment by George II after the Battle of Dettingen. The Honorary Colonel of the Regiment was General Templar, in whose command Cologne lay when Adenauer was dismissed, but who in 1951 was defeating the Chinese Communists in Malaya. Adenauer's solution was to persuade his old 'adversary' to accept what he described as the first presentation by a German Chancellor to a British regiment for many decades of a modern snuff-box in exchange for the Hohenzollern box – part of a famous collection formed by Frederick the Great. I was happy and relieved to negotiate this exchange.

In all his dealings with the Allied authorities he showed the same gift of simplifying a problem and reaching clear and usually helpful decisions. In the 1954 negotiations in London which resulted in German membership of NATO and the WEU, the other members present, including Anthony Eden, got very irritated with Mendès-France who, they felt, overdid his repeated demands for concessions to ease his path in the forthcoming French parliamentary debate. I had frequently to be the intermediary. One of these problems was to get from Dr Adenauer not only renunciation of nuclear weapons but many other concessions. Again, Adenauer was clear and straightforward, and authorized me to give Mendès-France, without any equivocation, the guarantees he required.

Although by the time he became Chancellor he had reached the age of seventy-nine, he was extremely fit. His house at Röndorf, on the *Rhöndorf* other side of the Rhine from Bonn, was on a hill, and it could only be reached by climbing about a hundred steps, which he used to do at a rapid pace until his death. Moving forwards into the Sixties, when he was finally persuaded that he had to resign, I was almost the last person to take official leave of him. He had spent a month going all round Germany saying goodbye, taking parades, etc. He had come straight from his farewell session with the German Parliament and dealt with several other visitors before it came to my turn. I thought I would find at least a slightly tired Chancellor. Not a bit of it. His first word was that I had not been to see him for a long time. This was all too true, since Anglo-German relations had been soured by the signing of the Franco-German treaty with de Gaulle and the latter's consequent veto on British membership of the Community. His second was that he very much wanted to talk to me about relations with the Soviet Union. I had assumed he would have five minutes or at most a quarter of an hour for me, and I was giving a lunch party shortly afterwards. But Adenauer settled down to discuss Mr Khrushchev, and Soviet policies, and the effect of the break with China, and what German policies should be during the next decade, exactly as if he were starting a new decade of political responsibility instead of finally resigning. When I had to leave him, he urged me to return to complete our conversation.

Although my responsibilities were technically restricted to Germany, this inevitably involved me to some extent in the post-war reorganization of Europe and much more in the building up of the Atlantic Alliance. One of my first trips abroad took me to the Coal and Steel Community in Luxembourg and to the Council of Europe in Strasbourg. The Labour Government had not joined the Coal and Steel Community and were not expected or indeed desired to do so at that time by Jean Monnet and Robert Schuman. We did, however, appoint as our representative to the Community a former industrialist, Sir Cecil Weir, who had played a major part in the post-war reconstruction of Germany. One of his major achievements had been launching what became the great Hanover trade fair. I found the Coal and Steel Community living and working on top of each other on one floor of a relatively small hotel in Luxembourg. The inspiration and the guidance still came from Jean Monnet, who expressed his confidence that once the enterprise was clearly successful, Britain would want to become a member.

The Council of Europe, whose brief was mainly cultural, and including human rights, was rather different, with a wider membership and a parliamentary assembly. We were full members, and it was the first of the major post-war European institutions, of which the new Federal Republic of Germany was a member. There was immense German interest and enthusiasm, and students and schoolchildren were taken in large numbers to Strasbourg to learn about it. Unfortunately it was not Ernie Bevin's favourite child, and he tried to keep its affairs to its Council of Ministers. He had never felt at home in the British House of Commons and did not take to international parliamentary institutions. He produced one of his most famous Bevinisms: 'If you open that there Pandora's box, you never know what Trojan Horses may come popping out of it.'

I went on to Stuttgart and Munich, where German federal institutions were flourishing under American and French encouragement. In Munich our Consul General took me to see an interesting new institution, Radio Free Europe, set up by the Americans to broadcast to Eastern Europe. For over two decades since my retirement from the Foreign Service I have been on the West European Advisory Committee of Radio Free Europe and Radio Liberty, which started a little later and broadcast to the Soviet Union, when it proved very useful to have had this early contact. Those were the days when Radio Free Europe was financed by the CIA, which naturally aroused a certain amount of criticism. This continued until the mid-Fifties, and may have been partly responsible for the way in which Radio Free Europe's programmes encouraged the Hungarian rising in 1956, without any prospect of Western help. Since then, Radio Free Europe and Radio Liberty have been financed openly on the American budget, and the only official control has been the Presidential nomination of the members of the Board of Independent Broadcasting which is responsible for them, together with the inclusion in their terms of reference of an important clause that their broadcasts should not be inconsistent with the policies of the US Administration. They have played a major role in keeping the democratic spirit alive in Eastern Europe and their rewards have been the tributes paid to them in 1989 by Walesa, Havel and countless others and the demand that they should 'stay on'.

Returning to the political scene in 1952, there was one big advantage in the delay over the European Defence Community. Since the German population were anything but enthusiastic about rearmament, there were the makings of a major political split between the two great parties, with the SPD opposing the Chancellor's European policies. There was the very natural feeling of many Germans, more especially in the SPD, that for Germany to join a European Defence Community would be to shut the door on any immediate prospect of German reunification. The delay therefore provided an opportunity to bring home to the German people that there was no immediate or indeed middle-term prospect of the Russians agreeing to reunification on acceptable terms.

The Russians helped us in the long run, despite some initial embarrassment, by opening an exchange of notes early in 1952. These were drafted on the Western side by a group consisting of myself and the American and French Ministers in London. Anthony Eden, who was a great stickler for detail and had the strange idea that these notes would find a mass readership, took the closest personal interest and at times nearly drove us to distraction by insisting on commas being adjusted and adjectives changed, as we thought, unnecessarily. My French colleague once said that he was at an advantage since Anthony Eden could not question his French, whereas we and the Americans had to satisfy in the same language the sometimes different requirements of our two countries.

The exchange went on for some time, and included eight notes in all. In 1952 Stalin was still in complete control and we were going through the most frozen period of the Cold War. Naturally the Russians took exception to the build-up of NATO and the prospect of a European

Defence Community. In one of our replies we rather overdid our account of NATO as a peaceful organization with other than defence objectives, giving the Russian drafters the opportunity to have a joke at our expense, saying that they were so impressed that they must ask what steps they should take to apply for membership. More seriously, however, the first Soviet note of 10 March has been attributed by some German historians to Stalin himself, therefore perhaps providing a serious basis for negotiations on German reunification. Since my retirement I have been in correspondence with Dr Rolf Steininger of Innsbruck University, who has written much on this. It is impossible to prove that something which was not done would not have achieved what other people say might have been achieved if it had been done. I am, however, quite confident myself – and, what is more important, Adenauer and the three Western Governments were all convinced – that this was not a serious offer on Stalin's part but rather a reaction to the success of the Lisbon NATO ministerial meeting early in 1952.

Stalin's plain purpose, as with the Berlin blockade of 1948, was to interfere with the process of West German membership of Western organizations. This time the procedure was the carrot rather than the stick, and the design was to halt the negotiations then in train to anchor Germany firmly in the West by the prospect of serious negotiations with Russia on German reunification. The exchange of notes was completed with a far better understanding inside Germany of what was really at stake. At the Four-Power Berlin conference of Foreign Ministers in early 1954, after Stalin's death, this whole question was gone into again. It was clear from Molotov's attitude that the Soviet Union was not prepared to accept the conditions without which neither the three Western protecting powers nor the Federal German Government itself could have accepted reunification: free elections under appropriate safeguards in both parts of Germany, and freedom of choice for the resulting government in its international position. What Molotov offered us was the kind of rigged elections that we had already seen in Eastern Europe immediately after the war and agreement between the Four Powers in advance as to what the international position of a reunified Germany would be – inevitably neutrality, armed or disarmed. In Anthony Eden's phrase, either would have been equally dangerous, because if a neutral Germany were armed, who was to keep her neutral? and if disarmed, who was to keep her disarmed?

Meanwhile, no progress was made by successive French Governments in getting the French Parliament to face up to the approval or rejection of the European Defence Community project. Foreign Minister after Foreign Minister, including Bidault and Schuman, constantly assured John Foster Dulles that all would be well, but the time was never right to risk a vote. We believed it never would be right, because of the objections coming from General de Gaulle while France was getting more and more involved in her great crises in Vietnam and North Africa, but above all at that time in Vietnam.

At this juncture, Stalin died in 1953. There was no obvious successor. The first would-be candidate was possibly the former Police Chief, Beria, who seemed to me to have a more open mind on the future of Germany than many of his colleagues. This was probably one of the reasons for his downfall after the popular demonstrations in Berlin in the summer of 1953. One of the immediate effects of Stalin's death was to inspire Churchill, then the most senior Western statesman, that his last duty to the world was to re-establish with what he called the new rulers of Russia the kind of working relations which he and Roosevelt had had with Stalin during the war. This idea horrified Eisenhower in Washington, Adenauer in Bonn and successive French Prime Ministers in Paris. It was anything but welcome to Eden and the Cabinet or to the Foreign Office. Eden, however, became seriously ill at this period, and I found myself having to bear some of the burden of dissuading the Prime Minister from pursuing his project. Eisenhower, having made his opposition very clear, had left it to Churchill to make his own decisions.

My arguments were really twofold. The first was that there were as yet no clear successors to Stalin in the Kremlin with whom one could 'do business'. It was not until 1955 that Khrushchev came to the fore as the acknowledged Soviet leader. In the meantime, such messages as Churchill was able to send to Moscow were handled entirely by an old leader, Vyacheslav Molotov, all too well known to us as such. But the second and even greater difficulty was that any success in creating this kind of new relationship with the Soviet Union would inevitably have put paid to or at least indefinitely postponed the existing policies, almost completed, for making the Federal Republic an important member of the Western community of nations. Adenauer strongly opposed Churchill's plans, which had little if any support in the British Cabinet. There was, however, reluctance to oppose Churchill openly, and he did, against all the available advice, insist upon sending at least one feeler to Moscow.

Luckily for the West, the Russians themselves, clearly requiring time to work out their own future after Stalin's death, were in no mood to embark upon discussions with the West, and least of all with only one of the Western leaders and he, at this stage, a less important one than the American President or even, for these purposes, the German Chancellor. Discouraged on all sides, the Prime Minister had to give up or at least postpone his project. This is regarded by some historians as another opportunity missed, but the Russians at that time were not thinking in terms of serious negotiations for German reunification.

The Prime Minister's position was not helped by events in East Berlin shortly after Stalin's death. The workers in East Berlin staged major demonstrations which had to be put down by Soviet troops. This was the first of many similar clashes, repeated later in 1956 in Budapest and avoided only with some difficulty in Warsaw. I recall taking the news of these events in East Berlin to the Prime Minister. I expected that he would be rather attracted by the idea of brave men standing up for freedom. On the contrary, he was – and quite rightly – deeply worried, no doubt feeling that, if the demonstrations continued, there would be demands for support from the West, more especially as Berlin was not then divided by a Wall, which it would be too dangerous to meet.

Churchill maintained that his ideas need not have interfered with our Western plans for the future of Germany, but I think he was alone in that view. At all events, he did not readily or completely give them up. He was particularly anxious that there should be a preliminary high-power meeting between the Western leaders to prepare the way for a possible summit meeting with whoever might by then have emerged as the Soviet leader.

At a crucial period, Churchill and Eden were both either ill or out of the country; Rab Butler was acting for the Prime Minister and in a sense for the Foreign Secretary, although Lord Salisbury was in charge of affairs in the Foreign Office. I found myself seeing a lot of Rab Butler at that time. To my surprise, although clearly his position was a delicate one, he would ask me what Winston or Anthony would have done in the circumstances, which gave me some understanding for the later reluctance of many of his colleagues to accept him as Prime Minister after Suez.

During this period Lord Salisbury and I went to Washington for talks with Eisenhower and Dulles. This meeting was designed to clear the way for a further meeting including the French, and if all went well, a Four-Power meeting later on including the Russians. Adenauer did not fit into this particular group of talks but was consulted at all stages. We had a lunch at the White House, at which I met my old Moscow friend, General Bedell Smith, then in a senior position close to the President. I had never been on official business in Washington, and asked Bedell Smith to tell me who the other people at the table were. When we came to Lyndon Johnson, who was then the Democrat Leader of the Senate, Bedell Smith said, 'That is the most important political figure in the United States, and anybody who wants legislation has to get it done through him. One day he will be the President.' His prophecy was fulfilled, although not in the way that Bedell Smith had expected. I recall also having pointed out to me my future American colleague in Bonn, George McGhee, one of the small group of non-professionals who have played such an active and successful role in American diplomacy. But it was not this that Bedell Smith had to say about him. He said, 'George is the kind of man we admire in America. Although the son of a millionaire, he made his own million before he was twenty-one.'

At all events, our visit to Washington should have given some pleasure to the Prime Minister, as it did lead on to a meeting between him and Eisenhower and the then French Prime Minister, Laniel, in Bermuda later that year. The Prime Minister was still recovering from illness. The great men were separated from their staffs in villas, with the rest of us in hotels, summoned as and when required. I was summoned to the Prime Minister on one occasion, and was puzzled by the questions he put to me. I was told that after I left he had remarked to John Colville, 'That was a very perceptive American official: he seemed to understand our point of view very well.'

Once again, however, the Bermuda meeting achieved its objective and did in fact provide the basis for a renewed Four-Power meeting at Foreign Minister level with the Russians in Berlin in the hard winter of 1954. Apart from the obvious advantage of renewing contact at that level with Moscow, one of our main purposes was once again to show German public opinion that everything possible was being done to explore the possibility of agreement with the Soviet Union before reaching decisions on the European Defence Community and the future of Germany, which must affect the prospect of German reunification.

The Berlin conference of 1954, at which I was the senior official with the Foreign Secretary, was in itself an interesting event. There had been no meeting with Soviet leaders at that level since 1949, marking the end of the Berlin Blockade. We had an old acquaintance in front of us in

Molotov. He had lost none of his ability to say no, and to argue every case to the bitter end. We were there for several weeks in what was a very, very cold Berlin, with what seemed to be less heating in our newly opened hotel than must have been available in Berlin during the airlift. At one stage during the negotiations Anthony Eden tried to bring matters to a head by presenting the next morning a detailed British plan for free elections in both parts of Germany. I had passed on his instructions to Michael Palliser, who was then working with me. He worked right through the night, and the next morning we had the Eden Plan, which was not accepted by the Russians but on which the Western powers could stand. Its main points were that elections in Eastern Germany not only had to be called free but, given the precedent of post-war elections in Eastern Europe, had to be guaranteed freedom with effective supervision, and above all that the all-German Government emerging from such elections should have freedom of choice in its international relations. We were prepared to accept a choice for the East, but I must admit that we were fairly sure in our own minds that this was the least of the dangers facing us. What Molotov refused in 1954 has been accepted by Gorbachev in 1990.

As always at such conferences, each of the Foreign Ministers gave at least one large party. Molotov's party was given at the palatial Soviet Embassy in Unter den Linden. My wife accompanied me to the reception. This was the first time that she had met Molotov since 1947. Unconfirmed stories about Mrs Molotov having been in trouble in Stalin's later years and even about Molotov having fallen under Stalin's displeasure had reached the West, but nobody knew the truth. As we moved forward in the receiving line, my wife used her rusty Russian to say that Molotov might not remember her, to receive the amazing reply, 'Oh no, I remember you well, because you remind me of the good days. You do not know what my wife and I have been through since then.' This was an astonishing statement from Molotov of all people.

At the conference table, however, Molotov did not thaw or unbend to anything like the same extent. Since we in the West were in full agreement with the German Government and were determined to go ahead to anchor West Germany in Western institutions unless the Russians were prepared, which they were not, to agree acceptable terms for German reunification, it was clear that there would be no return to Four-Power cooperation in Berlin. Some time was devoted to the Austrian peace treaty, but the time was not yet right, although it appeared that the Russians were more flexible over this than over the more important question of Germany. What was achieved in the conversations behind the scenes was agreement between Anthony Eden and Molotov over not so much the substance but the procedures for dealing with the Vietnam question. It was at Berlin that the foundations were laid for what became the Anglo-Soviet presidency of the joint Commission on Vietnam, which did useful work in the following years. At all events, after the Berlin Conference, no one in Germany could complain about the Western Allies and Dr Adenauer proceeding with existing policies at the expense of German reunification, and at that time, whatever some historians may say today, there was no disposition to give the benefit of any doubts to the Russians.

We were still waiting for the French Parliament to debate the European Defence Community – in the American case, in the hope that they would approve it, in our case, in the certainty that they would not. The French priority was their losing war in Vietnam. We had to wait for Mendès-France to come to power with a twin and rather unpopular policy, first, of settling the Vietnam problem with large concessions from France, and secondly, bringing to a head the European defence issue. Having got the agreement of the Chamber of Deputies to a Vietnam solution, he was then the first Prime Minister who put the European Defence Community to the vote, to find it rejected by a fairly large majority, as had been expected.

I think we in London were the only people who were not taken aback by this result. There was consternation and despondency throughout Europe, most of all in Bonn, where the Chancellor felt that this meant the complete collapse of all his European policies, but also to a considerable extent in Washington. A first step had been for the Prime Minister, now more or less recovered from his illness, to invite Mendès-France to Chartwell for a serious talk, at which I was present. Although I doubt whether they had met during the war, Churchill respected Mendès-France for his courage as a member of the French resistance, moving between France and London. Churchill welcomed him in his most courtly manner as 'Mr France', but went on to say that he understood he was an unusual French Prime Minister, who only drank milk. Mendès-France explained that this was a misunderstanding arising from his attempt to give a lead to the younger generation in France (who were beginning to drink too much Pernod and other spirits) to adopt a more simple lifestyle. 'Ah,' said Churchill, 'my doctors have also told me that I should adopt the simple life. And I do,

I do. I drink nothing but champagne and brandy, and I smoke nothing but cigars.' From this rather unpromising opening the Prime Minister gave Mendès-France the message that it was not enough to have brought matters to a negative vote in the Chamber of Deputies. Another solution now had to be found without delay and he looked for French cooperation in this task.

It was then for Anthony Eden to take up the torch, which he did to great effect. One Sunday he rang me at home with the proposal that he and I should go round the capitals of Western Europe to get things moving again and that we should start at once. As a good official I asked, 'But what do we go with, and what about the Americans?' Dealing with the latter point first, Anthony Eden, whose relations with Dulles were anything but good, replied that we now had the opportunity and the duty to take the initiative, since the Americans' preferred plans had collapsed. In reply to my first question he reminded me of the Steel–Roberts plan. His main concern was rightly that no time should be lost and that Mr Dulles should be given no opportunity to carry out his old threat of a massive reappraisal of American policy.

Mr Dulles was not best pleased, but had to leave it to us. The easiest meeting was our first, in Brussels, where the Dutch and Luxembourg Foreign Ministers joined M. Spaak. All of them being strong Europeans and worried about the future of Germany, they were in a state of some despondency. When Anthony Eden explained our plan, they were immensely relieved and had no complaint that it did not in itself advance the 'European' cause. The great thing was to find a way out of the very serious current crisis, and I think they would have jumped at almost any solution. At all events, they put their weight fully behind Eden and gave us a good start.

From there we went to see Dr Adenauer. I had never seen him in such complete despair. Whether it was the construction of Europe or the building up of a Western Germany as a preliminary to German reunification or the plans for Franco-German reconciliation, everything had collapsed around him. But he was always a man for getting rapidly to the kernel in anything that was put before him. As soon as Anthony Eden had explained his plan, Adenauer's spirits rose, and we left Bonn with his full support. Again, although a great European, he realized that this was not the moment to put the construction of a new Europe before the immediate problems.

Our next stage was in Rome, where we were not anticipating any major difficulties and indeed did not find any, more especially as the Italians were delighted that they and the Germans should join the Brussels Treaty, which would then become Western European Union. With NATO there was no problem, since Italy was already a member.

In Rome we coincided with Field Marshal Montgomery, who was on his way to talk to the Yugoslavs about the then unresolved problem of Trieste. As I had already been told that I should be going as Ambassador to Yugoslavia, I was extremely interested. The Field Marshal said he had been speaking to the Italians before going on to his friends in Yugoslavia. He then brought out a map and showed me exactly what should be done. A lot of it was rather detailed: I remember great importance attached to either giving up or keeping a lighthouse on one particular point. But having checked with the Field Marshal that these were the maps he intended to show to the Yugoslavs, I could not help remarking that they were Italian Ministry of War maps, and that this might not help him with the Yugoslavs. He changed the maps and did, I think, make a helpful contribution to the impending Trieste settlement. It had been reached before I went later in the year to Belgrade.

Our last call, obviously the most difficult, was Paris. We had left it to the last in the justified hope of having the full support of the five other countries. Mendès-France was in a difficult situation. He was not a very popular French leader, although he had temporarily acquired popularity through the Vietnam settlement. But he was in no mood to risk defeat in the French Parliament on German rearmament, on which most Frenchmen felt very strongly. As against this he realized – partly, no doubt, because of the message he had been given by Winston Churchill at Chartwell – that he could not postpone the issue yet again. Indeed, the Prime Minister had made it clear that if necessary we and the Americans would have to go ahead without France. So he was basically reconciled to having to go back to Parliament with an alternative, which could be based upon our plan as well as any other, but he argued with some justification that it was most important that he should be sure of a majority in so doing. In order to get this majority he therefore pleaded for a number of concessions, such as renunciation of nuclear weapons, some of which we felt Adenauer could be persuaded to accept, while others seemed to go too far. At all events, he agreed to come to a conference at Lancaster House in London in October 1954.

It was a major and successful conference at which I was privileged to serve as Anthony Eden's senior adviser. It resolved itself very largely into deciding not only how far one could go to meet Mendès-France but also how far his demands had to be opposed in order that he could explain in Paris that he could not get anything more from his allies. Adenauer was in very constructive mood. But Mendès-France wanted more, in the shape of assurances from Britain and, as far as possible, from the United States on the presence of our forces on the Continent. Although this had never yet been mentioned, it had always been a part of the British plan that we would commit ourselves to certain force levels on the Continent, as revolutionary a step for any British Government as the American move away from isolation to peacetime commitments in the North Atlantic Treaty had been for America. I think this is taken too much for granted today, in the light of so many other commitments we have had to make. At all events, Anthony Eden, again with his shrewd sense of timing and how to get things through the Cabinet, had waited until a solution was in sight. Then, at a small meeting of Ministers one night at Number 10, he got agreement to maintain under the Western European Union Treaty four divisions and the second tactical air force on the Continent of Europe. But we did include the escape clauses that, in the event of serious financial problems or of overseas requirements, we could withdraw some of the forces, but only with the consent of a two-thirds majority of the Western European Union and after consultation with SACEUR. When Anthony Eden returned the next day to the conference with this proposal, success was assured. Mendès-France felt that with this he could get a majority in the French Parliament. To make matters even better, our commitment led Mr Dulles to make a less far-reaching but also important commitment that American forces would also be left in Europe as long as the United States felt this was desirable and necessary.

The October conference ended on this happy note. British prestige stood at its highest point in Europe in the post-war period. This was also the height of Anthony Eden's success as a Foreign Minister. He had, in fact, had an annus mirabilis. There had been the Vietnam agreement providing that he and Gromyko should play important roles in future developments there; the termination of the crisis with Mussadeq in Iran; the Trieste settlement, bringing Italy and Yugo-slavia together again; the Suez settlement with Nasser; and this major European settlement.

Shortly afterwards I was summoned to Number 10 by Winston Churchill late one evening to check the speech he was to make in praise of Anthony Eden's successes in 1954. I need hardly say that officials did not write the drafts for Churchill's speeches, and were only required to check on facts. I reached a point at which I saw the Prime Minister looking rather anxiously at me, and I noticed that in the list of Anthony Eden's achievements, one was missing: Suez. Almost before I had opened my mouth to point this out, the Prime Minister said, 'I know what you're going to say, but I won't put it in. I don't regard it as an achievement.' I suggested that in that case it might be better to have no listings, but the fact remained that it was generally regarded as an achievement, and it would be considered very odd if it were not mentioned. This brought from the Prime Minister a very grumpy 'Have it your own way. But I still don't think it was an achievement.'

It was on this occasion that I noticed the trouble that the Prime Minister took over the choice of words in his speeches. I happened to look at my watch just as he was crossing out an adverb and trying to find another. He spent twenty-three minutes at a very busy time finding exactly the right adverb, and I think he tried about ten to a dozen during that time.

It was also on this occasion that, when the early editions of the morning papers were brought in to the Prime Minister between eleven and midnight, he looked at a cartoon which was based upon his own and Anthony Eden's performance during the year, when they had each been ill. It showed them having a race in bath-chairs along the front at Bournemouth with the Prime Minister clearly in the lead. He cheered up immensely at this. 'There, you see, they still think I'm better than Anthony.'

Indeed, it was one of the sorrows of that whole period that he was so frequently disappointing Anthony Eden by saying that he would be retiring and then not doing so. Apart from his own desire, which is that of most political leaders, to stay on a bit longer with a view to achieving certain things that the individual considers he can achieve better than other people, there was, I think, a doubt in his own mind whether Anthony Eden would prove as good a Prime Minister as he had proved a Foreign Secretary. Indeed, we now know that in the talks that took place from time to time on the timing of the hand-over, Churchill did try to persuade Eden to give up the Foreign Office in order to get more experience of home affairs. But Eden knew that the Foreign Office was his main source of strength, and he was determined not to leave his main base until he was Prime Minister.

20 | Tito's Yugoslavia
1954–7

I was not perhaps as excited as I should have been by the prospect of my first Embassy, to which we went in November 1954, possibly partly because, even as 'Number Two', I had had unusual opportunities, above all in Moscow but also in Delhi, each of them big and important posts, and also perhaps because of the very interesting time I had had in the Foreign Office, particularly during the last month leading up to the London agreements on Germany. But I cheered myself up with the remark made to me by the Permanent Under-Secretary at the Foreign Office, Sir Ivone Kirkpatrick, that the Yugoslav leadership under Tito was in his view one of the most intelligent in the world, and that whilst I might from time to time be irritated, I would never be bored. I found that both these pieces of good advice were fully borne out. Although our time in Yugoslavia was relatively short – just under two and a half years – it was a very agreeable and most interesting posting.

Yugoslavia at that time played a political role which was much greater than her size or historical record would normally have suggested. This was partly due to the personality of Tito, but also to the fact that Yugoslavia was at that time the only independent Communist country in Europe, apart from the maverick Albania. The break with the Soviet Union in 1948, although comparatively recent, was, I found, rather ancient history in the minds of the Yugoslavs. At a time when Khrushchev had only just taken over power in Moscow and when contact with the Soviet leaders still reflected Stalin's Cold War, the Yugoslavs provided an important window on the affairs not only of the Soviet Union but also of Eastern Europe generally.

The Yugoslavs had already developed what they considered a rather special kind of Communism, in that their factories and other institutions had much more autonomy than was the case in the planned economies of the Soviet Union and the Soviet satellites in Eastern Europe. The Yugoslavs were very proud of this system, which did indeed seem to have certain features which might act as a model for reforms in other Communist societies although this has not in fact proved to be the case.

I suppose as a sort of self-defence against pressures from the Soviet Union and possibly Bulgaria, the Yugoslavs had fairly recently joined with the Greeks and the Turks in a Balkan Alliance. This was on the face of it unusual, since Greece at that moment was under a king and Turkey had never been a particularly good friend of any Balkan country. There were, however, people in the West and some even in London who had the strange idea that the Balkan Alliance might be used as a sort of link joining Yugoslavia with the Atlantic Alliance, and assumed that one of my main tasks in Belgrade would be to forward this particular concept, in which I myself never believed.

It was important for Tito to develop a position in the world for himself and for Yugoslavia, which remained a Communist country and could not therefore join Western Europe but which equally was regarded as a complete heretic in the Communist world. Tito found the solution in becoming one of the main leaders of the non-aligned world. The major leader was Nehru in India, and Sukarno in Indonesia also played a less responsible leadership role. A younger disciple coming on the scene was Nasser, who had just become dominant in Egypt. Later on Castro had pretensions to be a leader of the non-aligned world, despite his close links with the Soviet Union. The major figures in this enterprise were, however, undoubtedly Nehru and Tito, with Nasser rapidly developing his prestige throughout the Arab world.

This aspect of Yugoslav policy was not very welcome to the US Administration, in which Dulles was dominant as Secretary of State. He and most Americans took the rather simplistic view that countries had to be either with or against them, and there was not much place in their philosophy for the non-aligned. On the other hand, Yugoslavia had broken with the Soviet Union and was very dependent at that time on American military and above all economic support, largely in weapons and wheat. The British position in Yugoslavia was a rather special one, and one which made the position of Ambassador particularly privileged and agreeable. We owed this to that small group who had been parachuted into Yugoslavia during the war and had suffered the same privations with Tito and his partisans in their heroic campaigns. The obvious names are those of Fitzroy Maclean and Bill Deakin and Randolph Churchill. They had certainly earned the friendship of Tito and his partisans to a much greater degree than the Soviet mission, who had not been so happy sharing the privations and problems of the partisan forces.

This had not, however, prevented Tito at the end of the war from becoming extremely anti-Western. There were great difficulties between Tito and the West, particularly over Trieste. His harsh treatment of the Serbian Royalist leader Mihailovic and of other defeated enemies in Yugoslavia also caused serious trouble. Above all, Tito provided extensive support to the Communists in the Greek Civil War when even Stalin seemed to be holding to his agreement with Churchill to treat Greece as within the Western sphere of interest. Once, however, the break came with Moscow, the Yugoslavs recalled their happier wartime relationship with the British, as I found in my dealings with Tito and his colleagues, who were then welcomed in London. The only fly in the ointment was the persecution of Djilas, once Tito's closest partisan comrade, for his criticism of the new Yugoslav establishment. This was especially resented in the Labour Party, where Nye Bevan and Jennie Lee were good friends of Djilas.

Yugoslavia's main problem, then as now, was whether a united Yugoslavia really existed. Of all the Versailles Treaty constructions, Yugoslavia was the most complicated. It was described as one country with six republics, five nationalities, four religions (including Communism!), three languages and two scripts. The only person regarded as a Yugoslav was Tito himself. Apart from him, the unifying forces were the Communist Party and the Yugoslav Army, although the army was largely officered by Serbs and Montenegrins.

One of the main problems for Yugoslavia was that each republic naturally wanted to have the same standard of living as the others, and factories which were working perfectly well in Slovenia and Croatia had to be duplicated in the entirely different conditions of Macedonia and Montenegro and even most of Serbia. This was, and remains, a great strain on the Yugoslav economy.

In these circumstances it was necessary for a British Ambassador to travel a lot in what was an extremely interesting and beautiful country. At that time we had Consuls not only in Zagreb, the second city of the

Republic, but also in Skoplje, the capital of Macedonia, in Sarajevo in Bosnia, and also on the Dalmatian coast at Split. In modern conditions these have now been reduced to one in Zagreb. We were also rather privileged to visit Brioni, the special holiday resort for Tito and the leading Yugoslavs. It had, before the war, been one of the most sought after resorts in Europe, and certainly the Yugoslav Establishment benefited from the old luxury. I was amazed to find so many of our Yugoslav contacts with their heads bobbing out of the very fine swimming pools at Brioni and obviously living an extremely pleasant life in the very good hotels there. Tito himself was established on a tiny island next to Brioni, where he very occasionally received major visitors but which we did not see.

Apart from Tito himself, who was most accessible, I found the other Yugoslav leaders quite as interesting and intelligent as I had been led to expect. My high-level contacts were mostly with Kardelj, a Slovene and the ideologist of Yugoslav Communism. At my first meeting with him I asked him to tell me a little more about the circumstances in which the Soviet Union had broken with Yugoslavia. He corrected me with a smile, saying that when I had been in Yugoslavia a bit longer I would put the question in the form of when Yugoslavia had broken with the Soviet Union, since they preferred to think of it in that light. After many talks with him, I gained the strong impression that the Yugoslavs were the Anglicans of the Communist world, and indeed Tito had some resemblances to Henry VIII. They regarded themselves as much more genuine Communists than those of Moscow, just as Henry VIII had regarded himself as a better Catholic than the Pope. I would not want to carry the resemblance too far, since Tito married only half the number of Henry VIII's wives and did not behead any of them, but in other respects he was a very similar ebullient, extrovert character with great attraction and yet obviously capable of pretty ruthless behaviour, both during the war and afterwards.

One of the more amusing figures was Mosa Pijade, who was a sort of elder statesman, his position having arisen largely from the fact that he had shared a prison cell with Tito for many years. Pijade had been a rather good painter and had studied in Paris. He was extremely quick-witted, and could be rather difficult in conversation. I had been warned of this, and when I first met him I thought I would choose a relatively neutral subject of conversation by asking him about his meeting with Winston Churchill on a recent visit he had paid to the United Kingdom. As he was not helping me very much, I produced the rather ridiculous statement that there were similarities and differences between him and Churchill. He was interested but not unduly complimented by this, and asked me to explain. When I said that he had started as a painter and become a politician whereas Churchill had started as a politician and become a painter, Pijade said, 'Oh, but there's another difference'; and when I innocently asked him what that was, he replied, 'I am a painter', which stopped the conversation.

We had already met in Paris when many of the Yugoslav leaders were there in 1946 for the Balkan peace conference. I was then told that several of the Yugoslavs who wanted an evening out said to Mosa that he must know the Paris nightclubs and perhaps he could take them to some of the better ones. Unfortunately his Paris had very much changed, and they spent about an hour or two looking for Mosa Pijade's old haunts, which no longer existed.

We often met but did not get to know Rankovic well, who ran the Interior Ministry and the Police, but we saw a certain amount of Tempo, the economic overlord, and of Colakovic, who was a sort of cultural overlord. They, with Kardelj, made up Tito's Vice-Presidents. The Foreign Minister, Koca Popovic, was a very interesting character. He came of a well-to-do Serbian bourgeois family. We had known his sister very well, who had been the wife of the then Royalist Yugoslav Chargé d'Affaires in Cairo before the war. Koca, like most of the Serbian bourgeoisie, had been educated in France, spoke excellent French, and was in many ways a brilliant French intellectual. He had joined the partisans and become one of the best generals in the partisan forces. As Foreign Minister he was rather dreaded by the Diplomatic Corps, since he suffered fools anything but gladly; and all diplomats at one time or another are apt to find themselves behaving foolishly to a Foreign Minister. I was lucky in that on the whole we always had fairly good relations.

I did more business, however, with his deputies, one of whom, Prica, afterwards became Ambassador in London and was the Yugoslav representative when diplomatic talks were held between the Yugoslav and the British, French and American Governments through their Ambassadors in Belgrade in 1955. The deputy from whom I got the most valuable information was Micunovic. He had been a General in the Yugoslav Secret Service, but was anything but secretive in what he told me about the Soviet Union. He had been Ambassador there and was to return in the latter days of Stalin and of Khrushchev. I found him as attractive as I found nearly all other Yugoslavs, with also very good judgement on the Soviet scene – a view which has been fully borne out by what I have since read in his excellent memoirs which, rather to the surprise of many Yugoslavs, were published in Yugoslavia even under Tito. Naturally, as a Communist, even though a dissident Communist, he had better access to ruling circles in Moscow than any Western Ambassador could hope to have, and his views, although usually critical, were correspondingly more valuable.

Since we were encouraging our cultural ties with Yugoslavia we also saw a lot of another amusing Paris-educated Serbian ex-bourgeois, Marco Ristic. My wife shared a certain amount of French culture with him and also what we discovered to be a shared boredom with folklore. It was Marco Ristic's duty on the many official occasions we attended to present Yugoslav folklore from each of the republics. It was very good but somewhat repetitive; and, as he pointed out to my wife on one occasion, he had to see it more frequently than she did. But he also introduced us to a rather deeper Yugoslav culture, and it was through him that we met the outstanding Yugoslav writer, Andric, who won the Nobel Prize for two or three of his excellent novels.

Another good contact was Vladko Velebit, who had a lot to do with the British. He also came from good bourgeois stock in Zagreb, and was afterwards a very successful Yugoslav Ambassador in London. Indeed, he became suspect in certain Yugoslav circles as too pro-British. His connection with Tito was an interesting one. In the mid-Thirties Tito had gone to Moscow as a rather junior, rising Communist. The non-Soviet Communists were all put in the same Moscow hotel, the Lux, and Tito was with the other leaders of the Yugoslav Communist Party. Stalin became as suspicious of foreign Communists as he was of his own Communists, and his purges extended to them. The result was that all the older leaders of the Yugoslav Communist Party were shot or disappeared, and Tito found himself the leader and had to return to Yugoslavia. Velebit, who was in the pre-war Communist underground, as a good bourgeois figure, was given the task of meeting Tito in Istanbul. He was looking out for some rather young and simply-dressed figure, but already at that time Tito was as interested in clothes as he remained for the rest of his life. Velebit told me that he had no problem getting Tito back into Yugoslavia because he looked far more bourgeois than he did himself. His only worry was that Tito insisted on wearing rather expensive rings, a taste which he shared with a less attractive figure, Marshal Goering.

There were many occasions when we dined in either big or small parties with the Yugoslav leaders, sometimes with and sometimes without Tito. We found on such occasions that they really remained, even ten years after the end of the war, a group of old partisans, fighting their old battles again together over dinner in much the same way as in England you might find members of football teams, or of the same school or college, assembling at dinners to talk about their old sporting battles. They used to joke and rag each other, always with respect for Tito but sometimes with less than respect for each other; and one of the more attractive features of these occasions was that they tended to forget that there were foreigners – myself and my wife – listening to all this.

Other occasions when one got to know the Yugoslav leaders in a similar way were at Tito's annual hunting parties. He had taken over all the old hunting lodges of the Yugoslav kings, and many others as well. I was told on good authority that whereas the last King of Yugoslavia had a maximum of six palaces, some small and one for each republic, Tito had thirty-eight houses he could use throughout the country. My Austrian colleague, who was a highly intelligent Socialist, described Tito as a 'typical nobleman of the old Austro-Hungarian Empire, living on and enjoying his wide estates, moving from country house to country house'; and there was certainly this aspect to Tito. I did not myself shoot, and found that the Diplomatic Corps whom Tito invited was, like Caesar's Gaul, divided into three. There was a small group of good shots; there was a small group like myself, who did not shoot at all; and there was a large group in the middle, including nearly all the Communist Ambassadors, many of whom ought really not to have shot but nevertheless thought they would 'have a go'. This made the occasion rather dangerous: indeed, after our departure, a French Ambassador was killed on one of these occasions, but there were no such misadventures in our time. We found that the evenings spent together with the Yugoslav leadership over barbecues were extremely rewarding, as clearly one got to know them even better in such circumstances than back in Belgrade.

Another place where one met the Yugoslav leaders, with the exception of Tito, was at the Sunday football matches. The Yugoslavs were very keen on football and had a good national team. I had the privilege of the equivalent of the Royal box, and even though I was less interested in soccer than they were I used to make a point of going to most football matches in order to meet them, again on occasions when they were at their most interesting. We had one great football occasion when Scotland came out to play Yugoslavia, and this was the occasion for one of our most successful cocktail parties, when various Yugoslav leaders, who we had not thought would wish to be invited specially, rang up to ask whether they could come. The match ended very appropriately in a draw, thanks to the brilliance of the Scottish goalkeeper. Another but less exciting sporting occasion was the Davis Cup match between the British, then rather better at tennis than we have since become, and Yugoslavia. There were also, on a beautiful lake at Bled in our last summer, the European rowing championships, when I am glad to say the British team did extremely well. This was not a sport at which the Yugoslavs especially excelled.

We were lucky enough to have quite a number of artistic events, which we very much encouraged, since Yugoslavia was at this time the only relatively open Communist country. The most important was a major Henry Moore exhibition, the first such exhibition in a Communist country, in most of which at that time art was still expected to be socialist and realist. There was immense interest, and when Henry Moore was asked to speak to a specially invited audience and the students were all encouraged to join us at the end of his speech, there was a mass surge of what seemed to be thousands of students invading the hall. The Yugoslav artists, as indeed we found many Soviet artists in far more difficult circumstances later, were extremely interested in modern art and very aware of and in touch with most modern developments. Henry Moore handled all this very well. My wife, being interested in sculpture, wanted to get him to talk about sculpture, whereas he seemed to be only interested in asking us about diplomatic life. Other important artistic visits were those of Beriosova and David Blair, then leading dancers in the Royal Ballet, who were to dance with the Yugoslav Ballet, and later, Benjamin Britten and Peter Pears. We also had a successful cinema month, which was opened by Anthony Asquith.

The arts in Yugoslavia also followed the old lines of division, in that in the Orthodox areas, Serbia and Macedonia, there was a strong tradition of painting based upon the beautiful frescoes in the many old churches, whereas in Croatia in the more Catholic north, the tradition was more one of sculpture, with the great sculptor Mestrovic as one of the great national figures. In Slovenia, which could well be part of Austria (as it once was), there was a remarkable opera house where we were taken to see a *Don Giovanni* which was of quite as high quality as anything in Vienna. When we said this to our host, the President of

Slovenia, he said that the unfortunate thing was that the Vienna opera house continued to recruit many of its best singers from Slovenia, one of the best ones at that time being Jurinac.

Since Yugoslavia was of considerable interest not only to Britain but to the Western world in general at that time, there were a number of important visitors. Two visits I recall particularly were those of the Belgian Foreign Minister, Paul-Henri Spaak, and the Norwegian Foreign Minister, Halvard Lange, each of whom I got to know well shortly afterwards when I moved to NATO. As a result of the Balkan Alliance we also had visits from the King and Queen of Greece and from the Turkish Prime Minister. Since the Greek and Turkish Ambassadors, both of them widowers, were among our best friends in Belgrade, we saw a great deal of the delegations on these occasions, which were designed, I suppose, on all three sides to keep the Alliance in being, without the ambition of putting any greater content into it.

A distinguished British visitor was Field Marshal Montgomery. As Deputy Supreme Commander in NATO, he rather wisely had created a role for himself outside the military headquarters where his position as a five-star General might have conflicted with that of his American superior, General Norstad, with only four stars. He had become a sort of roving ambassador for NATO, and had established a rather good relationship with Tito, having played some part in the Trieste Settlement shortly before our arrival in Belgrade. The story went (and Tito did not deny it) that at their first meeting Tito had been rather concerned lest the Field Marshal might want to bring him within the NATO fold. When Monty realized that this was the cause of the President's reserve, he at once told Tito that he would never dream of having Yugoslavia in NATO; and when Tito enquired why, he replied, 'Because you would be a bacillus in any alliance you were in. You should stay entirely on your own, but if you are in trouble, let me know, and I will draw my sword and come to your aid.' This was exactly the position that Tito wished to be in, and afterwards he was a firm friend of the Field Marshal, who paid annual visits to Belgrade.

On one of these visits I was invited to a lunch given for him by the Yugoslav Minister of Defence, General Gosniak. Apart from the Field Marshal and myself, there were twelve Yugoslav Generals. Monty, addressing the whole party, said that he had had some trouble recently with his political masters at NATO, at which I pricked up my ears. He went on to say that, having established a very happy personal relationship with one of the great soldier-statesmen of Europe,

Group photograph at presentation of letters to the then Soviet President Brezhnev with British Embassy staff and Soviet officials.

The author and his wife in the British Embassy after presentation of letters.

Nikita Khrushchev with the author and his wife at a British Trade Fair reception: with Reginald Maudling (Secretary of State for Trade), Furtseva (Soviet Minister of Culture), Mikoyan and Robert Maxwell also in centre.

Nikita Khrushchev with the author again at a British Trade Fair reception: with, from left to right, Lord Drogheda, Reginald Maudling, Soviet official and Mrs Maudling.

Nikita Khrushchev with the author at opening of British Trade Fair: Reginald Maudling speaking, and Patolichev (Soviet Minister of Foreign Trade) and Khrushchev, left.

The author and his wife with Nikita Khrushchev, Mrs Khrushchev and Furtseva in main box at Bolshoi Theatre for the Royal Ballet.

The author with the Patriarch
Alexei: Arnold Smith
(Canadian Ambassador)
behind.

The author meeting the
governing mayor of Berlin
(Willy Brandt), 1963.

The author seeing the Wall at the
Brandenburg Gate, 1963.

The author with the President of the
Deutsche Bank, Dr Hermann Abs,
1963.

The Queen's visit to
Germany, 1965. Arrival
in Bonn with HRH the
Duke of Edinburgh,
President Lübke,
members of the German
government, Michael
Stewart, British and
Commonwealth
diplomats.

The Queen's visit, 1965:
German dinner in Schloss
Bruhl.

The author and his wife in the Embassy residence, 1965.

The author in his Embassy office, 1965.

With Chancellor Erhard and George Brown.

Farewell in Berlin: with the governing mayor, Klaus
Schutz, 1968.

Farewell in Bonn: with the
President and Frau Lubke, 1968.

Anglo-German Königswinter
Conference in 1968, with Lilo
Milchsack DCMG and Sir Robert
Birley.

Marshal Tito, he had thought it was time he should establish a similar relationship with that other great soldier-statesman, General Franco. One could sense the ice descending upon the luncheon table at this point, but Monty carried on, 'You know, gentlemen, my NATO political masters would not allow me to do this,' at which point I saw the prestige and credit of the NATO Alliance rising high. Monty's hosts could not bring themselves to decide what to say, and the conversation was duly changed. Monty was too far away from me for me to intervene, but afterwards he said, 'Don't think they quite understood my reference to General Franco.' I said, 'On the contrary, Field Marshal, they understood it only too well. Of those twelve Yugoslav Generals, I think every one of them either fought with the Spaniards on the Republican side in the Civil War or had something to do with support for the Spanish Republicans, like Tito himself. So they were not at all happy about your comparison between Tito and General Franco.' 'Oh,' said Monty, why did nobody ever tell me?' But even this did not destroy his credit in Yugoslavia.

The visit of Nasser and Nehru to Tito in the summer of 1956 provided me with a short-lived role in what later became the Suez crisis. The issue at that time was whether Nasser would turn to the Anglo-Americans or to the Russians to finance the Aswan Dam project. I was instructed to do what I could to enlist the support of Tito and Nehru in persuading Nasser to accept the Anglo-American plan agreed between Eden and Dulles. They told me that was in fact Nasser's intention. Unfortunately – and this was the beginning of the Suez tragedy – Dulles withdrew the offer when he discovered that Congress would not support the Aswan project in addition to financial support for Yugoslavia itself. Yugoslavia was then given the preference, no doubt because Dulles' priority was the rolling back of Soviet communism in Europe and the rug was pulled from under the feet of Nasser and Eden.

I have left to the last the major visit to Yugoslavia during my time there, that of Khrushchev in the summer of 1955. Khrushchev, accompanied by Bulganin, who was still Prime Minister, had clearly wanted to reassure the world that there was a major change of Soviet foreign policy since he had taken over from Stalin. The two main indications of this were his readiness at long last to sign the Austrian State Treaty and the reconciliation with Yugoslavia. The last was not so much a concession to the West, since Khrushchev's aim was clearly to bring a former member of the Communist family of nations back into the fold. The Yugoslav approach to this was that as a non-aligned power with an independent policy in the world they would welcome the restoration of state relations with so important a country as the Soviet Union, but they were determined not to re-establish Communist Party relations as Khrushchev would have wished. Knowing as I did the general Yugoslav approach, I was not disturbed, as some people were, by the arrival of Khrushchev in terms of Tito's relations with the West. Clearly, better relations with Russia would encourage Tito to pursue his ambition as a leader of the non-aligned world, equidistant between East and West, but since this was his policy in any case, I did not see that this would weaken the Western position in Yugoslavia.

I had never seen Khrushchev before, although I got to know him very well later in Moscow. He arrived on what was in effect a 'pilgrimage to Canossa' in the eyes of the Yugoslavs, since there was no question of them having made any concessions whatever to encourage the visit. He made a very long speech at the airport. Tito stood by impatiently and very obviously refrained from taking up any of the olive branches offered in the speech, briefly saying that he was glad to see Khrushchev in Belgrade; and this indeed set the tone of the subsequent visit. There was a big party, to which all the diplomats were invited, at the White Palace in Belgrade. The Yugoslav hosts by this time were entirely indistinguishable in their attire and general appearance from any similar Western group. The ladies had all got new dresses from Paris and were looking very distinguished, and the men followed Tito in being extremely well dressed. A small group of Soviet leaders emerged into the gathering, led by Khrushchev, who in those days were anything but well-dressed: bell-bottomed trousers, I recall, were typical of their attire. The Russians looked at their Yugoslav hosts with horror, wondering into what capitalist world they had now come – not that they were not used to capitalists in their proper place, but the Yugoslavs, after all, had once been the prize pupils of the Communist cause. The horror was equally shared by their Yugoslav hosts, who could not believe that these were the people to whom they had been looking up only a few years before.

In addition to the major reception, there was a special room where the main Yugoslav hosts and the main Russian guests sat with some of the diplomats at a sit-down dinner. This had been so organized that the diplomats at the start of the meal consisted of the three major Western Ambassadors – of the US, UK and France – with the

Canadian Dean of the Diplomatic Corps. As the dinner proceeded we each of us in turn gave up our places to other diplomats, and when it came to my turn it was the Greek Ambassador who was to be introduced. Bulganin, who as Prime Minister played the main protocol role on the Soviet side, was told that this was the Greek Ambassador coming in. By this time he had drunk quite a lot, and he got up as if he himself were the host, gave the warmest of welcomes to the Greek Ambassador, and said, 'We are the two Orthodox here' – a statement which anything but pleased the Serbians present who, although they were not themselves practising Orthodox Christians, certainly regarded themselves as just as Orthodox as Bulganin or the Greek Ambassador. I saw the amazement on the face of the Greek Ambassador but unfortunately was on my way out and did not see what happened later.

There was then a return party given by the Russians, again in a Yugoslav palace, where again the specially favoured were in a little room, to which this time the diplomats were not bidden. We were all in a long gallery waiting for the party to end when we saw Khrushchev emerging with Rankovic, a big man, holding him up on his left, and Tito, also a big man, holding him up on his right. He had obviously drunk too much, and they marched him down this long gallery with the diplomats on each side. Khrushchev made the motions of walking but his feet rarely touched the ground, before he was taken down the stairs and deposited in his car.

More seriously, as was nearly always the case with Khrushchev, while he seemed to have failed in his major intention of bringing the Yugoslavs back into the orthodox Communist fold, he did succeed in establishing a new relationship with Yugoslavia, from which he certainly soon benefited greatly when faced with the Budapest rising the next year. Although we did not know it at the time, it is clear that he was in close touch with Tito about the arrangements to be made in Budapest, and it was with Tito's full knowledge and even probably agreement that Kadar was appointed to restore an orthodox Communist regime in Budapest.

The Suez and Budapest crises both came to a head while I was on leave and had learned of my appointment as Permanent Representative at NATO in Paris early in 1957. I visited NATO twice and found that the two crises had almost become interlinked.

Clearly, I had to see Tito on my return and I was determined to get my word in first on Hungary before he took me to task over Suez. I expressed my disappointment in the Yugoslav attitude, which seemed to have changed since the early days. I went on to say to Tito that I could not understand why Hungary under Nagy could not be allowed to be a neutral country leaning towards the East or indeed in the middle, like Yugoslavia, just as Austria was a neutral country leaning towards the West. Tito looked at me and said, 'I thought you had spent two and a half years in Moscow after the war, and still you put that question to me?' He added, 'You and I would not be talking here today if I had not liberated Belgrade myself and got the Red Army out of Yugoslavia and into Hungary as quickly as possible. Surely you realize that for the Soviet Union there is no such thing as "neutrality leaning towards", especially with a country which it has previously controlled.' My tactics were, however, effective – or perhaps Tito realized that I was as much opposed to the Suez adventure as he was – but at all events he did not refer to it on that occasion.

I certainly left Yugoslavia with very warm feelings towards the country and with a considerable admiration for Tito. As long as he was alive, Yugoslavia continued to play a role in European and indeed in world affairs which she would never have done without him. He did maintain an equidistant position between the Soviet Union and the West, and within the non-aligned group of countries, which grew bigger and bigger, he certainly tried to resist attempts by, for example, Castro, to swing the whole movement in the Soviet direction. Of course, Yugoslav national interests required this kind of policy if she was to maintain her role as an independent Communist country on the borders of the Warsaw Pact and continue to receive American assistance. Another important factor was that some million or so Yugoslavs left the country to work in what would now be the European Community and their earnings were very important for the Yugoslav economy, while Yugoslavia had become a major tourist centre for the West and in particular for the Germans, Scandinavians and British.

But in the light of hindsight, it does seem clear that Tito did not really unite Yugoslavia in the sense of merging the different republics into one Yugoslav entity. He did do something which great leaders very rarely do in providing for his own disappearance. The great question-mark for many years had been, 'What will happen when Tito goes? Will the old quarrels between the Serbs and the Croats immediately take over?' He provided a very complicated structure which did not allow any one of the republics or any one individual to have sufficient power or influence to take a leading role. The result was that his death did not create any major problem at the time. But the structure of checks and balances and constant changes of leadership which had ensured a decent transition was the very last recipe for dealing with the kind of economic and nationality problems which have beset Yugoslavia in recent times and which clearly require a strong leadership and the capacity for taking and then carrying out effective decisions. These are the problems now facing Yugoslavia, and clearly the solution offered by a strong leader in Serbia is unlikely to appeal to any of the other republics, least of all to the western, more developed republics of Slovenia and Croatia. It is indeed hard to see any early or ideal solution to these problems, which have prevented Yugoslavia from playing a leading part in the revolutionary changes in Eastern Europe, to which her earlier record of independence would seem to have entitled her.

21 | NATO after Suez

1957–60

We left Belgrade for Paris in February 1957 to take up my post as British Permanent Representative on the North Atlantic Council. At once I had to pick up again the threads of my work in London in 1954. It had not taken the British Government much more than two years to decide to trigger the escape clause in the WEU agreement, under which we could plead financial constraints for reducing our forces on the Continent. Although the decision rested with a two-thirds majority in WEU, it also required discussion within NATO, where SACEUR's advice was required and where the necessary financial expertise existed in the French Deputy Secretary General, Didier Gregh. To meet the NATO timetable I had to go almost directly from the Gare de Lyon to make the opening statement to the Council. It became a long-running issue, to whose solution the second Secretary General, Paul-Henri Spaak, made an important contribution.

I was lucky enough to also have some months with the first Secretary General, Lord Ismay, and to see with what skill he had established the right kind of 'family' atmosphere among civilians and military in what was still a very young and unique alliance, as well as setting up an effective civilian organization. I had worked with him at Yalta and throughout the war and post-war years under the Churchill Governments. Our last meeting had been at the important Lisbon Conference of the Atlantic Alliance in February 1952, where it was decided to bring the political Council from London to Paris, closer to the military headquarters which Eisenhower had established in France. Lord Ismay was at that time Secretary of State for Commonwealth Relations, but Churchill had sent him to Lisbon rather more in his capacity as his chief military adviser during the war, to follow the general proceedings under Anthony Eden. Pug Ismay and I sat just behind the Ministers, and Pug was scathing about running such important affairs by what he called a sort of town council; in fact, he got so indignant as the proceedings went on that he muttered to me, 'This is the last time that I ever have anything to do with this talking-shop.' But the members of the Alliance in their wisdom decided that Britain should have some compensation for losing the Council from London, and we were called upon to nominate the first Secretary General.

The choice fell upon Oliver Franks, who had so successfully built up the organization of the OECD, but he at once turned down the offer, whereupon Churchill decided that the right man would be Pug Ismay. Pug Ismay's sense of duty and his loyalty to Churchill were such that he accepted, very luckily for the organization, since no man was better qualified to set up this completely new and unique international organization. During the last few months of his period of office in 1957, I saw not only the splendid organizational results but also the complete confidence and affection that he enjoyed from all the member countries – although he had had some problems in his own country. He told me once of a visit to the north of England to explain this unique international organization to assembled dignitaries in Yorkshire. He was staying with one of them who, at dinner, after Pug had explained the whole thing to a large meeting, said that he had not wanted to embarrass Pug by the question he would now like to put to him, which was that he had been very interested in what Pug had said about the way the various national representatives worked together in the meetings of the Council, but could he perhaps say something about how the 'Soviet chappy' behaved at these meetings?

In the early months of 1957 NATO was digesting its first major crisis tests, Budapest and Suez, one straining East-West and the other West-West relations. NATO could not have been expected to intervene to save the Hungarians from Khrushchev's repression, but there was still considerable disappointment. Suez had left a greater strain, since two of the major members of NATO, Britain and France, had been completely out of step with all the rest and in particular with the United States. Local problems in Egypt were being settled more quickly than might have been expected, and the change of Prime Minister in Britain from Eden to Macmillan helped. In the very few months between the Suez disaster and my arrival in Paris, Macmillan had restored British relations with Eisenhower in Washington, but there was considerable bitterness in both London and Paris – especially in Paris – at what was regarded even by the opponents of Eden's Suez policy as abandonment by their major ally, the United States. I was glad to find that no one within NATO had taken seriously Khrushchev's threat to take military action, since it had so obviously been made only after it was quite clear that the British and French were already giving way under American pressure.

It was the political much more than the military aspects which dominated discussion of these issues in the NATO Council at that time. Fortunately, well before the Suez crisis, it had been realized that much more should be done to emphasize the political role of the Atlantic Alliance and the importance of political consultation in addition to building up an effective military machine. A group of 'three wise men' had been set up, consisting of the Belgian, Canadian and Italian Foreign Ministers – Spaak, Pearson and Di Martino – and their report was already before the Council. It has been rather forgotten, since it was subsequently updated by the Harmel Report of 1967. But it was in fact the 'three wise men' who, in 1957, laid down the overriding importance of effective political consultation between members of the Atlantic Alliance, and whose recommendation led to the development of the NATO council as the most effective and flexible organization for this purpose. This led on eventually to the use of the NATO machinery for assessment of the Soviet scene and to automatic Western consultation over all major exchanges with the Soviet leaders. All this has proved of great value in structuring the 'new and wider Europe' after the revolutionary changes in the Soviet Union, Germany and Eastern Europe in 1989–90.

This report more or less coincided with Lord Ismay's decision to retire after nearly five years in office. His successor was a major political figure, the Belgian Foreign Minister, Paul-Henri Spaak, one with the advantage of representing a smaller country and yet of having, with Adenauer, Schuman, de Gasperi and Jean Monnet, laid the foundations of the new Western Europe. As one of the authors of the three wise men's report, he came to Paris in the autumn of 1957 with, as it were, his own mandate for increasing the political functions of NATO.

On the military side, Eisenhower had replaced as SACEUR one of his old colleagues, General Gruenther, with another and younger American officer, General Norstad, who had also worked with

Eisenhower in the Allied Command in North Africa and throughout the war. During most of my time at NATO, I was working closely with Spaak and with Norstad, and I think both were inspired choices. Norstad was an airman who had throughout most of his career been engaged in staff work. This was held against him to some extent among the military, but it was in fact more important at that time to have a Supreme Commander with very good political antennae than a great fighting soldier. The latter solution had in fact been tried when General Ridgeway, fresh from his victories in Korea, had come to NATO, but he had proved to be the only unsuccessful appointment made by the Americans in a long string of very distinguished Supreme Commanders.

Spaak and Norstad were faced with major political problems concerning all three main European allies. I have already mentioned the perennial British problem of force reductions. The one concerning France was Algeria, and was confounded by the return to power of General de Gaulle in 1958. The problem concerning Germany was that of getting Germany effectively integrated into the NATO structure. This was all the more difficult because German public opinion remained anything but militarist. All this gave General Norstad great responsibilities but also considerable prestige. As I got to know him better, I used to tell him that he was the American Viceroy in Europe, which indeed was the position that he more or less enjoyed in security matters, particularly with the Germans. This did not make for the easiest of relations with Spaak who, although he admired Norstad, felt that from time to time he was getting drawn into political functions which should really have been those of Paul-Henri Spaak himself. However, they were big enough men to continue to cooperate effectively.

Returning to the British position, during my three and a half years at NATO, I not only had the problem of British force reductions, which took some time to settle, but also two other major political issues – Cyprus and the first Cod War with Iceland. One issue which has in more recent years caused major strains in NATO – the relationship between the United States and its European allies – hardly existed at that time, certainly not in the form to which we since became accustomed. America was still far and away the most important ally, both militarily and economically. This was fully accepted in NATO, and until de Gaulle returned to power there was no questioning the desire for effective American leadership.

The overall East-West relationship which was the main cause for the existence of NATO was going through a rather difficult period. Until the Hungarian crisis of 1956 Khrushchev, as the new and more liberal leader of the Soviet Union, had been a welcome change from Stalin. He had shown himself reasonably cooperative at his first summit conference in Geneva in 1955, and he had demonstrated his good intentions with the signing of the Austrian State Treaty and the restoration of relations with Yugoslavia. But all this had been put into question by his ruthless repression of the Hungarian revolution in 1956. Nevertheless, the general Western approach was that this should be regarded as a regettable aberration, in the same way that Suez had been a regrettable aberration internally in the Alliance, and that efforts should be made to get back to the more promising possibilities of a working relationship with a ruler such as Khrushchev who, unlike Stalin, was plainly very interested in the outside world and obviously anxious to discuss world problems with Western leaders.

The nuclear question was becoming ever more important, with the Russians moving towards greater parity with the Americans in the nuclear field, although by no means achieving it until the Sixties. There were also major doctrinal issues with the Alliance about its strategy, which resulted in the doctrine of flexible response which continued to hold the field in NATO for many years. Ideas were put forward on both sides during my time at NATO for nuclear-free zones in central and northern Europe. There was the plan of Rapacki, the Polish Foreign Minister, which attracted a certain number of people in the West. Norstad himself put forward alternative plans for nuclear-free zones which never, however, reached the status of agreed NATO positions. All this, especially under the strong impulses from the British Prime Minister Harold Macmillan, led up to the summit meeting with Khrushchev in Paris in 1960.

Although the Americans were still, throughout the Fifties and into the Sixties, much superior in nuclear strength, the West had to take account of major Russian advances in space under Khrushchev. Although these did not come to fruition until the early Sixties, the preparations began during the Fifties and this was a field in which the Russians proved equal and in certain limited respects even superior to the West. It tends perhaps to be forgotten that the Russians had long been expert in rocketry. Already about a century ago they produced very effective rockets before anybody else, and they had effective rocket launchers during the war. Insofar as rockets are in a sense a modern form of artillery, it is also well to remember that the Russians, even in the days of Ivan the Terrible in the sixteenth century, had, some people thought, the best artillery in Europe, which contrasted very much with their backwardness in so many other respects. They were also fulfilling the prophecy made to me in Moscow at the end of the war by the Polish Nobel Prize-winner, Parnas, in making great progress in the nuclear field, both civilian and military.

While Khrushchev was in general welcomed in the West as a pleasant change from Stalin, he was already showing himself a rather unpredictable and by no means easy sparring-partner. Unlike Stalin, he felt that the Soviet Union was getting strong enough to play a role, indeed to throw its weight about, in the Third World; and this was the period when he began his visits to India, Indonesia, Egypt and other Third World countries. It was also quite clear that any desire he might have for a stable relationship with the West in Europe and in the Atlantic area did not cover the rest of the world, where the Russians adopted the position that they were not giving up ideological competition nor support for national liberation movements, which was the formula for independence movements in what had formerly been the colonies of the Western European members of NATO.

Closer to home, it became clear during my time at NATO that Khrushchev was not satisfied with the position in Berlin as it had been left after the failure of the Russian blockade of 1948–49. Although this did not come to a head until the early Sixties, Khrushchev had, in 1958, already begun the second Berlin crisis, which was resolved in 1961 with the building of the Berlin Wall. There was therefore plenty to discuss at the Paris summit in 1960. Harold Macmillan had great hopes of this summit. Indeed, his attitude towards it had something in common with Churchill's strong desire for a meeting with the Russians after the death of Stalin, but with the advantage that this time there was an established and relatively new Soviet leader with whom to do business.

Even inside NATO there were personal initiatives from Spaak himself to establish contact with the Russians. I attended one or two lunches at which Spaak met the Soviet Ambassador in Paris, Mr Vinogradov, at which informal discussion was opened on the improvement of relations between NATO and the Warsaw Pact.

One of these lunches took place shortly after the collapse of the 1960 summit. This was the result of the unhappy U-2 incident, in spite of which Khrushchev had been determined to come to the summit. But once there, he was not a free agent and had to take into account the very strong feelings of the Soviet military and indeed of his colleagues in the Politburo. So there were no discussions in Paris, and the meeting broke up in such disorder that Harold Macmillan, at a small dinner that I attended at the Embassy at the end of the conference, was in deep despair, feeling, as politicians tend to do, that this 'last chance' to reach some kind of peaceful arrangement between the West and the Russians had been torpedoed by the U-2 affair.

At Spaak's lunch with Vinogradov I foolishly tried to improve the situation when Mrs Vinogradov was complaining about Eisenhower's refusal to apologize for the U-2 affair, while Vinogradov himself was almost saying that if only Eisenhower had been prepared to deny all knowledge of it, all might have been well. I told them the story of George Washington and the cherry tree which he cut down and how he had become famous throughout America for saying as a small boy that he could not tell a lie, suggesting that this had perhaps affected the handling of the affair. Mrs Vinogradov firmly replied that this time the cherry tree was Russian.

Turning to NATO's internal affairs, let me begin with what was I suppose the most important issue, that of bringing Germany fully into the Alliance. Here we were fortunate in having German Generals such as Speidel and Heusinger at the head of the German forces. Speidel, who had been a senior staff officer in Paris during the war, was a man of great tact and integrity who proved acceptable to the French in a very senior command at Fontainebleau. Franz Josef Strauss was also intelligent enough to see the importance of NATO for Germany, and although he was tempted later on to respond to French pressures under de Gaulle for separate Franco-German arrangements, particularly in the nuclear field, he never in fact gave way to them. No doubt the return to a crisis situation over Berlin helped a good deal in this respect. There was also a successful meeting of the NATO Council in Bonn in the early summer of 1957, and other important visits by the NATO Council to Germany during the three and a half years I spent at NATO, all of which helped to accustom both the Germans and the rest of NATO to the idea of Germany not only as a new member of NATO but as in effect the most important country on the ground for European defence.

Khrushchev's handling of the second Berlin crisis was very different from Stalin's handling of the Berlin blockade. He realized that he could not get the three Western powers out of Berlin by threats alone, and his tactics were a mixture of stick and carrot. The carrot was usually to persuade us that there could be some more appropriate and more modern arrangement than a continuation of occupation status, and later on he adapted this into a plan for a United Nations presence. The stick consisted of occasional unpleasant incidents in the Berlin Corridor, one of which led to the crash of a British Airways plane – not, however, actually shot down by the Russians. But the main part of the stick was the threat to turn over all Soviet rights in Berlin and indeed affecting Germany as a whole to the German Democratic Republic. During my time at NATO none of these issues came to a head, but they were all disturbing; and a conference was held in Geneva at which Selwyn Lloyd, with his American and French colleagues, got together with Gromyko to try, in vain, to find solutions.

I was most closely occupied with the particular British problems. The first and most difficult was the reduction of our armed forces stationed on the Continent. Spaak, not unnaturally as the Belgian signatory of the original treaties of 1954 and 1955, was rather indignant at our desire to change them so soon, and although he did show considerable statesmanship, my relations with him, which were fortunately based upon a friendship which had started in London during the war, had their downs as well as mostly ups. The downs usually came when he had not bothered to read the papers and came to Council meetings unbriefed. He was a man of great intelligence but had been used, as Belgian Foreign Minister, to operating with a very small staff of his own trusted advisers, and did not always make the best use of the international NATO machine. This was a matter of great concern to his British political deputy, an old friend of mine from Cambridge and the Foreign Office, Evelyn Shuckburgh, who found that he often had to come to me to find out what his chief, the Secretary General, had been doing. This was not, however, as simple a matter as it sounds. Members of the Permanent Council each spoke to him very confidentially about their particular problems, and if we had felt that they were going all round the Secretariat, we might not have felt able to do so. But Spaak and after him Joseph Luns, who had also been Foreign Secretary of a small country for a long time, had the same method of operation, which contrasted strongly with the Secretaries

General from bigger countries, like Pug Ismay, the Italian Manlio Brosio, and more recently Lord Carrington, who were more used to working within a bigger government machine, and to making good use of their international staff.

I benefited greatly, personally as well as officially, from the fact that Paul-Henri Spaak was pro-British, dating back to his wartime years in London, despite his disappointment at our not having grasped the leadership of Europe within the European Community, as he had encouraged Anthony Eden to do. His helpful approach applied also to his brilliant French Deputy for Economic Affairs, Didier Gregh, whose position was very important, since our case was based upon financial considerations. But the key figure in all this was really General Norstad, without whose advice we could never hope to get the two-thirds majority required within WEU. Norstad was a realist and determined to help us in any way he could, and I certainly regarded him as an ally. Our joint efforts were not, however, always well-received in London. The position of a member of the North Atlantic Council is a rather unusual one in that he is, like any other Ambassador, the representative of his country, but at the same time shares a collective responsibility as a member of the Council and to that extent feels, as I certainly felt, a duty not only to represent British views on the Council but also to press upon London, when required, the collective views of the Council in addition to reporting those of Spaak, Norstad and individual national representatives. On one of these occasions when I had accompanied Larry Norstad to a talk with the Chiefs of Staff in London I found myself summoned to Number 10 the next morning to be told that Lord Mountbatten had complained that I was supporting an American General against the British Chiefs of Staff. I was rather put out by this because, no doubt as a result of my days in India, I had always got on quite well with Lord Mountbatten. I was glad, however, to find that this complaint was not taken seriously by Harold Macmillan or by the Minister of Defence, Duncan Sandys.

Another unusual feature of the position of a Permanent Representative at NATO was that, although appointed by and in the last resort responsible to the Foreign Secretary, he was also working directly with the Minister of Defence and also to a certain extent with the Chancellor of the Exchequer. Looking back on that period, I probably had an even closer relationship with the Minister of Defence than with the Foreign Office, but not only over such matters as British troop reductions. Duncan Sandys, Minister of Defence for much of this period, had very strong views and seemed to me to be running the Ministry of Defence almost on his own, apart from his outstanding Permanent Under-Secretary, Sir Richard Powell. Fortunately for me, Duncan Sandys and I had joined the Foreign Service in the same year, and I had beaten him in the entrance exam. He always showed me a rather surprising respect and friendship. But this did not help me when Norstad came up with another proposal, which I supported, designed to help us over our force reductions.

We put this proposal to Duncan Sandys informally after a large dinner at Claridges at which Norstad had been the guest speaker. We went up to a special room with Richard Powell, and Larry Norstad explained that if the British Government would place Fighter Command, which at that time was not assigned to NATO, nominally under his command, this would make it easier for him to support our proposals for force reductions in other areas which were very much under his effective command. He made it quite clear that he had no intention of interfering in any way in Fighter Command. Duncan Sandys would have none of this, and kept referring to the decision taken in 1940 to turn down increasingly desperate French demands for additional British air squadrons to be transferred to support their losing battles in France: 'Had we given way, we should never have won the Battle of Britain.' Norstad and I kept on explaining that the situation was, we thought, somewhat different, and we obviously had the sympathy of Richard Powell, an outspoken civil servant, who finally made a rather ostentatious departure without having supported his Minister. Our proposal was eventually accepted, but too late to help us then with our force reductions.

We did, however, with the help of Norstad, Spaak and Gregh, finally achieve our objective without too much bad blood, and it was agreed that the numbers would go down from 80,000 to 65,000, but that the structure of four divisions and the second tactical air force should be preserved. It was my fate, however, to be plagued with this in one sense self-created problem, and I had to deal with it again as Ambassador to Germany not many years later.

The other two issues of special British concern were Cyprus and the first Cod War with Iceland. We did not ourselves take the initiative of bringing the Cyprus question before NATO, but Spaak, who thought of himself as a more or less independent senior political figure and not only as a Secretary General acting under instructions from governments, rather rashly offered his services as a mediator to the Turks and the Greeks. The result was disastrous from his point of view, since he lost the confidence of both sides. We, the British, were very much involved because it affected our position in Cyprus; but the issues were between Greece and Turkey, although in the event Macmillan played quite a big part in finding a temporary solution, which had eluded Spaak.

In the Cod War with Iceland we had very little sympathy within NATO, since it seemed on the face of it to be a case of a large country bullying a very small one. The fact that it was a rather major fishing country bullying a number of smaller British fishing ports was never fully understood by my colleagues. We made, I thought, the mistake of treating this matter mainly as a legal question and of leaving the negotiations in the hands of the Attorney General, whereas from the NATO point of view it was mainly a political issue which should have been dealt with by Foreign Ministers. At all events, we were not very successful in NATO, and I cannot claim to have had much success even within the group of countries who normally supported the British, who at that time consisted of the Canadians, the Norwegians and the Dutch.

The major event affecting the Atlantic Alliance during the late Fifties was the return to power in France of General de Gaulle in the summer of 1958. Up to that point there had been a succession of increasingly weak French Governments unable to deal effectively with the Algerian question just as their predecessors before Mendès-France had been unable to deal with the Indo-Chinese question. At one point the French wanted support within the NATO Council for their position in the Algerian war but did not press this, since it was also their case that the three Algerian Departments were part of Metropolitan France and they could therefore hardly press NATO to treat them as an international issue. All this coming on top of Suez made life rather difficult for the French within the Alliance.

When I first arrived in Paris in February 1957 there was no atmosphere of imminent crisis in France. Indeed, it was only two or three months later that the Queen paid a most successful visit to France as the guest of President Coty, in the course of which she also visited NATO. This visit was followed not very long afterwards by an equally successful visit from the Queen Mother and Princess Margaret, again as guests of President Coty. Under the surface, however, the Algerian crisis was building up and affecting the loyalties of the

French Armed Forces. The Commander of NATO Land Forces in Europe with his headquarters in Fontainebleau was a French General, Challe, whom we knew quite well. Like many of his colleagues he had fought in Algeria and was getting more and more critical of the failure of the French Governments to put down the Algerian rising. Indeed, it was General Challe and some of the other French NATO Generals who got involved in what amounted to a French military mutiny in Algeria, which eventually led to General de Gaulle's return to power in 1958, to prevent a takeover in Paris by the French Army from Algiers.

General de Gaulle's return obviously had a considerable effect on the French position within the Alliance. The General had never been happy over what he regarded as the subordination of France and other countries to the Americans, and was determined to make his feelings known. But for some time after his return he was still very preoccupied with the whole Algerian situation and with its aftermath, when the OAS were active throughout France and indeed tried more than once to murder him. I was told by someone close to him that, apart from more serious objections, he was always irritated at seeing the flags of the Americans and the other NATO countries flying at military headquarters on the road to Versailles which he often used. The first indication we had of his intentions was typical of de Gaulle. The French President in the autumn gave two major official banquets at the Elysée. One was for the Diplomatic Corps, which did not concern us. The other was for the French Corps Constitués, such as the Conseil d'Etat, and the international organizations in Paris. These were NATO, the OECD and Unesco. Invitations to this banquet used to go out before the summer holidays, but on this occasion we discovered that whereas Unesco and the OECD had received theirs, we had not, and did not. It was clear therefore that we were not regarded by de Gaulle as an international organization established in Paris. However, again following typical de Gaulle logic, when for some reason which I cannot recall there was a military parade down the Champs Elysées, we were all invited, as members of a military organization, I suppose.

Paul-Henri Spaak, who was a man of many parts, a former tennis champion with a deep French culture who had known de Gaulle during the war in London, thought he would try to bring the General round to a more favourable view of NATO, but he was entirely unsuccessful. General Norstad made the same attempt, with equally negative results. De Gaulle was always formally very correct with Norstad, although he did not always resist the temptation to drive wedges between him and Field Marshal Montgomery, who was Norstad's Deputy.

The Field Marshal's time at NATO came to an end in the late Fifties. General de Gaulle gave him a farewell lunch, which I attended. In the course of the General's speech, he made a long quotation from memory from Bossuet's sermon on the funeral of the great French soldier, Condé. He had chosen Condé specially because he had certain similarities with Monty in the care he took of his troops and the cautious way he approached campaigns in contrast to his equally great but more dashing contemporary, Turenne. As we left the party, Monty, quite rightly pleased with the occasion, asked me about Bossuet, who he was glad to learn was a bishop. It was typical of de Gaulle's courtesy and sense of occasion that he took the trouble to memorize such a long passage.

Another example of de Gaulle's old-world courtesy arose when, shortly after his return to power, he invited Winston Churchill to receive the *Médaille Militaire* at a ceremony in the courtyard of the Invalides. The *Médaille Militaire* is one of the greatest honours that can be given to a foreign statesman and the ceremony at the Invalides was indeed imposing. Although I am sure the main purpose was to thank Churchill for what he had done for France and de Gaulle during the war, there was also, I think, an element of satisfaction in showing that he, de Gaulle, was now the active President of France whereas Churchill was out of office and in rather poor shape. I was interested on a recent visit to Chartwell to see a photograph of de Gaulle, sent to Churchill at this time. To my surprise, the General was in civilian clothes, and the dedication was 'To my companion', which was a warmer phrase than would normally have been expected by outsiders to depict the Churchill–de Gaulle relationship during the war.

But more important than these personal tributes to a wartime colleague was de Gaulle's first major proposal affecting NATO. The military side of NATO in those days was technically under a committee of the Chiefs of Staff of all the member countries, with one or other of them elected as chairman for three years. But the effective military leadership came from the 'Standing Group' stationed in Washington, consisting of senior American, British and French officers. What were subordinate military commanders, the Supreme Commanders Europe, Atlantic and Channel, became better known figures than the changing chairmen of the military committee or indeed the members of the Standing Group back in Washington. De Gaulle complained that NATO planning and discussion did not take sufficient account of the outside world and in particular of the course of events in the Middle East, Asia and North Africa, nor of the very great responsibilities in those areas of countries such as the United States, Britain and France. His suggestion was that there should be a special group set up of these three nations to take an overall view and in effect to 'supervise' general NATO policy. He plainly intended this to be part of the NATO structure. Considering the warm relationship later established between General de Gaulle and Adenauer, it is amusing to recall Adenauer's horror when he first heard of this proposal which left out in the cold such major NATO countries as Germany and Italy, where there was much indignation. My German colleague, Herr Blankenhorn, was round to see me to express Adenauer's concern within a few moments of the story having leaked. The smaller powers were equally indignant.

It was clearly impossible for the Americans or ourselves to go down this road. We found an alternative suggestion in separate planning groups for different areas of the world – for example, one for South East Asia and another for the Middle East – but not as part of the NATO structure. We said that even under the existing NATO machinery it would be quite possible to discuss these and other problems intelligently without necessarily excluding our NATO partners. But plainly de Gaulle was more interested in establishing the principle than in the actual discussions, and although tripartite talks did in fact take place away from NATO headquarters in Paris, it was clear that de Gaulle was not interested in using the machinery already existing within NATO. His many problems in Africa and in the renewal and revival of France itself were such that France remained within the NATO military structure, although not as a very active member, for some years to come, and it was only in the mid-Sixties that he felt the time was ripe for him to insist upon the removal of NATO from France.

As an example of General de Gaulle's attitude to NATO, I recall a lunch to which I was invited by Admiral Nigel Henderson, who had with considerable initiative got permission to sail up the Seine in a barge, moor it alongside the then NATO buildings at the Trocadero, and make this his residence in Paris. He told me he had invited a great friend of his, a French Admiral, to lunch; and would I kindly be careful as he was a strong Gaullist and would not welcome criticism of the General. I did not in fact have any opportunity, because the French Admiral himself opened the conversation with attacks on General de Gaulle. It turned out that on de Gaulle's return to power the French Admiral, who knew him well from wartime days, had gone to congratulate him. When asked what he himself was doing he explained that he had a temporary NATO assignment pending his appointment to command the French naval forces at Brest. This drew from de Gaulle the comment, 'A NATO assignment? You have also become a traitor?'

In 1959, we went to Washington for the tenth anniversary of NATO and also visited Strategic Air Command in Omaha. The Omaha meeting produced a shock. We assembled in the morning to be addressed by General Curtis Lemay, a very powerful figure indeed. We were amazed to hear that his Strategic Air Command was almost incapable of effective action; we were left with the impression that insofar as he could get any of his aircraft into the sky at all, they were unlikely to cause any harm to the enemy. We broke for coffee, after which the conference resumed with Curtis Lemay taking an entirely different line, explaining what a marvellous force he had. It turned out that he was also receiving a Congressional committee on the same day; the briefs had been mixed up, so that we had received the address intended to get more money out of Congress.

At Denver we got another picture of NATO's problems, looking across the Arctic at the Soviet Union, which is what the American-Canadian Command was set up to do – a Command whose importance tended to be rather overlooked by the Continental European members of NATO. Our Canadian visit covered Ottawa, Montreal, Quebec and a short visit to the Dew Line, where a radar screen was being established. On our previous American trip we had been regaled for the most part with large American steaks; at Quebec, where we were entertained by the famous regiment of the Vingt-Deux, Paul-Henri Spaak and my Continental colleagues were much cheered by a magnificent French-Canadian lunch. We moved back to Montreal to be entertained by the already quite well-known and later (during the Olympic Games) even more famous Mayor of Montreal, Jean Drapeau. We were told that M. Drapeau would be a little late, but he finally arrived, and in a flood of old-fashioned French-style eloquence described our Secretary General Paul-Henri Spaak as a 'gift of God to humanity'. At this stage, I'm afraid, much as we liked Spaak, it was very hard for the members of the Council to keep straight faces, and even harder when within a minute or so M. Drapeau explained that he very much regretted that he was unable to stay to host our dinner because of other engagements. For quite a long time afterwards we ragged Spaak with the thought that although a gift of God to humanity he did not rate M. Drapeau as his host at dinner.

Spaak used to tell a story against himself of the war period when he was explaining the war situation to the Americans in his then imperfect English. Some of them commented that he looked like Churchill but spoke English like Charles Boyer, the French film actor. Why, asked Spaak, had they not compared his looks to those of Boyer and his eloquence to that of Churchill?

Our Council meeting the next summer in 1960 was more dramatic. It took place in Turkey and coincided with the Turkish military revolt against the Menderes–Zorlu Government. We arrived at Istanbul and were surprised to be kept waiting rather longer than we expected at the airport by the polite Turkish Foreign Ministry official. Finally we set out and reached the bridge which normally took one across the Golden Horn, to find that it was shut. Our Foreign Office guide got out to speak to the military in charge, and it was quite plain that they were not prepared to open the bridge for him. This was the first intimation we had that Istanbul was under military control. We then went all round the Golden Horn to come, in our case, to the British Embassy by the back route, just escaping a major demonstration dispersing under fire from the large Taksim Square.

We discovered on arrival at the Embassy that the Turkish Government had been deposed by a military coup and that there was a curfew preventing anyone moving about in Istanbul excepting the members of our conference, which was to be held some distance away in the University, which had also been closed. Those now in charge had arrested the Prime Minister, the Foreign Minister and the President, but they decided that the NATO meeting should go ahead, and even released the President to entertain us to lunch, whereupon he returned to confinement. The programme included a flight to Ankara and then a trip by sea to Izmir with a visit to Brusa. These duly took place with Selim Sarper, the former Turkish Permanent Representative at NATO, now the Permanent Under-Secretary in the Turkish Foreign Office, acting as host in the place of his Minister under arrest. The whole programme was duly completed, and we left from Istanbul airport in the usual way. It was one of the most eerie meetings I can recall. There was nobody on the streets during the whole of our time there. Later on, and not so very much later, the unfortunate Menderes and Zorlu were hanged, and many of our Turkish diplomat friends got into serious trouble. Plainly, however, the Turkish military had wished to make it clear that Turkey remained firmly committed to NATO.

There were also two major summit meetings during my time at NATO. The NATO Council could meet at any level – either Permanent Representatives, which was the usual thing week by week, or Foreign Ministers, or other Ministers or, on special occasions, Heads of Government. In order to revive confidence after Suez and Budapest there had been such a meeting with Eisenhower and other Heads of Government attending in Paris in December 1957. Indeed, that was the only meeting I can recall attended not only by the Heads of Government as well as Foreign Ministers but also by Ministers of Defence and of Finance. There was another similar summit meeting with Eisenhower in 1959, after which there were relatively few until recent years.

One of the most attractive features of the NATO post was the close cooperation which grew up not only between the civilians and the military but also within the Council itself. Pug Ismay had started a custom, which was continued by Spaak and I think goes on to this day, of weekly lunches for the Permanent Representatives, at which discussions could take place informally on subjects which were not ripe or suitable for official treatment in the Council. We also saw a great deal of each other socially, and this created a very definite community spirit within the NATO Council.

I was relatively junior (Grade II) compared to some of my colleagues, and I discovered afterwards that Pug Ismay had been insisting, but without success, that I should be upgraded to a Grade I Ambassador to keep me on a level with them. Many of them could almost be described as elder statesmen, particularly the Dutch, who in my time were always represented by ex-Foreign Ministers, Stikker, who afterwards became Secretary General of NATO, and Van Kleffens. We had a very senior American Representative in Randolph Burgess, who was also accredited to the OECD, and outstanding Norwegian and Canadian Representatives. Our doyen, although one of the youngest of the Ambassadors, was André de Staercke, who had made a name for himself as what we would call the Principal Private Secretary to the Regent, Prince Charles, in the post-war period in Belgium.

Life in Paris as a NATO Permanent Representative was particularly agreeable because one did not have the responsibilities of a national Ambassador dealing with the many sections of French society and the many visitors from home who expected to be looked after by their Ambassador, but at the same time it was open to us to move out of the NATO circuit occasionally and to meet French friends. We made the most of these opportunities. I found the work at NATO very congenial because, although living in a most agreeable foreign capital, one remained part of the Whitehall machine, operating very closely with the Foreign Office, the Defence Ministry and the Treasury and also in touch with the Prime Minister. I had to go to London at least once a month, and I had on my staff not only Foreign Office officials but defence and finance officials as well.

NATO itself was not only adding the function of political consultation to its normal military and strategic tasks but was also broadening its interests by the appointment of a scientific adviser on the same level as the political and economic deputies. This brought to NATO from time to time the most important scientific figures in the different Governments – in our own case, Lord Zuckerman, who was, however, sceptical of what could be achieved in his field by an international defence organization.

Apart from close contact with the Secretary of State for Defence and his civil servants, I naturally saw a good deal of the Chiefs of Staff, who came to Paris from time to time, and also of the British Standing Group, who came more frequently. We were then appointing for the first time a Chief of Defence Staff, following an idea of Lord Mountbatten's. He had, however, wanted somebody else to get the job worked in before he took it over himself, and the first holder of this office was a Marshal of the Air Force, Sir William Dixon. In Washington we had Admiral Sir Michael Denny at the Standing Group, then the Senior NATO defence body. Whenever Denny and Dixon arrived in Paris, we not only had our work in NATO but also 'night work' in taking them round the best Paris nightclubs.

The late Fifties were one of the most interesting periods in what is now the rather long life of NATO. It was a period of growth and development from a mainly military organization into one dealing with political consultation, preparing the way for NATO as the best instrument for consultation between member Governments, even in areas for which NATO itself had no responsibility. Above all, it was building up its position as the place in which consultation would take place not only for defence against the East but also for negotiation with the East, a role into which NATO has certainly grown in subsequent years, with such success that its continued usefulness has been taken for granted by all concerned, including former adversaries, with the ending of the division of Europe and of Germany in 1989–90.

One of the dangers affecting our work in NATO was that we might have become a rather too inward-looking 'club', which I think on the whole we successfully avoided, but we had to be rather careful in our dealings with our fellow diplomats outside NATO. I served with a distinguished Ambassador in Paris, then Sir Gladwyn Jebb, who was an old friend but had thought that he might combine the roles of Ambassador to France and to NATO. After General de Gaulle's return we ageed that he was lucky not to be responsible for NATO as well as for France. But there was a tendency in the NATO world to speak with perhaps less than the appropriate respect for our 'local' Ambassadors, which some of them resented. The very distinguished and intelligent wife of our American colleague, Mrs Burgess, resented having to give way to the US 'local' Ambassadress, Mrs Houghton, pointing out that her husband, as American Ambassador to NATO and the OECD combined, had greater responsibilities than the Ambassador to France. The Burgesses, the Houghtons and the Norstads, and many Americans working with them, became close friends, adding greatly to the enjoyment of life in Paris, as close friendships with American colleagues in Moscow had contributed so much to our enjoyment of the somewhat different social and official conditions there.

All in all, I was very happy at NATO and hoped I would be left there. The day came when I was taking Selwyn Lloyd, then Foreign Minister, to Le Bourget after a NATO meeting and was listening with great pleasure to his comments that it was time that diplomats were left rather longer in their posts, which indeed was desirable at that time. He obviously sensed my enthusiasm, and said, 'But this doesn't affect you. You are going to Moscow.' I argued with him that one should not be sent from NATO to Moscow, and that, although I and my wife would personally be happy to go back there, the Russians had published a book in 1948 about the British Embassy in which I and my wife were almost the villains of the piece, and it did not seem to me that we were likely to be welcomed back. I mentioned to him the sad case of George Kennan, who had returned to Moscow as Ambassador but, when he made an unfortunate remark at Berlin Airport, had instantly been declared persona non grata. Selwyn Lloyd said he thought that I would find that things had changed in the days of Khrushchev, as indeed proved to be the case. But I should have been happy to stay at NATO rather longer than the three and a half years that we spent there before returning to Moscow in the autumn of 1960.

22 | Khrushchev
1960–62

On our departure for Moscow in October, we again had the privilege of an RAF Britannia which, following tradition, was filled with frozen foodstuffs to a value of £1000–2000 to be put into the Embassy deep-freeze on arrival, essential for diplomatic entertaining in conditions less favourable for the privileged, which covered the Diplomatic Corps and journalists, than when we had left Moscow in 1947. Thanks to the ingenuity of the staff of our Copenhagen and Moscow Embassies, these 'iron rations' successfully survived an unexpected overnight diversion to Copenhagan and the temporary collapse of the Moscow Embassy deep-freeze.

My wife and I were both immensely interested in coming back to Moscow under the reforming and relatively 'liberal' Nikita Khrushchev, whom we had last seen in Belgrade in 1955. Having displaced Malenkov and then defeated Molotov and the 'Anti-Party' Group in the mid-Fifties, by the autumn of 1960 he was firmly in the saddle. He had startled the world, and above all the Communist world, by his denunciation of Stalin at a Party Congress in 1956, although the actual speech, well-known outside, had still not been published inside the Soviet Union. He had also shown his good intentions in East-West relations at the 1955 Geneva Summit, by finally completing the Austrian State Treaty and by the reconciliation with Tito.

During my previous Moscow experience, from Yalta to the Berlin blockade, Khrushchev had been almost the only member of the Politburo diplomats never met. For much of this time he was the 'boss' of the Ukraine, bringing it back under the Soviet yoke after the war by 'Stalinist' methods. In fact, in the Diplomatic Corps in Moscow he was at that time nicknamed 'The Butcher of the Ukraine'. His transformation into the relatively liberal, progressive and extrovert leader of 1960 came to me – and, as I subsequently gathered, also to himself – as a major surprise. His earlier record in the late Thirties as Mayor of Moscow and constructor of the famous underground system, as one of the younger generation elevated to high rank to replace Stalin's murdered colleagues, had also been tough. Entirely self-educated, like Ernest Bevin, whom he resembled in some respects, he had great intuition, common sense and an earthy sense of humour. I think myself that he had realized through his intelligent family, including his son-in-law Adjubei, the editor of *Izvestia*, that there was a new generation of educated young Russians who could not be treated as Stalin had treated the peasants whom he had thrown into factories and disciplined into a semblance of hard work by the roughest methods, including imprisonment and even execution.

Khrushchev shared Peter the Great's curiosity about the outside world and, unlike Stalin, was the world's greatest tourist-statesman. He and Bulganin, Prime Minister in the early years when Khrushchev was only Secretary General, had not only paid their famous visit to Belgrade in 1955 but had also been to most Western capitals, including a rather rumbustious visit to London under Anthony Eden's premiership in 1956. This was the occasion when George Brown lost his temper with Khrushchev at a Labour Party lunch and Khrushchev retorted that if he were in England he would vote Conservative. He had been fascinated by his first visit to America and excited by the immense success of American agriculture, in particular by American corn crops, which he decided to introduce into the Soviet Union – not, as it turned out, very successfully. The great sights of America, and in particular Hollywood, had a great appeal for him. His last and recent visit to Paris had unfortunately been cut short by the U-2 crisis.

One of his main interests, again completely unlike Stalin, was in the Third World. Stalin had never felt that the Soviet Union was strong enough after the war to embark upon any very positive, as distinct from propaganda, policies in the Third World, and he had concentrated more upon consolidating and strengthening the Soviet position in Eastern Europe and, to a lesser extent, in neighbouring areas in the Mediterranean and Black Sea. But Khrushchev was not only an entirely different and much more optimistic character than Stalin, he was also lucky enough to be leading the Soviet Union when the standard of living, low though it was, was improving; when he was able to give at least the privileged part of the population rather better housing; and above all when the Soviet Union was making its mark in the world in space. It was under Khrushchev that the first Sputnik went up; and during our time in Moscow the first space astronaut, Gagarin, went into space and received a fantastic welcome back in Moscow.

All this strengthened Khrushchev's conviction that the future really did lie with the Soviet Union. He coined the slogan that the time had come to catch up with and overtake the Americans. The more sceptical Muscovites reacted with the quip that it might be all right to catch up with the Americans but that the Russians must on no account overtake them, because if they did everybody would see the patches on the seats of their trousers. When we were driving in the Embassy Rolls-Royce to Leningrad just after the great Kremlin reception for Gagarin, we had to stop at one of the only two filling stations then available on the whole 700-kilometre route, and what should have been the automatic pump was out of action. It takes some time to fill the tank of a Rolls-Royce by hand, time enough for the driver of a jeep to comment to a friend: 'How typical. Yesterday we received Gagarin back from space. Today we can't even fill the tank of the British Ambassador by modern methods.'

This was very much what Khrushchev was up against, as Gorbachev has been since. But this did not really affect his Third World policies. By this time it was fairly clear that the Soviet Union, although getting stronger not only in space but also in the nuclear field as well as modernizing its conventional forces, intended to avoid actual conflict with the West and particularly with America in the Atlantic area. But he always made it clear that peaceful co-existence, which was his slogan, revived from Lenin, did not apply to either ideological disputes or to what were termed 'national liberation movements' – in other words, support for any former or still colonial countries in the Third World.

Khrushchev's tourism therefore included such important centres as New Delhi, Djakarta and Cairo. The relationship with Nehru was always kept on a basis of mutual interest – for example, a shared hostility to China – without any kind of ideological background, but Khrushchev had great hopes of a close relationship with Sukarno's Indonesia and, closer to home, with Nasser in Cairo, based on Soviet support for the Aswan Dam. Similarly, as the countries of Africa became independent, starting with Nkrumah's Ghana and some of the neighbouring former French colonies, the Russians showed keen interest and at once promoted these countries, not to the full status of members of the Communist community, but to aspirant Socialist membership. This led on shortly to the special relationship with Cuba, even though Castro was not originally a Communist himself. Although economically and strategically dependent upon the Soviet Union, he has also tried to emulate Tito's role as a Third World leader.

There was, however, another side to this happier picture. The second Berlin crisis, opened by Khrushchev in 1958 and which had been part of my NATO agenda, was still with us in sharper form. More and more East Germans were leaving for the West via Berlin. This was draining the GDR of its best experts. Khrushchev could not allow it to continue indefinitely, although he did not want to risk the consequences of a second Berlin blockade. He was balancing against the dangerous threat of handing over Soviet rights to the GDR what he hoped would be an attractive solution for the West – turning the whole of Berlin over to the United Nations as a sort of special enclave. I don't think this was ever a popular concept with the GDR, who regarded East Berlin as their capital, but Khrushchev no doubt thought he could impose it upon them if necessary. However, it was certainly even less attractive to West Berliners, who had got used to strong economic support from Bonn and to their Three Protecting Powers and, above all, to being able to rely upon the strength of the United States. They did not regard the United Nations as an adequate substitute.

This Berlin crisis, which was long drawn out and lasted until the building of the Berlin Wall in August 1961, imposed a considerable strain upon East-West relations. It justified John Kennedy's comment, after Khrushchev had subjected him to a bullying session in Vienna in 1959, that we were in for a long, cold winter. And of course the strains were to increase in 1962 with the Cuban missile crisis. So with all his *bonhomie* and despite a very deep and genuine improvement in the lot of the Soviet population as well as in the social and working conditions of diplomats and the foreign press in Moscow, Khrushchev was in some ways a more dangerous and less calculable actor on the international stage than Stalin had been or than Gorbachev was to be two decades later. This alarmed his own colleagues as much as it did his Western adversaries.

Khrushchev's problems lay not only in East-West relations but perhaps even more seriously from his point of view in the deterioration of Soviet relations with Mao's China. The most important thing happening in Moscow when we arrived in the autumn of 1961 was a major Communist Party conference, attended by the Chinese Prime Minister although not by Mao Tse-tung himself. Khrushchev's version of Glasnost did not go nearly as far as Gorbachev's today, and little news emerged from this conference. It was, however, clear that things were not going well between the Russians and the Chinese and, as we now know, Mao developed a great contempt for the 'boorish' Khrushchev and in particular for his fears of nuclear war and consequent reluctance to allow relations with the USA to deteriorate too far. More concretely, Khrushchev had for his part begun to reduce vital Soviet aid for China and to withdraw Soviet advisers. China was not then a nuclear power, and Mao talked rather wildly about paper tigers and in terms of nuclear war being acceptable to bring about the world triumph of Communism. Khrushchev would have none of this. He saw very clearly the dangers of a nuclear world, and indeed one of his major contributions, although not himself much of an ideologist, was to modify basic Marxist-Leninist doctrine, which had previously been that there had to be a world conflagration between the capitalists and the Socialists, provoked by capitalism in its death throes, in order to ensure the final success of Communism.

The tension between Mao's China and Khrushchev's Soviet Union grew in the early Sixties, although it was some time before the degree of the tension became obvious. Already in Irkutsk on Lake Baikal, one of the few permitted areas for diplomats to visit in Siberia, the local people were beginning to talk critically about China. The much smaller number of diplomats who went to the Pacific, travelling to Japan by the one approved port at Nakhodka, reported that there people spoke of very little else but the Chinese menace. I first realized that things were going badly between the two great Communist countries when I invited the Rector of Moscow University to a party for the first British exchange students attending Soviet universities. Encouraged no doubt by the vodka or whisky, he described his Chinese students as a formidable lot, hard workers with no time for distractions, not even drink. They were, he said, as dedicated as Soviet students had been in the Revolution. Then I realized that there was real trouble between the Soviet Union and China, and before very long this became obvious to the whole world.

One of the more difficult issues in the Third World during the early Sixties was the future of the Congo, where Dag Hammerskjold was trying to work out a United Nations solution to maintain the unity of the country, then divided between various rival leaders. One, Lumumba, had his name given to a new university in Moscow for students from Africa. Perhaps the Russians did not realize that the students from Africa were less disciplined than their own students and did not always understand the limits placed upon their demonstrations. On one occasion, the Lumumba students, encouraged to demonstrate against the Belgian Embassy, almost destroyed it and very nearly killed the Ambassador and his staff. From then on demonstrations against targets of this kind were left to Soviet students, and the Lumumba students were diverted to friendly demonstrations at Cuban or approved African missions. Ghana and Nigeria were among the first newly-liberated African states to set up missions in Moscow. Nkrumah was welcomed there with open arms and his Ambassador, John Elliot, added a new and valuable dimension to our local Commonwealth consultations. It became clear that African students had their 'racist' problems in the Soviet Union, so much so that I sometimes wondered whether Western interests would not have benefited from a system of British Council scholarships for African students to the Lumumba University rather than to the University of London.

The greatest black African country, Nigeria, took its time over its relations with the Soviet Union, which under Khrushchev tended to pick out the bigger Third World countries for favours. The most frequent Third World visitor to Moscow during my time was Sukarno from Indonesia, who enjoyed special favours. No foreign planes were allowed into Moscow without Russian pilots aboard and preferably, in the case of major invitees, the Russians liked to send their own planes to fetch them in. On one of his trips round Europe, Sukarno was travelling in a chartered SAS plane with some pretty SAS air hostesses, and successfully insisted on using this aircraft for his Moscow visit. He arrived in the middle of the summer when nearly all the theatres were closed. But for Sukarno the Russians had decided that they would bring the Bolshoi back from the Caucasus and the Baltic to put on a performance of *Swan Lake*, to which the Diplomatic Corps was invited, as usual at some twenty-four hours' notice. We were rather more surprised to be disinvited at twelve hours' notice. We discovered that Sukarno had complained that he had seen *Swan Lake* often enough and would prefer to go to the Circus. No Western visitor, however important, would have behaved in this way; but Sukarno duly went to the Circus and the Bolshoi dancers resumed their summer holidays.

Indonesia, however, was a great disappointment to the Russians. Having had a lot of American aid, they got rid of their local Communists, rather roughly, and moved out of the Soviet orbit. Later on the Soviet Union had a similar experience in Egypt, and the only one of the major Third World countries with whom Soviet relations have remained close is India. The Soviet Union had to content itself in the Third World with two important but smaller 'satellites' in Vietnam and Cuba. Vietnam fell naturally under Soviet influence as a secular enemy of China and as a country increasingly dependent upon Soviet military and other aid. In the early Sixties interest in South-East Asia was centred upon Laos, the most delightful but the weakest of the three components of former French Indochina. Under the terms of the Geneva Settlement, the Soviet Union and the United Kingdom were Co-Presidents in the Indo-Chinese peace negotiations, and I found myself negotiating with a distinguished and attractive Soviet official, Pushkin. We were in a sense respectively spokesmen for two countries, never mentioned, the USA and China, while Vietnam proved much more effective than any of us in bringing Laos under its influence.

The most important of the Soviet Union's Third World commitments, however, turned out to be Cuba. This was too close to the United States to be welcome in Washington, and was no doubt intended to become a model for Communist takeovers throughout Latin America. Castro, however, like Tito in Yugoslavia, had accomplished his own revolution without any help from the Russians. He had not started life as a Communist and on the whole the Cubans, even when they did sign on as members of the Communist Party, were less disciplined than the usual Soviet satellites. My wife and I met a group of important Cubans in Stalingrad in the autumn of 1962, shortly before the Cuban missile crisis. We were all the main guests in the local hotel, and the Cubans had obviously got bored stiff with the normal Soviet official programme by this time. When they discovered that I spoke a little Spanish and came from Argentina, they treated me almost as a lifelong friend. It became clear as we spent an evening together that they were not at all happy in what they regarded as the very austere surroundings of even Khrushchev's Soviet Union, and were determined to remain if they could a rather distinct part of the Soviet world alliance.

My first year in the Soviet Union saw the culmination of the second Berlin crisis. Normally speaking, the negotiations with Khrushchev on this crisis would have been conducted by the three Western Protecting

214

Powers in Berlin, as they had been at the time of Stalin's Berlin blockade. But General de Gaulle had taken the view, which may well have been right, that to negotiate on our absolute rights in Berlin was a sign of weakness and that we should not attempt it. The Americans, on the other hand, with our support, felt that the matter was too serious and the risks too great for such treatment, and that we had to see what could be done. The result was the negotiations had to be left to the Americans, who had a very good Ambassador in Tommy Thomson, who got on well with Khrushchev. This, however, made things difficult for him, since he bore the whole responsibility and, without our help at the negotiating table, had to remain in the closest contact with his British, French and German colleagues. My German colleague, Herr Kroll, was a controversial diplomat who had had a successful career previously in Yugoslavia, where I had known him slightly, and above all in Japan. He had established a close personal relationship with Khrushchev, whom he resembled in temperament. Adenauer kept him in Moscow because of this personal relationship, in the hope that the time might still come for the Federal Republic to embark upon serious negotiations with the Soviet Union. On the other hand, he did not enjoy the confidence of his Foreign Minister, Schröder, nor of his Foreign Office.

The fact that we were not engaged in the official negotiations did not mean that we were in no way concerned. Almost every time that I met Khrushchev – and we met frequently – the question of Berlin would come up, and I had to be careful not to take a personal position which might embarrass the American negotiations. The two most vivid and important conversations I had with him came shortly before the building of the Berlin Wall. The first was in June 1961, when the Royal Ballet was in Moscow for the first time, their proposed post-war visit having been a victim of the Cold War. Khrushchev and several of his colleagues came to the *Sleeping Beauty* performance, and my wife and I were invited into the Soviet equivalent of the Royal box and also to a sit-down supper, again in the box, at the end of the performance, but not, as I had expected, with our leading performers. I was subjected, in the presence of Gromyko and Mikoyan and other Soviet leaders, to a lecture from Khrushchev lasting over an hour on the necessity for solving the Berlin question. This was his major attempt to persuade me that his United Nations solution was the right one.

My second experience was less pleasant. I was at a diplomatic reception, as it turned out, a day or two before the Berlin Wall was built. We in Moscow had no inkling that this was in the wind, and indeed very little seems to have been known even in Berlin. Khrushchev, who must have assumed that I did know what was about to happen, suddenly told me that Major General 'So-and-so' had just been appointed to command the Soviet troops around Berlin. Even Khrushchev was not in the habit of supplying foreign Ambassadors with military information of this kind; I was too surprised to react, even when Marshal Gretchko was summoned to confirm the information. This annoyed Khrushchev, who went on to say that Major General 'So-and-so' had re-established order in Budapest in 1956, which made me sit up but did not call for comment. My failure to react resulted in Khrushchev losing his temper and telling me that he could destroy my country with eight nuclear bombs. It was clearly time to respond, so I said that since my country was a relatively small island perhaps six would be enough, but that the Royal Air Force could then destroy Moscow and many other major cities of the Soviet Union. Typically, Khrushchev suddenly changed his mood, and said, 'Well, maybe you are right. Let's have a drink.' In the light of hindsight, Khrushchev was clearly warning us not to take military action in response to the building of the Wall, which indeed neither we nor the Americans were in a position to do effectively.

During the crisis months I had a talk about Berlin at a Kremlin reception with Kozlov, Khrushchev's Number Two and as such reputed to be a hardliner, whom we diplomats rarely saw. When I expressed concern about the Berlin crisis, he told me that it would be resolved peacefully. The Soviet authorities regarded Europe as divided after the war by a line which they would have wanted further west and we no doubt further east. While we would make trouble for each other on the other side of the line, this would never be carried so far as to risk a war. Berlin was admittedly a circle on the Soviet side, but the same principle applied.

The building of the Wall ended the Berlin crisis, and it was some months before we moved on to the next major political crisis over Cuba. It was very typical of Khrushchev to have started something in 1958 which he plainly intended to end very differently. But it was also very typical of many of Khrushchev's ventures that he nevertheless did achieve, although in quite a different way from that intended, his major objective of preventing the exodus from East Germany, even though the solution was on the surface more humiliating than he or the GDR would have wished. Behind the Wall the GDR developed into the Soviet Union's leading economic partner, although plainly one with feet of clay, as became clear with the breaching of the Wall and German unification in 1989–90.

My last meeting with Khrushchev was in many ways the most important and revealing. With the second Berlin crisis settled for good or ill with the Wall, it was generally understood that Khrushchev wanted to complete his 'tourist' visits to Western Europe with Bonn. Indeed, in 1962 he sent his son-in-law, Adjubei, there to prepare the way. But nothing had actually been arranged, and the Berlin Wall had not improved the climate for such a visit. My farewell call on Khrushchev was very shortly after the Cuban missile crisis, and he knew that I was going as Ambassador to Bonn. I thought that for once I would have a very short time with him as he was obviously exhausted after the strains of the final week of the Cuba crisis. But, rather like a battery recharging itself, he began to talk and talk, and what I thought would be a quarter of an hour's farewell ended in a two-hour meeting. I had one piece of business, to persuade him to formalize the purchase of a British chemical plant. He at once said to me, 'You know, there are six chemical plants we want, and there will certainly be one for you, don't worry; and there will be one for the French and one for the Italians and also one for the West Germans.' And then, he added with a little grin, 'There'll be two others for whoever gives me the best terms.' This led him on to philosophize about the capacity of the West Germans, of whom he had a much higher opinion than of his GDR allies, only seventeen years after their complete defeat, to produce chemical plants at all. And then he talked at length about Germany, without any reference to 'militarists' and 'revanchists', which were the terms then normally used by Russians about Germans. His theme was how much Russia over the centuries had owed to the Germans, who had developed so much of the Russian economy, what a remarkable race they were, and how much he was looking forward to seeing West Germany for himself. In the event, he never got there, but his attitude was a very interesting illustration of the ambivalent attitude of Russians towards Germany – on the one hand, naturally angry and bitter about what they had suffered in the war and concerned for the future, but on the other, full of admiration for the best German qualities and anxious to benefit from them.

It was the Cuba missile crisis which prevented Khrushchev from seeing the Federal Republic of Germany and it was the main event in my two years' service in Moscow. It has always been regarded as the most dangerous crisis in East-West relations since the Berlin Blockade, and one which nearly led to nuclear war. As seen from Moscow, the crisis was less alarming, since it was clear that Khrushchev had never intended it to reach such proportions. The crisis had been building up for some months and most of the 'action' was in Washington or Cuba itself. My own experience related to the last week of the crisis. As I was about to leave Moscow, there were many farewell parties and I was seeing a lot more of Soviet leading personalities than I would normally have done in such a short time. Also, there was a new American Ambassador, Foy Kohler, who had just arrived, with another series of parties, so that he and I were in close touch with the senior Soviet officials.

It was quite clear that the Soviet leadership, which can always manipulate its publicity and has to give a lead, positive or negative, to its own people, was not building up to a major crisis. Indeed, there was no news whatever in the Soviet papers about what was going on in and around Cuba. During that last week, which happened to be a calendar week, it was not until the Thursday that anything public appeared in the Soviet press, and then in the form of an exchange of messages on the front page of *Pravda* between Bertrand Russell and Khrushchev. Russell had decided that it was his duty to call upon Khrushchev to save the peace of the world and Khrushchev was of course only too happy to oblige, so that the Soviet public realized at one and the same time that if there had been a crisis it was now over.

This came just after Khrushchev had sent his first reply to Kennedy, in which he had climbed down and offered to remove the Soviet missiles from Cuba. This had been followed by a second message which, it was suggested, had been imposed upon him by his colleagues, who thought that he was selling the horse too cheap, in which he reminded Kennedy that he also had problems with American missiles in Turkey and Italy and the United Kingdom, which he thought should be removed at the same time. This not unnaturally shook Washington, where Kennedy and his entourage had been on twenty-four-hour watch for several days, and created an impression that perhaps Khrushchev was playing with them. It was then that Robert Kennedy saved the situation by proposing that they should reply to the first letter and ignore the second.

By a strange coincidence, during this crisis week a famous American bass, John London, was in Moscow, singing the title role in *Boris Goudonov*. Khrushchev, who must have seen *Boris Goudonov* many times, went to see it yet again, obviously because an American was singing, so that this could be duly announced on the front page of *Pravda* the next morning. Not only did he go to see *Boris Goudonov*, which lasts about four to five hours, but he then gave John London supper afterwards. Again, all this was in the papers to show that relations with the United States were perfectly normal.

On the Saturday, when, as we now know, the crisis was over, I received a message from Harold Macmillan for Khrushchev. In the days of Stalin it would have been easy to get hold of people in the Soviet Foreign Office and in the Kremlin to receive such a message at any time, but the Russians had become great weekenders and there were delays in finding duty officers. I was not worried, because the crisis was over, but on the other hand a message at that level should not be delayed. I happened to turn on the Soviet wireless and was relieved to find that it was playing Beethoven's *Ode to Peace* rather than martial music.

The question arises how such a serious crisis had come about. Khrushchev obviously feared that the Americans were going to invade Cuba, and putting missiles there seemed an effective way to prevent this. He must have expected that this would become known to the Americans. He was clearly prepared for protests and I think myself counted upon a showdown at the United Nations, where he could put his own complaints about US missiles in Turkey and Italy. He had, indeed, on more than one occasion when I had met him talked about going again to the United Nations in the autumn, although his previous and very notorious visit when he smacked his shoe on the desk was not exactly a happy precedent.

What he had not taken into account was American superiority at sea and Kennedy's decision to stop Soviet ships taking missiles to Cuba. During the crisis week in Moscow, Soviet officials frequently came up to me almost gibbering at this unexpected development. Surely as an Ambassador representing such a naval power as the UK, I must agree that it was an act of war to interfere with ships at sea in peacetime? This had ruined Khrushchev's plan, and incidentally shaken what confidence his colleagues had left in his judgement. This must have contributed to their decision to oust him from power in favour of Brezhnev in 1964, although there were also internal problems behind their successful coup.

But again, as in the case of the Berlin Wall, what appeared to the world as – and indeed was – a considerable public setback for Khrushchev, was not entirely a disaster for him. His first objective had been to protect Castro from American invasion, and in the general agreement with Kennedy he got an American commitment covering this and therefore achieved his objective, although not in the way he intended and at excessive risk. Nor, indeed, did he get much thanks from Castro, who felt that he had been treated as an object of Soviet policy rather than as a valued ally. Nor was it long before Khrushchev achieved his secondary objective, the removal of US missiles from Turkey and Italy, which had in any case become Kennedy's objective also. At all events, it was far more agreeable to be in the eye of the hurricane in Moscow than it must have been to be in Washington above all, or even in London, where there really was serious fear of nuclear war.

There was another important factor which must have influenced Khrushchev's thinking, as it did that of Kennedy in Washington. This was the Penkovsky spy affair, which meant that the West knew the limitations of Soviet nuclear rearmament and Khrushchev knew that we knew. This takes me back to my arrival in Moscow in the autumn of 1960. I was sitting in my study, rather busy, one evening, when my secretary came in to say that there was a British businessman who insisted on seeing me. As I was working rather against time, I suggested that he should return the next day. Luckily, as it turned out, I did see him, for this was Greville Wynne, who had come to tell me about his links with Penkovsky.

Penkovsky had been a senior member of the prestigious State Committee for Scientific Cooperation and worked closely with the influential Gvishiani, Kosygin's son-in-law. One of the Committee's main purposes was to ferret out information about arms and high technology. The staff were allowed and even encouraged to make foreign contacts. Penkovsky had in this way got in touch, first of all with the Americans and Canadians, who did not react, and then with the British, who did, his particular contact being Greville Wynne, a freelance British businessman who came out to see what contracts he could get in the Soviet Union. The whole story of Penkovsky has been told elsewhere, and I need only record here that arrangements worked very successfully for a considerable time under which he provided us with extremely valuable information, on his official visits to London, or through Wynne and other contacts in Moscow. He had good connections in the higher ranks of the Soviet Armed Forces and knew the Soviet figures for Soviet nuclear arms production, which were at that time much below those of the United States. I am sure that neither

220

the Americans nor the Russians were contemplating a nuclear exchange, but Penkovsky's information ensured that Khrushchev could not indulge in diplomatic nuclear blackmail, more especially in the Caribbean, where the Americans also had obvious naval superiority and geographical advantage. So much has been written of Soviet successes in espionage matters that it is well to remember that they also had their failures, and probably the Penkovsky case was more important than any of the admittedly numerous Soviet success stories.

23 | The Soviet Union Revisited

Inside the Soviet Union, Khrushchev had made life infinitely better for the Soviet people in ways other than their slowly improving material conditions. Above all, he had opened Stalin's concentration camps and liberated many millions of their inmates. Although he did not change the Soviet system to prevent KGB arrests in the night, in fact such horrors for the most part ceased and the Soviet population was no longer under the constant fear of a knock at the door at night, followed by the Gulag. The psychiatric hospital was, however, a growing threat for some of the more independent. Rather surprisingly, Khrushchev did not earn as much respect and gratitude from the Soviet people as he deserved. Many of them preferred the more dignified leadership of Stalin, a mass murderer, to what they considered Khrushchev's shaming behaviour with his shoe at the United Nations.

Foreign diplomats enjoyed, by comparison with the Stalin era, easier contacts at all levels. There were many major commercial and cultural exchanges, but oddly enough very little British political contact at high ministerial level. The only senior Minister who came to Moscow was the then President of the Board of Trade, Reginald Maudling, for the opening of a British trade fair. This applied equally to other Western Embassies and left the Western Ambassadors to conduct relations directly with Khrushchev. This made life much more interesting and pleasanter than it might otherwise have been, for with him personal contact was much closer and more continuous than could possibly be the case with a leader such as Gorbachev, functioning under similar strains and stresses to those of a Western

President or Prime Minister. Khrushchev loved meeting people. He loved giving parties; he loved going to parties. There were very few months when one did not meet him at least once a week at some party for a long conversation. Apart from Khrushchev himself, I had an initial surprise when presenting my letters to the Head of the Soviet State. This had, in my earlier experience, been a mere figurehead and the occasion purely ceremonial. I was warned, however, that the new 'Head of State' was a more active and important personality called Brezhnev, who took a keen interest in international affairs and would keep me behind for a longish talk after the ceremony. It was in fact an interesting conversation and serves as a reminder that the Brezhnev who ousted Khrushchev in 1964 was very different from the doddery leader still in office two decades later.

The general impression I now have, looking back at that time, is therefore one of a sort of Golden Age compared with my first period in Russia under Stalin, with extremely close relations with Khrushchev and many of his colleagues, and a constant succession of visitors to Moscow. Indeed, during our first year there we entertained 6,000 people in the Embassy which I do not recollect doing in any other Embassy. On the cultural front we had during that time the Old Vic; the Royal Ballet, for the first time; Lord Harewood, coming to organize a special Russian contribution to the Edinburgh Festival; a major film festival with British films; and many other lesser events. On the economic side, we had not only the first British but the first of all major Western trade fairs, which became quite a feature of relations with the Soviet Union at that time. There were also visits from scientists, doctors and members of other professions, which were very welcome to me as Ambassador since it was in this way that one could meet their Soviet opposite numbers, who were ready to come to the Embassy to meet such distinguished visitors and to include the Ambassador in their return hospitality.

Throughout the crisis months in 1960–61 over Berlin we were much more active in Moscow with more agreeable commercial and cultural exchanges. The first British trade fair in May 1961 was a major undertaking, although looking back on it one cannot claim that it did a great deal for Anglo-Soviet trade, which has ever since been rather overtaken by Soviet trade with West Germany above all, but also with Italy and France. It was, however, a great success at the time. There were many important British industrialists who came to Moscow, and the fair provided an opportunity for useful talks between Reginald

Maudling and his opposite numbers in the Soviet Union, Kosygin and to a lesser extent Mikoyan in the Politburo and Patolichev, the Minister for Foreign Trade. As in everything else, however, Khrushchev had to take the leading role. At the opening of the fair he turned up with several of his colleagues. When the moment came for departure, I was expecting to see at least two big cars turn up, and was amazed to find one small Soviet car which looked about big enough for Khrushchev alone. He insisted on all of his colleagues piling into it with him. This was an extreme example of one of Khrushchev's characteristics which must have been irritating to his colleagues. Not only did he attend every party he could, but he was an eager host himself, and on all occasions he was accompanied by most of his Politburo colleagues, who got little opportunity to open their mouths. They must have heard all his best stories so many times. I cannot help thinking that one of the driving forces behind the decision to get rid of him in 1964 was the determination not to have to go to all those parties; at all events, under Brezhnev they did not do so.

Apart from his personal contacts with Harold Wilson, Mikoyan never played a big part in British-Soviet relations. Indeed, he nursed a grudge against us, going back to an event in the early days of the revolution in the Caucasus, when British forces had played some part in the establishment of temporary bourgeois regimes. Mikoyan's brother had been one of a very famous group known as the Forty Baku Commissars who were shot and, although we had had nothing to do with this, he held us partly to blame.

Kosygin was younger than Mikoyan, and for the outside world the most important of Khrushchev's colleagues, not only as Prime Minister but as a sort of economic overlord, always accessible to major Western industrialists, among them Paul Chambers of ICI. He already had in mind the sort of Perestroika reforms on which Hungary was then embarking and on which Gorbachev has staked his future. Although Gorbachev has had plenty of economists to advise him, he has lacked a senior colleague with the economic capacity combined with the political weight of Kosygin. But Kosygin also had his problems. Once, when asked why he was not propelling the Soviet Union forward at the same pace as Hungary, he is said to have replied that it was relatively easy for a small boat like Hungary to turn round in a short time, especially when it could rely upon the Soviet Union to bale it out if it got into trouble, but it was far more difficult to turn round a huge tanker like the Soviet Union, who could not rely upon any outside saviour. One of our first lunch parties in 1960 brought together Kosygin and Paul Chambers and, at my farewell interview with Khrushchev in 1962, I received his assurance that ICI would get their contract for a chemical plant.

Khrushchev himself took a keen interest in economic matters, including the improvement of Soviet housing. Under Stalin the emphasis had been on large over-decorated blocks of flats with a wedding cake appearance. Khrushchev simplified Soviet construction, and Moscow had a big building programme, with great cranes a major feature of the skyline. The quality of these buildings was not very high, and when a Swiss expert summoned by Khrushchev pointed this out to him, he at once agreed, but said that the demand for houses was such that he had to try to meet it soon, and hoped that they could be replaced with better quality buildings in due course.

Turning to culture, we were lucky to have as the Minister for Culture and I think the only woman member of the Politburo in the whole period of the Soviet Union, a rather remarkable lady, Furtzeva. She was the wife of a senior Soviet diplomat, Firyubin, who had been my colleague in Belgrade. She was close to Khrushchev and had a considerable influence in cultural matters. On one occasion she told me that she had found some remark of mine at a social gathering so interesting that at their next meeting she had informed Khrushchev and his Politburo colleagues. I still cannot recall what I had said to her, and could hardly ask her to remind me! On another she advised my wife against showing a well-known 'kitchen sink' film of the early Sixties at the Moscow Film Festival because it showed Britain in a bad light. She was naturally concerned with such major events as the visit of the Old Vic, which came shortly after our arrival, and the Royal Ballet, which came in the summer of 1961. This was preceded by a solo visit of Nadia Nerina in the autumn of 1960, who was much admired in the Russian classical ballets and through whom we met Ulanova and the Moscow ballet world within a week or two of our arrival. When she returned with the Royal Ballet in 1961 she had as great a success with *La Fille Mal Gardée*, a ballet which was new to the Russians, as Margot Fonteyn had in *Sleeping Beauty*.

One of our main contacts with Furtzeva came with the visit of Lord Harewood, the first member of the Royal Family to come to the Soviet Union since the war and a welcome guest at the Embassy. Furtzeva handled the visit with the right balance between the respect due to a junior member of the Royal Family and that due to his own wish to be treated as a professional musical 'impresario'.

We were able to pick up some of the cultural contacts we had had in the mid-Forties, but discovered that by the Sixties each Embassy's contacts were strictly rationed. One of our contacts was, not unnaturally, the Professor of English at Moscow University, Olga Akhmanova, whose royalties on the many million copies of her English-Russian dictionary had made her a rouble millionaire. However, she remained a dedicated Communist, living in a small flat in what had been her old bourgeois family home. She and her sister, married to a retired army officer, and a light comedy actress, married to a Jewish intellectual, made up our short but agreeable and interesting quota of 'private' families we could visit.

We managed also to see a number of modern Soviet painters and sculptors now quite well known abroad – their work, although officially disapproved, was collected in Soviet intellectual circles and by diplomats like ourselves. We of course knew George Costaki, whose collection of early and mid-nineteenth-century Russian art has become world famous. It covered every wall and filled every cupboard of his Moscow flat. Khrushchev, under some pressure to encourage modern Russian art, reached the point of agreeing that some of the Costaki collection should be shown in Paris, only to reverse this decision after attending and being shocked by an exhibition of contemporary Soviet painters.

Khrushchev was not, I think, personally interested in art to anything like the same extent that Stalin definitely had been, although sometimes with unfortunate results. But he had an infinite capacity for surprise; his self-education had, as in the case of Ernie Bevin, produced results. Once I had a message for Khrushchev from the Prime Minister, Harold Macmillan. Such messages were usually delivered personally, but just as I was getting in my car to go to the Kremlin there came a last-minute message from London not to deliver the message personally, I assume to avoid any possible publicity. It was too late to cancel my appointment. So I duly arrived, apologized to Khrushchev for wasting his time, handed him the message and was about to take my leave. Khrushchev, however, had other ideas, saying that nobody ever came to see him for less than an hour and if I left so rapidly his people would think we were going to war. So I was pressed to sit down, while he put the message unopened on the mantelpiece. Khrushchev then mentioned that he had just recovered from a bout of flu, which at that time amounted to letting me in on a state secret. This had given him the opportunity to re-read *War and Peace*, which he did every year. I did not, frankly, believe him. But he then went on to recite a famous passage about the hunt on the Rostov estate; and when I checked on my return to the Embassy, he had reproduced the longish passage pretty accurately.

My turn came next when he asked me what I had been reading recently. I had just been reading a book by Turgenev, which opens with a description of a snow-covered field in the Ukraine and a small peasant boy. The minute I mentioned the name of the book, Khrushchev said, 'Oh yes, I know that book. There's a small boy on a snowy field – and you know, that boy might have been me.' So obviously he had read that book too, and suddenly I saw a very different Khrushchev in front of me. We went on like this for about an hour. I cannot conceive of any Western Prime Minister in a similar situation behaving as he had done.

There were other less agreeable meetings – for example, the one before the building of the Berlin Wall – and then there were some that fell between these extremes. One I remember very vividly was on the occasion of a visit by the Roumanian Prime Minister. There had been a major meeting in the Kremlin, followed by a great reception to which all the Ambassadors had been invited. When I arrived I ran into one of our correspondents, who said Khrushchev had just made a speech in which he was very rude about the British, talking about a mangy lion who had lost his teeth and his tail. As I entered, determined to remain extremely cold, a rather hot and embarrassed Khrushchev came rushing in. On these occasions the Ambassadors were often placed in a circle which Khrushchev would go round. He came straight to me, and said, 'You're angry with me.' I suggested that I had every right to be. He said, 'Well, you know me, I say these things. I don't really mean them. You mustn't take this too seriously,' and continued to show me his most friendly side. In the course of conversation, which had moved on to shooting, I asked him whether there were still bears in the Soviet Union. 'Bears?' said Khrushchev. 'Of course. I am a bear. Look.' And he proceeded to give me a bearhug, picking me up in his arms before sending for drinks and asking to be forgiven. So what was to have been a display of coldness on my part turned out to be one of the most friendly public meetings I ever had with Khrushchev.

One of the frustrations of diplomatic life in Moscow in the Sixties which had not existed in the immediate post-war period was the restriction placed upon travel. Large parts of the Soviet Union were out of bounds for diplomats and for journalists: for example, the only places in the whole of Siberia to which we could go were Nakhodka, and then only *en route* by sea to Japan, and Irkutsk. The great capital of Siberia, Novosibirsk, was not then visitable, largely, I imagine, because it was the site for the great centre for Soviet academics at Akademikgorod. The British Week there in 1978 was not even a gleam in the eye in the Sixties. If one wished to go more than forty kilometres outside Moscow one had to notify the fact forty-eight hours in advance, which gave the Russians the opportunity to say that there were difficulties – no hotel rooms, for example, or whatever excuse they chose to give. This had forced upon us similar restrictions in the United Kingdom against Soviet diplomats. I must confess to some surprise that these restrictions were not removed in the early years of Gorbachev's rule. I once complained to Kuznetsov, who was then a friendly Deputy Foreign Minister. He replied with a smile that even the one-third of Russia that we were allowed to visit was surely larger than the whole of the United Kingdom.

Nevertheless, we did see a lot of the Soviet Union, individually and in groups. The Soviet authorities themselves organized trips for the Diplomatic Corps at least once a year. The first of these visits in my time was to Central Asia in 1961. Unfortunately I had to go back to London for the Soviet trade fair, but my wife went and afterwards wrote a very interesting account of the trip. The second such visit, the following year, was to the Ukraine, including Yalta and the Crimea. We went first to Kiev, which had been well rebuilt after the wartime destruction we had seen fifteen years before. We were entertained in the eighteenth-century Palace of the Tsars, but the room in which we dined was very obviously in the style of a century later. When my wife pointed this out to the Chief Minister of the Ukraine, he said that this could not possibly be so, as the rooms had all been redecorated exactly as they were; but he sent for the expert in these matters, who was deeply embarrassed at having to adjudicate between his Chief Minister and my wife, since he had to explain that they had indeed restored it exactly as things were but that this particular part of the palace had been assigned to a member of the Imperial family in the nineteenth century, who wanted to have a few rooms in contemporary style.

We were taken to a large communal farm which specialized in dairy cattle and milk production. The head of the farm gave us the total milk production figures for the 800 cows and for the 500 individually-owned cows, the latter figure being much higher. We went on to

Sebastopol, which had only just been restored, having suffered a great deal of wartime damage. As the headquarters of the Soviet Black Sea Fleet it was still out of bounds to all the Naval Attachés in Moscow. The Russians had overlooked the fact that my neighbour in the bus in which we went round the port, the new Turkish Ambassador, was an Admiral, even better equipped than his Naval Attaché might have been to take it all in. Our next stop was Yalta, where we were shown the Livadia Palace where the Crimea Conference of 1945 had taken place. Our guide was somewhat taken aback when she discovered through a minor correction on my part that I had been at the conference.

I had been so impressed by my wife's account of the Diplomatic Corps' excursion to central Asia that I was determined to go on my own with my then Private Secretary, Anthony Loehnis, now a distinguished banker. We added Bokhara to Tashkent and Samarkand. Under Tsarist and Soviet rule material standards had much improved in relation not only to the past but also to neighbouring Moslem lands. Mistakes have been made, especially in constantly changing nationalist policies, with which Stalin was closely concerned, and also in economic policies, where excessive emphasis upon cotton production has had repercussions on the water tables and largely emptied the Aral Sea. We were taken to a concert by an Uzbek singer recently returned from imprisonment, which rapidly became a manifestation of Uzbek nationalism. However, nationalism in Moslem central Asia then seemed to me a more long-term danger for the Soviet Union than nationalism in more 'developed' republics with some tradition of independence, such as the Baltic or Caucasian Republics or, most important of all, the Ukraine.

Apart from many visits to Leningrad and the historic cities around Moscow, my wife and I also paid two interesting visits to Georgia and one to Armenia, which had only just been opened to diplomats in 1961: I was, indeed, one of the first Western Ambassadors to go to Armenia. We went with letters of introduction to the Catholikos from Nubar Gulbenkian, and saw that he was still very much the respected father of his people. Armenia was the only republic in the Soviet Union in which there were no Russian high officials. Plainly, the Russians trusted the Armenians, whose only alternative was neighbouring, and unfriendly, Turkey. Even in Georgia, which also took a line of its own, there were still Russians in key positions in the Ministry of the Interior and in the Police. Even in 1962 we still found portraits of Stalin in the offices of most of the senior officials.

Although Khrushchev was a 'liberal' Tsar, especially in contrast to Stalin, this did not apply to his treatment of religion and more especially of the Orthodox Church. Stalin had much improved the treatment of the Church and even appointed a Patriarch, partly because he saw the advantages for Soviet foreign policy in the Near East. Khrushchev, however, had a strong prejudice against the Orthodox Church, and one can only describe him in this context as a persecuting Tsar, although his 'persecution' was not obvious in such major centres as Moscow or Leningrad. It was said in Moscow that when Khrushchev became the acknowledged leader there were three seminaries in all Russia. He closed one of them in Odessa, and was said also to have closed a second, which would have left only one for the needs of the whole of the Soviet Union.

Churches in Moscow and tourist centres were restored, even if mainly as museums rather than what were termed 'working churches', but this does not seem to have been the case throughout the Soviet Union. On one of our visits to Zagorsk, the main centre of the Orthodox Church near Moscow and a great place of pilgrimage, an old lady in the crowd whispered to me that we should not be taken in by the large numbers at Zagorsk; she came from Sverdlovsk, a large town in the Urals with more than a million inhabitants (where Yeltsin started his Party career), and it had until recently had only two working churches, one of which had just been closed.

This did not, however, mean that the major ceremonies of the Church at Easter and Christmas were not carried out with great magnificence, both as regards the raiments of the officiating priests and the splendid singing. Since there were very few working churches, they were always crowded. At the big festivals, they were usually surrounded by police, who came in useful, enabling diplomats like ourselves to push through the crowds into the church but whose main function, I think, was to try to prevent too many Russian citizens from trying to get in after us. It was interesting to see, however, in the milling crowds outside, that although there were occasionally anti-religious demonstrations, there were usually quite a number of younger and middle-aged people who were obviously coming with a full sense of devotion. It must be admitted, however, that the great majority of the worshippers were old. A visiting British cleric who had been in Russian churches before the war, when asked for his impressions, replied that, glad though he was to see the churches so full, he was sorry to see that they were still full only of old people – to which he received the reply that they could not be the same old people. It might indeed be asked how, in such circumstances, there were so many worshippers. One of the reasons was that at the time of the Revolution, when there was very strong anti-religious fervour, the younger and middle-aged parts of the population were so occupied with the Revolution, while at the same time keeping themselves alive, that their children were left to be brought up by religious grand-mothers.

In 1962 we were lucky enough, towards the end of our stay, to have a visit from the Archbishop of Canterbury, Dr Ramsay. My wife and I were invited to most of the services and ceremonies, and had the pleasure of entertaining the Patriarch and his senior entourage at the Embassy. Seeing them walking up the splendid staircase of the mid-nineteenth-century Embassy building in their robes was one of the finest sights that I can recall in Moscow, apart from the view of the Kremlin across the river. The Archbishop's reception at Zagorsk was equally splendid, and in the Moscow Cathedral I was privileged to be invited with him behind the Iconostasis during the service in his honour.

There was no Protestant church in Moscow for the members of the Diplomatic Corps. We in the British Embassy were part of the diocese of the Bishop of Fulham, and were visited either by him or by an Anglican chaplain resident in Helsinki. During the rest of the year my fortunately large study was used for morning services every Sunday which, since we were in foreign parts, were usually well attended, not only by the British but by other Protestant expatriates in Moscow. The Bishop of Fulham raised with me the question of getting back, under Khrushchev's supposedly more liberal regime, what had been the old pre-Revolutionary British church in Moscow, not far from the Embassy. It had been turned, like many Orthodox churches, into a block of flats, and the chances of getting it back for our purposes were very slight. I pointed this out to the Bishop, who reproved me and said that one of my main functions in Moscow should be to plant the flag of Christ opposite the Kremlin. I replied that, whilst as a private individual I might have been happy to try to do so, I did not think I had been sent to Moscow by Her Majesty's Government with this as my main task.

The Orthodox Church seems to have benefited from Gorbachev's liberal regime, and celebrated its Millennium with great pomp and dignity. There are even disquieting signs of the Orthodox Church attracting the support of Russian nationalist movements such as Pamyat.

The state of the Church in the Soviet Union naturally leads on to icons, which have long been one of our special interests. Considering the active persecution of the Church during the early Revolutionary period and the horrors of successive civil wars and of the Great Patriotic War, it was amazing to me how many icons had survived and how many Soviet citizens who could not have been particularly religious were still happy to have an icon in the usual corner of their one room. Fortunately, Marxism-Leninism has always taken the view that whatever was good under past systems before Marxism-Leninism existed need not be dismissed. This meant that one of the best rooms in the Tretyakov Gallery in Moscow was devoted to medieval icons, and similarly magnificent icons were to be found in the museums and churches in Leningrad, Tiflis, Vladimir, Souzdal, Pskov, Rostov and other historic cities. There was a brisk black market in icons in the Diplomatic Corps of Moscow. We in the British Embassy, like the American Embassy, were very careful not to get involved in anything under the counter. It might have been supposed that the strains of the long-drawn-out crisis over Berlin and the rather shorter Cuba missile crisis would have adversely affected the personal positions of the American and British Ambassadors. But in fact my own, and even more, the American Ambassador's relations with Khrushchev remained extremely good. When we were each offered a very large and obviously important icon, we were advised by the Chief of Protocol himself to send it to the Tretyakov Museum which he was confident would give us a certificate declaring that, good though it was, it was not of museum quality and could be exported. There were also some foreign collectors who managed to make very remarkable collections and get them out of the country, which must have required a blind eye from the Soviet customs. The general interest in icons, purely from an artistic point of view, increased during our time in Moscow to the extent that one of the old churches in Moscow, which had been associated in the Middle Ages with the greatest icon painter, Rublev, was restored neither as a working church nor as a museum but as a centre for icon restoration.

One of the privileges of life in Moscow, which we tended to take rather for granted, remained easy access to the very good theatre, ballet and music in general. Foreign diplomats, or at all events Ambassadors, continued to be given privileged treatment as regards tickets for all the major events. Although at times one groaned slightly at having to see *Swan Lake* for the fourth time in three months, the quality of performances was always very high, although by this time the British, American and other ballet companies outside the Soviet Union were on much the same level with rather more enterprising and less conservative productions. It was the absence of any new ideas in either the ballets themselves or in Soviet productions which led rising stars like Nureyev, Makarova and Baryshnikov to defect, to the great advantage of Western ballet.

Although there were no longer great composers in Russia, as Shostakovitch and Prokoviev had been during our first stay, there were still great performers, such as the violinist Oistrakh and the pianists Gillels and Richter and many others who could stand comparison with any performers in the Western world. While we were in Moscow John Ogden gave us the pleasure of a British victory in the famous Tchaikovsky Competition.

It was rather easier than it had been in the Forties to establish not very intimate but still closer relations with the Soviet artistic world, whether in the theatre, the opera, ballet or cinema, although the better modern painters remained rather underground and one had to be more careful for their sake. The theatre was of high quality in the sense that a great range of classics, both Russian and foreign, were performed and usually well acted. Again, there was a lack of novelty, both in the productions and the choice of plays. One of the problems was that Soviet actors are civil servants with prescriptive rights to the parts they performed.

For security reasons we had been compelled to bring with us a British military staff for the kitchen, dining and reception rooms. We had been worried whether there would be effective cooperation between them and the remaining Soviet bedroom staff. In practice all went well, although our Soviet staff had a far better time, since Soviet trade union rules ensured that they were never working over weekends or after five o'clock in the afternoon, when we were very happy indeed to have our British military staff to deal with essentials. The only major problem which I recall between them related to the use of what was then our one washing machine. Our British staff had somehow acquired prior rights to this machine, and the Soviet staff asked us to get them a separate one, taking it for granted that we would order one from Britain.

Since, at that time, the Soviet press was full of the new achievements of Soviet science, not only in space with Sputnik but even on the ground with new washing machines, frigidaires and cars, my wife thought that we would at least test out the wonders of modern Soviet domestic science, however sceptically. Our scepticism was nothing compared to that of our Soviet staff, who were horrified at the suggestion of buying a Soviet washing machine.

A personal Ambassadorial visit to GUM secured the allocation, on the usual Soviet system of privilege for senior personalities, of one of the manager's stock of washing machines. Within a week it had broken down. A second was obtained which lasted for the best part of a fortnight. On our third visit the manager, almost before we had opened our mouths, had handed the rouble value of the machine back to us. I could not help wondering what happened to the unfortunate Soviet citizens who had waited, probably a long time, even to get on the queue for their washing machines. This, I think, was typical of the whole Soviet system of priorities. For priority projects, like putting the Sputnik up in space or the defence programme or even a large car plant like that put up by Fiat, no expense or effort was spared. But when it came to washing machines or other consumer goods, there was no such priority pressure, least of all from the persons who really mattered such as Kosygin or Khrushchev himself.

I would not want to end this sketch of diplomatic life in the Soviet Union under Khrushchev on this sour note. There had been great improvements, psychological, social and material, by comparison with Stalin's post-war years. There were times when Khrushchev's lapses from 'liberal' behaviour or some of his dangerous initiatives in foreign affairs seemed to reverse his reforming course or to set the alarm bells ringing. But there was never a dull moment, which is rare in diplomacy. Totally different though he was from Gorbachev in character and conduct, he certainly opened the way for Gorbachev's substantive reforms, and I am glad to see that he has received due credit for this.

24 | Bonn

1963–8

I took up my last post in Bonn in February 1963 during a bitterly cold winter with even the Rhine frozen outside our windows, reflecting the state of British relations with de Gaulle and Adenauer after de Gaulle's recent veto upon British membership of the European Community, thus bringing to a halt Ted Heath's negotiations, which had been proceeding well in Brussels. The bottom had fallen out of Selwyn Lloyd's original plan under which I was to have the agreeable task of consolidating Anglo-German relations on the basis of our joint membership of the European Community. Man proposes, but in this case Charles de Gaulle disposed. He was emboldened to take this arbitrary step, resented by all his EEC partners, by Adenauer's signature of the Franco-German Treaty. As a result Adenauer's stock in London had slumped dramatically as compared with the mid-Fifties when I had been in such close contact with him over German membership of NATO and WEU. Fortunately the German Government also contained such important personalities as the Economics Minister, Erhard, responsible for the German economic miracle, and the Foreign Minister, Schröder, who were not happy about the exclusivity which Adenauer seemed prepared to accord to his relationship with de Gaulle. To secure ratification – to de Gaulle's indignation – a protocol had been added by the German Bundestag to the Franco-German Treaty, insisting that the treaty must be placed within the framework of Germany's other international commitments and in particular of NATO.

My first months in Germany were taken up outside Bonn with visits to the eleven Länder, or States of Germany, and their politically important Ministers-President; also with getting myself into the picture in Berlin, where I had a second residence and where I held the unusual position for a diplomat of Head of British Military Government. This went together with maintaining contact with the Soviet Ambassador (and in effect 'Viceroy') in East Berlin, Abrasimov, in our joint capacities as heirs of High Commissioners sharing Allied rights and responsibilities in Berlin. A further unusual diplomatic responsibility, which took up much time and provided much interest and happy personal contacts, was the close relationship with the British forces in Germany and in particular with the two Commanders-in-Chief, Army and Air, as well as with the GOC in Berlin.

What unfortunately was missing in these early months was any personal contact with Chancellor Adenauer. But he had already been forced by his Liberal partners in the Coalition Government to resign half-way through the then four-year term of the Government within six months of my arrival. This had resulted from his ill-advised project of following Heuss as President, given up as soon as he realized the very limited powers of the Federal President.

For me as British Ambassador, the succession in the autumn of 1963 of Erhard, who was very well-disposed towards Britain, as indeed towards the other non-Community countries in northern Europe, with an excellent and also pro-British Foreign Minister in Schröder, was a great boon. Adenauer's relationship with Schröder had been anything but good, although between them they had really created the CDU. It was a post-war development of the old Weimar Centre Party, of which Adenauer had been a prominent member and which had been Catholic. Schröder and others had brought in the Protestants from the north of Germany, to the extent that the CDU was about fifty-fifty Catholic and Protestant, this having been assisted by the large influx of Protestants into the Federal Republic from East Germany. In Bonn, which had been an entirely Catholic town when I studied there in the late Twenties, the relationship was sixty per cent Catholic and forty per cent Protestant, reflecting similar changes both ways throughout the Federal Republic.

Both Erhard and Schröder wanted to see the United Kingdom in the Community. Some people in London expected them to use the great economic weight of Germany to overcome French opposition. Since this opposition, however, came from General de Gaulle himself, the chances were extremely slight. Nor did I consider it in our long-term interest to prejudice Franco-German reconciliation, already under strain after Adenauer's departure. On one of his visits to Bonn, de Gaulle referred to treaties, with one treaty obviously in mind, as roses which soon faded and lost their bloom. The EEC issue and de Gaulle's opposition remained with us during my five years in Bonn and created similar difficulties and strains for Anglo-German relations in 1967, when Harold Wilson and George Brown revived the British application to join the EEC, relying on the support of the Big Coalition Government under Kiesinger and in particular of Brandt and the SPD, with as little hope of success as under the Erhard and Schröder Government.

The two other major issues with which I was concerned in Germany were Anglo-German trade and the German Ostpolitik. Germany was so obviously a major British market that it was with Germany that we began a new policy of organizing British Trade Weeks on the Continent. The first such Week was on a relatively small scale in Munich. This was part of a policy of getting away from the old zonal post-war organizations of Germany, when British influence had been in North Rhine-Westphalia, Lower Saxony, Hamburg and Schleswig Holstein, and French influence in Bavaria and Baden Wurttemberg. I found myself encouraging British cultural and economic activities in the south, just as I found my French colleague was increasingly active in such traditionally pro-British centres as Hamburg and Hanover in the north.

The then Lord Mayor of Munich was a rising young Socialist politician called Vogel. He had a brother who was a rising CDU politician in the Rhineland. When I paid my first visit to Munich, I found Vogel rather weary. It was during the carnival period, which goes on for many weeks in Munich, and as the new Lord Mayor he was expected to attend every one of the carnival balls which, as he explained to me, meant staying up to three o'clock in the morning on almost every night of the week. However, he was most helpful about the British Week, as indeed was the then CDU Minister-President of Bavaria, Herr Goppel, whom I also got to know very well as the years passed. Since Ambassadors are not always good prophets, I like to recall that I saw in Herr Vogel at that time a potential candidate for the post of Chancellor in Bonn, if and when the SPD should push the CDU out of what then seemed to be permanent office. Herr Vogel has not actually become Chancellor, but he did become an unsuccessful candidate in a Federal election and he has for some years been the rather successful party leader of the SPD in Bonn.

I pride myself similarly on having picked on Herr Kohl, on a later visit to the capital of his home province of the Rhineland Palatinate in Mainz. In the absence of Altmaier, the senior of the German Ministers-President, our host for the evening was a then little known but considered locally a promising young Minister of the Interior called Helmut Kohl. I then made a mental note that here also was a potential Chancellor candidate, which to the surprise of many people he did in fact become. As Chancellor he has proved a great survivor, seeing off a more brilliant rival in the late Franz Josef Strauss, and presiding over the unification of the two German States in the early Nineties.

Returning to British trade policy, the successful experiment in Munich was followed in the spring of 1964 by a much more ambitious 'British Week' in Düsseldorf. British business was much more ready to put on a show in the north, which was known to it, than in the south, which at that time was associated more with holidays. Indeed, one of my failures in Germany was in an attempt just before I left Germany, when the time had come round for another major British Trade Week, to have it held in Stuttgart. I argued that Stuttgart was the right place because of its modern industry, with important firms like Daimler Benz and Bosch and a great concentration of small and medium-sized private businesses, which are one of the main strengths of the German economy. I was met with the preference of British exporters for a British Week in Hamburg. When, against my better judgement, I went to Hamburg to suggest this to a city which regards itself as almost English, the city fathers were amazed at the proposal that Hamburg needed a British Week. They reminded me of our saying about taking coals to Newcastle, but reluctantly agreed, and I hope the Week, which took place after I left, was successful, if redundant.

I was never sure how successful these British Weeks were in the long run in promoting British trade, but they certainly did a good deal for the general British position in Germany and presumably in the other European countries where they were held. They were developed later on a smaller scale into British export promotions in large stores throughout Germany and into encouraging British firms to exhibit at the very many trade fairs throughout Germany, ranging from the great, universal fair in Hanover to food and consumer goods fairs in Cologne, motor and book fairs in Frankfurt, toy fairs in Nuremberg, fashion fairs in Munich and Düsseldorf, and food, fashion and electronics fairs in Berlin. British-German trade developed well during the Sixties, better than in the more difficult Seventies after our entry into the Community but also, alas, after the oil crisis and menace of recession. British industry proved itself capable of producing goods for one of the most selective markets in Europe, although we also relied on investments in Germany, which were then greater than German investments in Britain, and a little later upon our oil exports to balance the books. German firms then establishing themselves in the UK found themselves very much at home and, like Japanese firms, had little trouble with labour relations, then considered one of the major burdens affecting British industry.

Since we were likely to be kept out of the European Community for some years, it was important to promote closer relations with the Federal Republic in every other field. One method was to revive the Western European Union, which had become rather dormant. This was welcomed by the Germans. We had one or two meetings at ministerial level, where topics of general European concern were discussed, but with the passage of the years and the renewed interest of the Wilson Government in joining the Community, the WEU revival ran out of steam. The French, later in the mid-Eighties, in their turn revived the Western European Union when they feared that Germany might be looking too much to the East. Once again, it proved difficult to find enough for Western European Union to get its teeth into, since the topics with which it could deal are mostly and inevitably handled in NATO and other organizations. But it has proved and will no doubt prove again a valuable European institution, more especially since it has been strengthened by the accession of Spain and Portugal. It may have an important role to play in the remodelling of European security around a united Germany and the free nations of Central and Eastern Europe and with such great changes in the Soviet Union itself.

Anglo-German relations were flourishing, particularly in the universities, despite the absence of any special arrangements on such an imposing scale as those under the Franco-German cultural agreements. We did benefit greatly from post-war institutions, which had grown from strength to strength, in particular from the Anglo-German Königswinter conferences, still inspired by their founder Lilo Milchsack, which provided and still provide 'Forty Years On' more intimate high-level and inter-disciplinary exchanges, covering all political parties, than any other similar international gatherings. Another has been Wilton Park. Originally established for the re-education of German prisoners of war selected as potential leaders of the new democratic Germany, it developed into an Anglo-German, then a European, and now a worldwide conference centre, but always with an Anglo-German core. The British Council had successfully taken over the work of the post-war 'Brücken' or 'Bridges' all over the British zone. It was a major tribute to their success that the headquarters of the British Council in Cologne remained in the offices of the Cologne 'Bridge', which were for many years placed at the disposal of the British Council by the Cologne authorities on the same favourable terms as in the more privileged occupation days.

We continued to benefit, although perhaps not quite so obviously by the Sixties, from the major part we had played in the reorganization of the German trade unions after the war; from the considerable role played by Sir Robert Birley and other British educationalists in the restoration of the German educational system to its old high standards after the excesses of the Nazi regime; and from our contribution to the development of German press, radio and television. Successful press proprietors and other media personalities took pleasure in reminding me of those early days and had not forgotten those who had helped them. When a Royal Commission on trade union reform in the UK visited Germany in the mid-Sixties, I invited the then Head of the German Trade Unions, Rosenberg, to meet them at dinner. After reminding him of all he had told me about the help the German unions had received from the British TUC after the war, I suggested he now had a good opportunity to 'return the compliment' with some good advice to our Royal Commission. Rosenberg, who had spent some time in the UK and was very pro-British, replied that he would like to do so, but that it might prove too expensive. He did not want there to be another war, won by the Germans, to improve the British trade union system. 'We trade unionists,' he explained, 'are very conservative with a small "c".'

But in spite of all this the British position in Germany had suffered, as compared with that of Germany's two other major allies, the United States and France. Obviously we could not compete with the Americans on the economic front or indeed in terms of German dependence on the US for defence. But what had been a rather subordinate French position in the early post-war years, even down to Germany's entry into NATO and WEU in 1954–55, had changed very much for the better. This went back to the French realization in the late Forties that there was no longer any prospect of restoring Franco-Russian relations, as they had hoped to do at the end of the war in order to keep Germany 'under control', followed by intelligent and far-reaching French initiatives such as the Coal and Steel Community in 1948 and even in this context the unsuccessful European Defence Community initiative in the early Fifties, above all the European Economic Community, in addition to a most ambitious programme of professional and youth exchanges. Since the United Kingdom had not felt able to join in any of these ventures, and the core of these new European institutions lay in Franco-German reconciliation, the Federal Republic had inevitably become more closely engaged with France than with the United Kingdom, which had certainly not been the case in the immediate post-war period nor indeed at such major turning points as the Berlin airlift in 1948–49 or the NATO-WEU settlement of 1954–55. The UK had become very much the third in the allied trio rather than the second.

Pending our membership of the Community, we had to work at improving our bilateral relations as well as developing our common interests with the Germans, particularly in NATO and over security questions, where the French were the odd man out. There was also the important developing field of East-West relations, where British and German interests were then similar. The immediate priority was the bilateral relationship. When I arrived in Bonn in 1963 it was already some years since the first post-war State Visit to the United Kingdom of the first President of the new democratic German Federal Republic, Heuss, without any return visit from the Queen. The Heuss visit had probably been premature, insofar as British public opinion was not yet ready to welcome a German President, even such a delightful and obviously democratic character as Heuss. There had even been a hostile demonstration from the students at Oxford. But the fact remained that the Queen, by this time, had paid State Visits to almost every country in the world, and if HMG did not advise Her Majesty to visit Germany soon, all our efforts in other fields might be wasted.

This was particularly important because of the special position that General de Gaulle had acquired in Germany, partly on his visits, on one of which he had rather surprisingly insisted upon his partial German ancestry, a field in which the Queen could obviously outplay him with ease. American Presidents had also been to Germany, and there had been, above all, the most successful visit in the summer of 1963 of President Kennedy, which is best known for his famous phrase, 'Ich bin ein Berliner.' When I pointed this out to London, I had a sympathetic hearing from the then Foreign Secretary, Rab Butler, whom I had first known as Parliamentary Under-Secretary in the Foreign Office before the war, and it was rapidly agreed that such a visit should be made. State Visits, however, take some time to arrange, and the Queen's visit took place in 1965 under a Labour Government with Michael Stewart as Foreign Secretary.

I had not previously been concerned with any State Visits and did not realize the immensely detailed work which went into them, particularly into a visit of such political importance as this one. It was to be one of the longest State Visits that the Queen had ever paid, one of ten days, to cover much of the Federal Republic. One of the first problems which arose concerned the Queen's and also Prince Philip's many relations in Germany. There had recently been a State Visit from the King of Greece who, with his wife, also had many relations among the German princely houses. Since Prince Philip was much involved in these family matters, he sent me a message explaining that there had been great protocol difficulties during the King of Greece's visit when members of the former German ruling houses, who had no position in the current Republican protocol, had found themselves seated at dinners below relatively junior German officials. Prince Philip suggested that I should explain the position to the German President, Herr Lübke, and say that the Queen would understand if her relatives were not invited on any formal occasions.

President Lübke was a very decent man of clear and firm views but without a broad vision. He had been selected in a hurry when Adenauer turned down the Presidency himself, and had many good qualities without being on the same high level as other German Presidents, such as Heuss himself or Richard von Weizsäcker. He was greatly helped by his intelligent wife. One of his qualities was that he knew his own mind. When I put Prince Philip's suggestion to him he at once told me that this would not do. He came from the Sauerland in the mountains behind Cologne, whose inhabitants are famous for the hardness of their heads. In the Sauerland, he explained to me, it was a tradition when, if I wouldn't mind his putting it this way, a girl of the country came back after it did not matter how many years, her relatives must be invited to meet her; and there was no doubt about the Hanoverian origins of the British Royal Family. He could not therefore possibly fail to invite her relatives to meet her. I found myself between the hammer of Prince Philip and the anvil of President Lübke.

Luckily, by this time I had got to know the late Prince Ludwig of Hessen, who had married a Geddes and knew Britain well. He had a keen interest in music and had translated the librettos of Benjamin Britten's operas. For my purposes the important thing was that he was well in with Buckingham Palace and also seemed to be accepted by other German princely families as an authority whose opinion on anything affecting the British Royal Family should be respected. He produced the solution, which was that the German 'royals' should only be invited when the Queen visited their own particular parts of Germany – the Hohenzollerns in Berlin, the Hanovers in Hanover, and so forth. Any small protocol difficulty could therefore be got round in a way that would not have been possible with a large number of princely invitees at the same party. I think the solution in Bonn itself was to invite only those who were going to be hosts to the Queen on the rare occasions when she was 'off duty'.

This did, however, create another difficulty. Prince Philip's relatives, who were all in western Germany, had come quite well out of the war and were in a good position to entertain the Queen in suitable style in their great houses in Baden-Wurttemberg and the Rhineland. The Queen's direct relatives were the Hohenzollerns and the Hanovers. The Hohenzollerns had lost all their palaces, and the then head of the house lived relatively modestly in Bremen. The Hanovers had been hard hit by the withdrawal of the Allied forces to the Elbe at the end of the war, since some of their best houses were in the area then occupied by the Russians. The Queen had some breaks in her ten days, dining at Wolfsgarten with the Hessens and at Langenburg with Prince Philip's sister, then spending part of a weekend with Prince Philip's other relatives, the Badens, at Salem.

The Germans discovered a very good solution to what could have been a major problem in a ten-day visit of constantly changing residences. After their first nights on the Petersberg high over Bonn, where HM gave her party for the President, a special train was made up, in which she and her suite went round Germany. This saved a great deal of time and stress, and proved a most successful arrangement. Another problem arising from the length of the visit was the necessity to submit an unusually large number of speeches for the Queen, suitable for the different places in which she had to make them. The third of her speeches was in Koblenz, just before crossing the Rhine to be the guest of the Hessen Government at Wiesbaden. She happened to be crossing the Rhine at precisely the spot where Marshal Blücher had crossed on his way to join Wellington at the Battle of Waterloo. Our speech writer in the Embassy introduced a very diplomatic reference to the spot where, in a period of Anglo-German military cooperation, a great German general had crossed the Rhine on his way to help his British allies. There was no mention of Waterloo or the French. This did not prevent the French General in Koblenz from saying afterwards that he had had the greatest difficulty in restraining himself from leaving the meeting in a huff; and I was told that even so good a friend of this country as General Catroux, then Marshal of the Legion of Honour, refused his invitation to the Queen's birthday party at the British Embassy in Paris, all because of what they regarded as a veiled reference to Waterloo.

In Berlin, the Queen not only gave reassurance to the Berlin population but took a parade of the British garrison, as she had previously taken a major parade of the British and Canadian forces in the Federal Republic.

For me, one of the most important features of the Royal Visit was not so much the reception of the Queen in Germany, which I knew would be most enthusiastic, but getting the story back on television to the United Kingdom. Those were the days when British television was still full of films and pictures of jack-booted Nazis and escapes by British prisoners of war, and when some British correspondents in Germany were still under guidance from their head offices in London to report unhappy rather than satisfactory developments in Anglo-German relations. It was therefore important that the British public should see for themselves what sort of people their allies in the Federal Republic now were. They could hardly fail to get the message that the new German democracy had nothing in common with Hitler's Third Reich.

The Queen ended her visit in Hamburg. The city fathers, who were, as has almost always been the case, Socialists since the war, but very much to the centre, arranged for twenty of the leading citizens to be received by the Queen at a special guest house on the Alster Lake in the middle of Hamburg. At that time one of the most famous footballers in the world was Uwe Seeler, captain of the very successful Hamburg and German national football teams and highly regarded for his sportsmanship and good character. I knew he was likely to attract more attention in the popular British press than most other citizens of Hamburg, however worthy. The Socialist city fathers were less than enthusiastic to include him, but I stuck to my guns, with the results I had anticipated.

I had originally suggested that HM should start her visit by sailing into Hamburg, but the Federal Government correctly decided that the visit should start in the capital, Bonn. Her Majesty's departure from

Hamburg at night with HMS *Britannia* fully illuminated and escorted by British and German naval vessels was an unforgettable sight. The Queen's visit had more than fulfilled our highest expectations, and established a sure foundation for Anglo-German bilateral relations.

25 | Berlin and Ostpolitik

1963–8

General de Gaulle's exclusion of the United Kingdom from the European Community and the inability of the Germans to change this situation, as they would have liked to do, was the most negative feature of my five years in Germany not only for Britain but also for the EEC itself. One of the most positive features, which made its contribution to the successful development of Anglo-German bilateral relations, was Germany's Ostpolitik. At Königswinter meetings throughout the Sixties, the main thrust of the German participants was to press the British, despite French opposition, to maintain their determination to join the Community, while the main thrust of the British was that the Germans should follow the lead of their Western allies and repeat in the Soviet Union and Eastern Europe their successful policy of reconciliation in the West. We used to joke that throughout this period the leading participants at Königswinter, although absent, were General de Gaulle and Nikita Khrushchev.

It is often thought that the German Ostpolitik began with Willy Brandt towards the end of the Sixties. This was not the case. There had been a progressive development which, to a limited extent, went back as far as Adenauer. It gathered strength under Schröder in the early Sixties and in the 'Big Coalition' of Kiesinger and Brandt in the mid-Sixties. Adenauer had himself been to Moscow in 1956 and established relations with the Soviet Union as a major exception from the then German policy of having no diplomatic relations with any country which recognized the GDR. In return for this he had obtained the repatriation of a number of Germans from the Soviet Union. Above all, this had put him on speaking terms with the fourth of the major powers responsible for All-German affairs and for Berlin. He certainly had it in mind to go beyond this, and had a deeprooted belief that increasing tension between the Soviet Union and China would influence the Soviet Government towards a more accommodating policy with Germany in the West. But since Adenauer's first priority was to anchor Germany firmly in Western European and Atlantic institutions, he had in fact little or no opportunity for developing a positive Ostpolitik before his enforced resignation in the summer of 1963. It was, however, significant that at my farewell meeting with him he wanted to discuss the Soviet Union and more particularly the effect of its increasingly difficult relations with China.

The main factor which pushed West German Governments into a more positive Ostpolitik was the Berlin Wall in the summer of 1961. This meant that the GDR had to be accepted as a fact of life, in addition to the Soviet Union itself. It was by then becoming more and more of a burden on Germany's otherwise successful policies in the Third World to maintain the Hallstein Doctrine in its stark simplicity, which meant breaking off relations with any country which entered into relations with the GDR. One of the main examples of this was in Yugoslavia when I was Ambassador there in the mid-Fifties. My first German colleague, Herr Kroll, was succeeded by a well-known FDP politician, George Pfleiderer, an attractive character who made it clear to me that his main objective was to put more warmth into German relations with Yugoslavia, as the first step in a new policy to be extended to the other nations of Eastern Europe. His efforts were, however, ruined when Tito, to my mind injudiciously, recognized the GDR, whereupon Pfleiderer was removed from Belgrade and relations with Yugoslavia broken off.

The new German policy was also influenced by the emphasis which General de Gaulle was himself putting upon his relations with the Soviet Union, more especially as he was not above hinting when displeased with Bonn at the possibility of France resuming her traditional relations with Russia at the expense of Germany. De Gaulle's general idea was to take Germany by the hand, introduce her to Moscow, and in effect to control German relations with the Soviet Union. This, however, had little attraction for the Russians, who saw more advantage to them from the German economy than from the French and had never shown any tendency to conduct their relations with any country through a third country. Since the United States and the United Kingdom at that time were also attaching considerable importance to improving their relations with the Soviet Union and Eastern Europe, it became increasingly clear to German political leaders that Germany's interest lay in joining in these moves to the East.

There was also in Germany an increasing realization that the theory on which German Eastern policy had hitherto rested that European reconciliation would only come about through German reunification was no longer valid, if indeed it ever had been. Instead, politicians in Bonn gradually turned to the opposite principle that it was through European unity that German unity could be re-established. Once this principle had been accepted, as it was after the Berlin Wall, together with the realization that the GDR could no longer be completely ignored nor its separate statehood denied, the way was open for an active German Ostpolitik.

This began with Gerhard Schröder even in his days as Foreign Minister to Adenauer but continued to a much greater extent after Adenauer's departure in October 1963. Schröder could work on the same wavelength with the new Chancellor, Erhard, and with the general sympathy of the FDP as well as of the SPD opposition, which was then more naturally interested than the CDU in the GDR where the main strengths of the Socialists had traditionally lain. Schröder felt, however, that it would be wiser to begin with what he must have thought was the easier task of creating a relationship with one or two of the East European states who had not suffered as much as others from Hitler's Germany, and then moving on to Poland and Czechoslovakia. But he found himself limited in most cases to trade agreements rather than restoration of political relations. The Germans did not find it easy to rid themselves of the effects of the Hallstein doctrine and were also faced with constant difficulties over the inclusion of Berlin in such agreements.

Meanwhile, non-official channels were also active, in particular the Churches, the SPD and big industry. The Lutheran Church arranged meetings with Protestant Churches in the East, and this was followed up by similar moves from the German Catholic Church, more especially directed to their fellow Catholics in Poland. The SPD could not easily find opposite numbers in the Warsaw Pact countries, and were therefore restricted to what were never very satisfactory exchanges with the official SED in East Germany, uniting Communists and Socialists. German industry had probably the easiest task, since there was increasing demand for West German products throughout Eastern Europe, including the Soviet Union. One of the main protagonists in this activity was Herr Beitz, then the head of Krupps.

The difficulty was that the Soviet Union regarded these approaches to some of its 'satellites' in Eastern Europe with anything but sympathy. The Russians felt that this was an attempt to weaken the Warsaw Pact and did not encourage a favourable response from any of their allies, at that time still under their effective control. In conversations with the Soviet Ambassador to the GDR, with whom I had meetings every few months in Berlin, he expressed himself with great scepticism and even hostility when I commended this new German attitude towards the East. His line was that the Germans had to make major concessions, and I recall in particular one of his phrases, 'to abandon all nuclear pretensions' (of which I myself had never seen any sign) before their new Ostpolitik could be considered sincere.

One of the main issues was the question of frontiers, particularly with Poland, which had been moved westwards under the agreements reached between Stalin and Churchill. The Poles were not unnaturally fearful that the Germans as they became stronger might put forward claims to their old territories in what is now western Poland, where there was still a large German minority. While West German Governments had no thought of raising the frontier issue, which in any case directly concerned only the GDR, they did find it difficult to make the kind of declaration which would satisfy the Poles without possibly causing difficulty for themselves with a large number of their new citizens, who had come from the East. Schröder's well-meant attempts to enter into normal relations with Poland and Czechoslovakia therefore met with resistance.

When the Erhard–Schröder Government was succeeded in 1966 by the Big Coalition, with the CDU Chancellor Kiesinger supported by the SPD leader Brandt as Foreign Minister, Kiesinger himself took over the Ostpolitik and tried to mollify the Russians with a major declaration renouncing once again any intention to change German frontiers by other than peaceful means. The influential State Secretary in the Ministry for Foreign Affairs, Dr Carstens, paid an important visit to Moscow to reassure the Russians. But judging by the reactions of my own contact, Abrasimov, in Berlin, all this was without any noticeable effect. 'Revanchism, militarism, determination to change frontiers, and nuclear pretensions' were still the main themes of the replies to my attempts to reassure him on German intentions.

Looking back on this period, it seems clear that the mistake made by the German Governments of the early and middle Sixties was the attempt to deal with their Ostpolitik piecemeal, thus giving the Soviet Union the impression they were trying to detach the East European countries one by one. The other problem was the inability of any German Government at that time to recognize the existence of the GDR. It was therefore not until Brandt, with the increased status of Chancellor, decided to advance simultaneously on many fronts that progress could be made. He negotiated at one and the same time with Moscow and with the Poles, who were the main problem countries in Eastern Europe, and accepted the existence of the GDR, while at the same time the three Western protecting powers negotiated with the Soviet Union on the status of Berlin.

Once it was clear to the Russians that they were not being left out, and also that the result of all this would be a new status for the GDR, the German Ostpolitik gathered strength and resulted at the end of the Sixties and in the early Seventies in West German treaties with the Soviet Union and with Poland, normalizing their relations, and in the Four-Power agreement over Berlin, together with the important West German recognition of the GDR, not quite as an independent state but nevertheless as a state with which West Germany had a special relationship. Relations with the GDR were conducted, not through the Ministry for Foreign Affairs but through the Chancellor's office, and what were in practice the respective diplomatic representatives in East Berlin and Bonn were never so described.

In terms of Germany's relations with her main allies in the West, the completion of the German Ostpolitik was an important step, although the French had to accept that from then on Germany would be conducting her own relationships with the Soviet Union and indeed as time went on would be a more important partner for the Soviet Union than France or for that matter the United Kingdom, especially in the economic field. This complex of West German agreements went far to reassure the Russians, the Poles and the Czechs that the Federal Republic had no intention of reopening the issues of the frontiers, although it continued to maintain that only a united Germany could make final and binding agreements.

From the Soviet point of view, probably the most important result of these arrangements with Bonn was to ensure stability in Eastern Europe and to legitimize the gains which the Soviet Union had made at such vast cost in the Great Patriotic War. For Germany's Western

250

allies the agreement over Berlin was of major significance. So much had been left at the end of the war without any written documentation. This was above all apparent in regard to the surface access routes and facilitated the Berlin blockade. Meanwhile, a great body of what we in England would call case law had arisen over Berlin and was generally accepted on all sides. Above all, the Russians had never departed from their own responsibility to deal directly with the three Western powers over all matters concerning Berlin, although this had been put in question, before the Berlin Wall, by Khrushchev's threats to hand over Soviet authority to the GDR.

In the periodic meetings I had with Abrasimov I found that he would from time to time raise some complaint, usually on what we both realized was a relatively minor matter. I would have liked to be able to reply that this was covered by a specific article in an agreement, but had to fall back on case law. The Russians have never had much understanding of case law, and had they then been disposed to be awkward I do not think they would necessarily have accepted my answer. There was therefore every advantage in having everything affecting Berlin cleared up in a written agreement, which has stood the test of time. There has been no threat to the Western position in Berlin or to West Berlin itself since the agreement of 1971.

In the early Seventies, I was asked by the leading Italian magazine on international affairs, *Affari Esteri*, to write an article on the Ostpolitik and the Berlin agreements. This was afterwards republished in a number of British and German papers. My view was favourable. This drew down upon me the criticism of old friends in the CDU, who maintained that the SPD Government had given away a great deal and could have obtained a better return from the Russians. My own conviction, now as then, is that Brandt gave nothing away which had not already been lost through the war, and that West Germany, as well as the West in general, gained at least as much as the Soviet Union and her allies did from the resulting stability in Eastern Europe, which led on to the Helsinki CSCE agreements and to the general reduction in tension which was already apparent in the early days of Brezhnev and became even more obvious under Gorbachev.

My old friend Dr Carstens, who had moved on in the world since I had first known him as State Secretary to the Ministry for Foreign Affairs, becoming first the parliamentary leader of the CDU and later the Federal President, did not dissent from my general conclusion but added – and here he may have been right – that a rather tougher negotiation, which he assumed the CDU would have conducted if in power, might have resulted in a slightly more favourable settlement from the German point of view. But in effect no CDU Government has called the Ostpolitik in question, and I still regard it as one of the major successes of German and Western post-war policy. With the revolutionary developments in Central and Eastern Europe in 1989 it is not the West which is now in danger from the East, but rather the other way round. Without the German Ostpolitik of some two decades ago they could hardly have taken place at all.

German Ostpolitik naturally brings me to Berlin, which was one of my main responsibilities during my five years in Germany. Berlin was relatively quiet during the mid-Sixties. But I and my two Western colleagues made a practice of visiting Berlin at least once a month, and we tried to arrange our visits in such a way that one or other of us would be in Berlin covering most of the time. This also enabled us to arrange meetings with Abrasimov once a quarter.

When I arrived in Berlin in the early months of 1963 it was recovering from the immediate effects of the Berlin Wall and settling down to what many people regarded as its rather reduced circumstances. It was no longer one of the main crisis centres in Europe, which had at once alarmed but also exhilarated the Berliners. Willy Brandt was still Governing Mayor of Berlin but he had by no means settled down since the Wall and was in a state of considerable depression. No doubt the erection of the Wall and the inability of the West to do anything about it was largely responsible for this, as was also his failure to oust Dr Adenauer in the Federal elections of 1961. I found it difficult to interest him in the routine questions which required discussion between the Governing Mayor and the Allied authorities. He had, however, a great capacity for rising to occasions; and two such major occasions during his latter years as Mayor were the visit of the American President, John Kennedy, in 1963 and that of the Queen in 1965. Each of these visits contained a large element of morale booster for Berlin, and both were entirely successful. After Erhard's resignation in 1965 Willy Brandt was able to get away from Berlin, and he became Foreign Minister in the Big Coalition Government under Kiesinger. The change in him was extraordinary. From a rather despondent and discouraged personality, from whom I could get little response in any general discussion, there emerged an effective and active Foreign Minister with whom it was easy to do business. He did not lose interest in Berlin, and his successors, Albertz and Schütz, certainly listened to Willy Brandt in Bonn.

Apart from these two major visits from the President and the Queen, Berlin remained relatively quiet. There was fortunately no crisis comparable with either the blockade and airlift or the Berlin Wall, but from time to time we had what would elsewhere have been minor problems but which in Berlin could always escalate into major ones. One was known in Berlin parlance as the 'tail-board crisis'. This arose when the East German authorities, who were allowed to look into Allied trucks bringing troops and supplies into Berlin in order to check that everything was as it should be, insisted that the tail-boards of high American lorries be taken down in order that they could more easily count the American troops inside. The Russians, who seemed reluctant to exercise their authority over the East Germans, did not respond to American suggestions that they should intervene, whereupon the American Commander refused to take the tail-boards down and debarred himself from moving into or away from Berlin. There was here the making of a serious crisis. Eventually, the East Germans gave way, and the lorries proceeded with their tail-boards still high.

A similar situation arose in regard to the entry of Western official cars into East Berlin, which had become more of a problem since the building of the Wall. The GDR guards at Checkpoint Charlie, which was the only entry into East Berlin used by Allied vehicles, following the same logic as that of the tail-board crisis insisted that they should be able to check who was actually in the cars. My American colleague, who was going to visit his military mission in Potsdam, refused to show any identity document, and as a result his two Western colleagues had also to deprive ourselves of any visits to our own military missions in Potsdam. Attempts to get this matter settled through the Russians had no success. On the British side we never took these 'theological' issues quite so far as the Americans, and eventually a system was worked out which stood the test of time, in which the Western Ambassadors, or senior personalities, would show their special identity cards from inside the car with all the windows tightly closed so that no East Berliner could handle them in any way. This got us into and out of East Berlin satisfactorily but never got us as far as our military missions in Potsdam in the GDR.

A more important and potentially difficult issue was the crash of a Soviet plane into one of the lakes in the British sector of Berlin. Since it was a very modern Soviet fighter, the RAF were anxious to get as much information as possible. We were able on one pretext or another to delay its return to the Russians for some forty-eight hours, which enabled them to acquire all the information they needed.

At that time there were still four remaining Four-Power institutions in West Berlin. The most important was the Air Centre, where a Soviet officer joined with his British, French and American colleagues in controlling traffic in the air corridors. The best-known was the prison at Spandau, which at that time housed three remaining prisoners – Hess, Speer and Von Schirach. I have written about this in Chapter 7. The third was a Soviet information centre, which has long ceased to function and did not cause us any problems at that time. The fourth was the Soviet War Memorial on the British side of the Brandenburg Gate, which meant that we had to make arrangements for Soviet guards of honour to march in and out of the British Sector every day. This was in an uninhabited part of Berlin, and no serious problems arose. But every now and again some little problem arose concerning Soviet citizens resident or doing business in West Berlin, and it was on such issues that I had my exchanges with Abrasimov on British case law.

The main problem in Berlin in the late Sixties was the economy. While there were lots of young people in Berlin – mainly students and younger Germans coming to Berlin to avoid military service or even to get special marriage allowances – and an ever increasing number of older people, the middle generations were missing. This meant, for example, that in the vast Siemens works in Berlin, then employing some 40,000 people, there were few if any ambitious young managers in their forties, since such people preferred to work at Siemens' establishments in Munich or Erlangen. There was also at that time a reluctance on security grounds to employ foreign workers in Berlin. This saved the city from the many problems which have since grown up in dealing with the very large Turkish minority which now occupies a whole quarter of Berlin and has turned that part of Berlin into one of the larger Turkish towns in the world.

The Berlin economy depended then, even more than today, on subventions from the Federal Republic, through which Berlin could remain the largest single German industrial city and the greatest metropolis between Paris and Moscow. The high standard of living in West Berlin as compared with the East was maintained. The food department on the top floor of the local Harrods, the Kaufhof des Westens (KDW), was then as now even better stocked and even more impressive than those at either Harrods or Fortnum & Masons. A lot of trouble was also taken to maintain Berlin's cultural importance. It had long been famous for its theatre and its music, and although Munich was a competitor, my own personal feeling was that Berlin remained the cultural number one in Germany, as indeed it should have been, with its historic past and all the assistance it received.

What unfortunately was never achieved was to turn Berlin into a natural meeting place between East and West, even to the limited extent achieved by Vienna in rather different circumstances. We on the British side had to make a special effort to interest British businessmen, who were then very active throughout the Federal Republic, in trade with Berlin. Large conference centres were started, which ensured Berlin a prominent position in staging trade fairs. Major theatre companies like the Old Vic, the Royal Shakespeare and the Royal Ballet performed in Berlin as well as in West German cities. The two universities, the Free University in the American sector and the Technical High School in the British sector, also maintained a high standard and on their merits attracted young people from the Federal Republic.

Towards the end of my time in Germany the problem of student unrest arose, having been brought to Europe from Berkeley in California. The first university affected in Germany and I think in Europe was the Free University in Berlin. More extreme movements on the streets such as those associated with the names of Rudi Dutschke and later Cohn-Bendit had not yet come to the fore. I wrongly thought that student unrest, which was perhaps natural in a university dealing mainly with the arts and social studies such as the Free University in the American sector, would not affect the Technical High School in the British sector, which was largely concerned with medicine and science. The unrest did spread, although to a lesser extent, as it also spread to most German universities.

In Berlin, as 'Head of British Military Government', I had to keep in close touch with the GOC and the three British regiments in Berlin. The position of GOC was also unusual, in that the Major General who held the office had a responsibility on the military side to the Commanders-in-Chief at Rheindahlem in what the British in Berlin persisted in describing as the British Zone, and on the political side to me. He also had a political deputy, a Minister in the Foreign Service, who again had a direct responsibility to the General in Berlin and to me as Ambassador in Bonn. Like almost everything else in Berlin, the situation was on paper peculiar, but it worked satisfactorily in practice, with only one exception, well before my time.

My position as Head of the British Military Government in Berlin naturally leads to my other unusual responsibility for a British Ambassador, of maintaining close contacts with the British Forces in Germany. The two Commanders-in-Chief, Army and Air, had their headquarters at Rheindahlem in North Rhine Westphalia, two or three hours by car from Bonn. We had an institutional relationship whereby the Minister in the Embassy and one of the secretaries sat on various committees, discussing matters of joint interest to the Forces and to us at the Embassy. I had regular meetings with the Commanders-in-Chief, either in Rheindahlem or in Bonn, which I very much valued.

The first Army Commander-in-Chief in my time was General Caassels, who had distinguished himself in command of the British division in Korea, and went on to be Chief of the General Staff. We only spent a short time together in Germany. His successor, General Stirling, encouraged close relations with the Embassy, even to the point of inviting me to take the salute as the Queen's Representative at special military occasions such as the Queen's birthday parades in Düsseldorf and in Berlin and special regimental occasions throughout Germany. I valued this not so much for the ceremonial as for the opportunities it gave me to keep in touch with so many units of the British Army in Germany.

One of the problems affecting the armed forces in Germany was their relationship with the local population in the areas where they were stationed. Our forces, unlike the French and the Americans, were in the north of Germany, where the general attitude of the population is more reserved, indeed rather English, making it more difficult to establish close relations than it was for the Americans in Bavaria or the French in Baden. Another difficulty was that when our regiments invited local Germans to mess nights, as they did, the display was so much more splendid than anything which the rather austere new German Army could put on that many of even the wealthier Germans felt that they could not return such hospitality in any appropriate way. There was also the language problem. Since our 60,000 or so British troops and airmen in Germany were far and away the most important 'tourists' we had there, it was important that they should be able to play their part in improving personal relations between the two countries. Many of the senior British officers during my time were well aware of this, and the Commander of the First British Corps in Bielefeld, General Mogg, made successful efforts to encourage first of all, the learning of German, and secondly, exchanges of hospitality between British troops and the Germans in the areas of his wide command.

The more serious problems that the Commanders-in-Chief and I had were back in London, where governments were constantly under pressure to save foreign exchange and to reduce the number of our troops in Germany. These pressures became greater under the Labour Government after 1964. One of the ways devised to reduce our foreign exchange expenditure was to persuade German forces, still in their early period of equipment, to purchase British military and civil material. Although we were up against major competition from the Americans and later also from the French, we were successful in certain fields. We and the Americans had 'offset' agreements with the Germans under which they committed themselves to spend specific sums of money on such purchases. Every year we had great arguments about the fulfilment of these offset agreements. The trouble was that German purchasers, whether in the armed forces or outside them, always had the feeling that anything put forward under an offset agreement must inevitably be of rather lower quality or higher price. My own feeling is that we would not have lost much if we had never had any offset agreements at all. We had to continue with this practice throughout my period in Germany, and once a year they brought tension into Anglo-German relations. I remember a great battle to persuade the German Post Office that we had the kind of equipment they needed, and which indeed they eventually bought later when it was no longer offered to them under an offset agreement.

At least once a year senior Treasury Ministers would descend upon Bonn to bring pressure to bear upon the Germans. The Conservative Chief Secretary, now Lord Boyd-Carpenter, was followed by later visits from Labour Ministers, the most senior being Jim Callaghan; then Chancellor of the Exchequer, the whole issue having been taken up a rung from the Chief Secretary. Throughout this period we were trying to persuade the Germans to buy equipment for which they sometimes had no real need at all.

We also, in my view, missed the bus in the nuclear field. At that time (the early Sixties) we were ahead of other countries in Europe. The Germans had hardly begun, but on the other hand, as a major industrial nation, were interested in civilian uses of nuclear energy. A high-powered British delegation came out and dined with me in Bonn on their way to see Siemens in Munich. They took the line that this visit would be largely a waste of time because Siemens would not know very much about nuclear technology and would have very little to give them. I pointed out that surely the object of the operation was to get Siemens interested in such a way that they would at least be prepared to cooperate with us and/or buy some of our equipment. When our delegation returned to see me again in Bonn, they explained how right they had been in thinking that there was nothing to be learnt at that time from Siemens. It was hardly surprising that only a few years later the Germans were selling more civilian nuclear stations to the rest of the world than we were.

One very important project, the Tornado aircraft, which I believe is the biggest single example of Allied cooperation in arms production, did, however, start in my time – and might indeed have ended almost before birth had it not been for the personal relationship that my Air Attaché had with the then Head of the German Air Force, General Steinhof. This relationship arose from the fact that they had been together in an engagement in the Mediterranean in which the General had suffered great burns to his face, afterwards put right by the famous surgeon Mr Mackindoe in England. I heard through some grapevine that the German Ministry of Finance, after the initial agreement that the British and the Germans would begin work on the Tornado, were having serious doubts about the eventual expense and were likely to persuade the Federal Government to abandon the whole plan. My Air Attaché was able, through his personal relationship, to go straight to General Steinhof, and I think this was largely instrumental in the decision to go ahead with the Tornado.

The next Commander-in-Chief after General Stirling was a brilliant soldier, General Shan Hackett, with whom I worked even more closely. Shan was also a distinguished writer and scholar who afterwards became the head of King's College, London. He had an interesting relationship with Denis Healey as Defence Secretary. At the end of his more critical letters he was careful to add a postscript saying that he was writing, not in his capacity as a British General commanding the British Army of the Rhine but as a NATO General commanding the Northern Army Group, with the duty of informing the British Defence Secretary of the situation as he saw it, just as he would have informed the Ministers of Defence of any of the other countries involved in the Northern Army Group.

He and I were, however, faced with a major problem in my last year, 1967–68. The Government had reached the decision to reduce the

British forces in Germany from four divisions to three. We were afraid that this would mean the disbandment of the division to be withdrawn. We therefore worked out an arrangement under which the fourth division, when it left Germany for a base in the north of England, would remain technically under General Hackett's command, which meant that it had to remain in being. In addition, its heavy equipment was to remain in Germany so that the personnel could be moved back at very short notice.

26 | Diplomatic Departure

1968

Our last posting in Germany was personally a happy one. We felt closely involved in the development in the Federal Republic of stable democratic institutions in addition to its economic miracle and remarkable cultural restoration. British-German relations were improving so notably that Lord Home could later describe them as based on total trust and confidence. We made good and lasting friends and were fortunate in being able to lay the foundations for a continued connection with German affairs, economic and political, in London after my retirement in 1968.

There was one major disappointment, for which neither the Germans nor the British were responsible, the exclusion of Britain from the European Community. Although the giants of the post-war years, Churchill, Bevin, Adenauer and even Stalin, had left the stage, there were still major figures handling German affairs. I began in Bonn early in 1963 under Harold Macmillan as Prime Minister, Rab Butler as Foreign Secretary and Ted Heath as Minister for Europe, and continued in 1964 under Harold Wilson as Prime Minister with Michael Stewart and George Brown alternating as Foreign Secretaries. On the German side after Adenauer's forced retirement in 1963, there were Erhard as Chancellor, Schröder at the Ministry for Foreign Affairs and Von Hassell at Defence, followed in 1966 by Kiesinger as Chancellor and Willy Brandt at the Ministry for Foreign Affairs, with Schröder at Defence and with Helmut Schmidt, Schiller and Franz Josef Strauss playing increasingly important roles in finance and economics.

Taking our own leaders first, I had known Harold Macmillan when

I was at NATO in the late Fifties, and had been with him at the dinner at the British Embassy in 1960 which followed the collapse of the Paris Summit talks with Khrushchev after the U-2 incident. He was hard hit by this, and felt it was the end of a chapter and that it would be extremely difficult to re-establish the working relationship with Khrushchev which had begun at Geneva in 1955. During my succeeding two years in Moscow there had indeed been few high-level contacts between the British and the Russians, but Harold Macmillan had always taken a keen interest in the Soviet Union, and was greatly concerned with the two major crises of the Berlin Wall and Cuba. He was an understanding and courteous chief, always ready to discuss the position when I was home on leave and to give full consideration to the many communications we sent from Moscow. But by the time I went to Bonn, the end of his long administration was in sight.

Although it was the Conservative Government and in fact Harold Macmillan and Rab Butler who had decided on the Queen's visit to Germany, by the time HM came in 1965 the Labour Government of Harold Wilson and Michael Stewart was in power. It was Michael Stewart who accompanied the Queen on most of her visit. It was not, however, until he changed places with George Brown that Harold Wilson decided to revive the British application to join the European Community. George Brown was not the most popular of Foreign Secretaries with all my British diplomatic colleagues, although I myself had no trouble and was indeed kept at my post in Bonn for six months after the usual retiring age of sixty. George Brown had been close to Ernie Bevin as a young man in the Labour Party and the trade unions when I was Principal Private Secretary, and this helped me to hold my own when it came (as it sometimes did) to argument.

His aim was to be another Ernie Bevin, and as he had a much better education and a very quick mind, he could have succeeded. At his best, he was a good Foreign Secretary, particularly on the most important issues of foreign policy which were then in Europe and the Middle East, but he lacked many of Bevin's qualities, including Bevin's human touch and Bevin's sense of personal responsibility. This sometimes created unnecessary problems with his German opposite numbers, Schröder and Willy Brandt, whom he tended to treat as an inexperienced 'new boy' in the select company of Western Foreign Ministers. In Germany as elsewhere there were some, although relatively few, of the incidents associated with George Brown's moods. But they never in my experience affected his negotiating skills. If the pro-

gramme demanded a start at nine am, he was always down punctu-
ally, waiting for the car at five to nine, and then conducting important
conversations with his German opposite numbers with complete
mastery of the subject.

There was no doubt about George Brown's full commitment to the
policy of getting Britain on the second attempt into the European
Community or about his commitment to an even-handed policy in the
Middle East. But even his energy and insistence could not overcome
General de Gaulle's opposition to our renewed European application,
although the effort was in my view worth making if only for the good
effect it had in the Federal Republic and other Community countries.

On the German side, Erhard will, I think, be judged more
favourably by history than he was at the time of his Chancellorship.
Adenauer had always feared that Erhard would not make a successful
Chancellor, and he was proved right. But it was Erhard more than any
other man who had set Germany on the path to the economic miracle.
He it was who took the decision to free the economy and to reform the
currency, when even the Americans, who were responsible for his
appointment, were by no means convinced that such policies could
succeed. He also ensured that the German economic miracle was
based not only on the market economy but on what was rightly called
a social (not a free) market economy, thus preserving a balance
between the two sides of industry which has not been so successfully
achieved in any other Western country and remains a model to this
day.

Erhard also took a much broader view of Germany's international
position than Adenauer, and felt that it should not be so exclusively
based on Franco-German reconciliation, important though this was.
He looked also to America and Britain and to the Nordic countries,
and was a strong supporter of Schröder's foreign policies, which were
similarly oriented.

Schröder was a complete contrast: he was thoroughly businesslike.
One knew exactly where one was; when he could be helpful, he was;
and when he could not, he explained this very clearly. As far as I was
concerned, he was always friendly and well-disposed. But Schröder
did not suffer fools gladly, and he was apt to treat some of the
backbenchers in his own party as such. On one occasion when we were
talking together at a party, a rising CDU backbencher passed and
greeted Dr Schröder with more than a simple 'Good evening', to
receive the very cold reply, 'Can't you see I'm talking to the British

Ambassador?' I could not help feeling that that was one vote that Schröder might lose when it next came to a major vote in the party.

He had the intellectual qualifications for Chancellor, and he was a successful Foreign and later Defence Minister, as he had been a good Minister of the Interior. There was a brief period during the negotiations for the next Chancellor and the next coalition after the fall of Erhard in 1966 when Schröder seemed on the point of reaching agreement with Franz Josef Strauss in a coalition under their joint leadership. I was extremely surprised on my only visit to Bayreuth to see them both together receiving plaudits from the crowd in an interval of *Tannhäuser*. This unlikely combination did not, however, come about. When Schröder was put forward as the CDU candidate for President, he did not get a majority, which hardly surprised me as his many qualities did not include popular appeal. Schröder remained an active promoter of good Anglo-German relations, and until his death in 1989 continued to support the *Deutsch-Englische Gesellschaft* (German-English Society) and the Anglo-German Königswinter conferences.

I have already written in the Berlin context about Willy Brandt. The two other outstanding SPD politicians in my time were Helmut Schmidt and Schiller. Schiller was Minister of Economics, and ran a very successful double-act with Franz Josef Strauss as Minister of Finance. I had good relations with each of them, and Strauss has already featured in previous chapters. He and Helmut Schmidt were the two most brilliant German politicians of this period, but Strauss was too flamboyant for North German voters and failed in his one attempt to become Chancellor. It was only after I left Germany that Helmut Schmidt became one of the most outstanding Chancellors of the post-war era, to be compared with Adenauer. His English was perfect, as befitted a native of Hamburg, where he had made his reputation in local government. He was a good friend of Britain, and as strong a supporter of the *Deutsche-Englische Gesellschaft* and the Königswinter conferences as Gerhard Schröder. In 1980 he and Margaret Thatcher attended the thirtieth-anniversary conference in Cambridge. Margaret Thatcher opened with the quip that she had had to become Prime Minister to be invited to this prestigious conference although Helmut Schmidt had been to seventeen Königswinters. Helmut Schmidt later became disappointed in what he considered the reserved British attitude within the European Community, as he also became disappointed in the policies and behaviour

of American Presidents, with the result that during his close cooperation with Giscard d'Estaing, as French President, and after retirement,
he came to believe more in bilateral Franco-German cooperation than
in a wider approach. One fault that he shared with Schröder was a
certain arrogance, and this again led to his lack of popularity within his
own party, where he was in any case regarded very much as a man of the
right, with the result that it was through lack of support in the SPD that
he finally had to give up the Chancellorship.

Another outstanding CDU leader with whom I came into contact
was Richard von Weizsäcker, to my mind the most distinguished
President of the Federal Republic, of which in a sense he became the
conscience. I knew him first as my CDU contact in organizing Königswinter conferences, later as Governing Mayor in Berlin, and then as
President, in which capacity he maintained his strong connection with
Königswinter and a firm, but at times critical, friendship for Britain.

At the next level, I was dealing with outstanding civil servants, such as
Carstens and Lahr, his economic opposite number in the Ministry for
Foreign Affairs, who fought hard for us in the Community, and Karl
Gunther von Hase, later a very popular and successful German Ambas-
sador in London, then spokesman for the German Government, later
Secretary of State in the Ministry of Defence, and eventually Head of the
Second German Television. In retirement we have worked very happily
together over Königswinter conferences, Radio Free Europe-Radio
Liberty and the European Media Institute. These easy and excellent
working relations in Bonn were repeated throughout the country in the
Land governments, with whom we also had many dealings, and more
especially in Berlin.

Bonn was not a place where one saw a great deal of one's colleagues,
as one had in Moscow or Belgrade. But this did not apply to relations
with the American and French Ambassadors, with whom I shared many
responsibilities in Berlin and on 'All-German questions'. My American
colleague, George McGhee, was one of the small number of non-career
American diplomats who have held a number of diplomatic posts and
become as expert as any career Ambassador. He had previously been
Ambassador to Turkey, and had long periods of service in senior posts
within the State Department. I found him a good colleague and close
friend in Germany.

He had to operate in a period when German Governments were
beginning to feel, as indeed they had every right to do, that the Federal
Republic had become an important independent member of the West-

ern European political family and was no longer a 'client' state relying on the favour of the United States. There had by then developed the split within the CDU between the Atlanticists, looking mainly to the United States, and the Europeans, looking mainly to General de Gaulle's France. All this made life more complicated than it had been for earlier American Ambassadors. George McGhee understood this and operated successfully in the new situation.

My first French colleague was an old friend, Roland de Margerie, with whom I had worked together in the Secretariat of the Supreme War Council in 1939–40 under our then Prime Ministers, Daladier and Chamberlain. He was succeeded by another French diplomat, François Seydoux, a German specialist, with whom relations were inevitably difficult because of General de Gaulle's attitude to our membership of the community. On one occasion he complained – not to me, but to Dr Winnacker, then head of the great chemical concern, Hoechst – because I had been invited to make one of the main speeches at the annual meeting, which Hoechst always held in their great new hall near Frankfurt, with an audience of over two thousand people. Dr Winnacker had invited me precisely because he was dissatisfied with General de Gaulle's policy of keeping us out of the Community. I was careful not to criticize the French in my speech, but nevertheless Dr Winnacker later told me that he had received a letter from the French Ambassador asking why he had not been invited instead of me, to receive the reply that such invitations were decided by Dr Winnacker. This prompts me to record how accessible and friendly I found German industrialists and bankers, whose role in the Federal Republic was most important. Despite all my efforts, Anglo-French relations even in Germany were bound to be strained as long as de Gaulle kept us out of the Community. One of the French correspondents, de Kergorly of the *Figaro*, wrote an article accusing me of striving to undermine the French position in the Federal Republic. This was untrue, and I was angry. I complained through my Press Attaché, to receive the response that I should have been flattered because he had emphasized the skill with which I was doing this!

I had always been lucky in the high quality of my British colleagues in every post in which I had served with some overall responsibility, beginning in Moscow at the end of the war. This was particularly important in Germany, where the Ambassador was so constantly on the move, apart from dividing his time between Bonn and Berlin. Many went on to senior posts and three were among my successors as

Ambassadors in Germany. There were two I must mention, the first my Personal Assistant Nancy Orpe, who supported me magnificently and put up with me from 1951 until I retired in 1968, and the second Lance Pope, who gave me a great advantage over all other Ambassadors in Bonn. He had been a prisoner of war in Germany and after the war stayed on to become what would have been described in the Far or Middle East as an Oriental Secretary. He knew everyone in Germany – industrialists, trade unionists, in all political parties – and they all knew and trusted him. Many people in such a position would not have resisted the temptation to become a bit of an 'éminence grise' and to give the impression that they were really running British policy in Germany. This was never the case with Lance Pope.

Our last weeks in Germany in the spring of 1968 were spent in goodbye visits in the Länder, in Berlin and in Bonn itself, where we gave a farewell garden party ourselves. We were met everywhere with genuine friendship and warm hospitality which reflected the happy state of British-German relations. Asked at a press conference for parting impressions, I summed up the two decades since the war in saying that had anyone told me in Moscow in 1945 that only twenty-three years after the war the Atlantic Alliance would have united Western Europe and North America, that Western Europe would have re-established its economy so successfully and have made such progress towards greater unity, and that British-German relations would have resumed the warmth which had been usual before the two world wars, I should have dismissed such a prophecy as fantastically optimistic. I was indeed fortunate to have had the opportunity, in a career where end results do not always reflect diplomatic endeavours, to play some part in all these great developments and to have ended it so happily in a stable and prosperous Germany so far removed from Hitler's Third Reich, with which my official connection with German affairs had begun less happily in 1937.

In his great speech in Berlin in 1963, President Kennedy made his own optimistic prophecy that the time would come when Berlin would again, 'be joined as one – and also this country [Germany] and this great continent of Europe – in a peaceful and hopeful glow'. He concluded that, 'the people of West Berlin could then take sober satisfaction that they were in the front line for almost two decades'. We have seen his prophecy fulfilled nearly three decades later in a way and at a speed which he could not have foreseen. As a diplomat who worked for these goals in London, Moscow, Belgrade, NATO, Bonn and Berlin and afterwards throughout an active retirement, I count myself fortunate to be able to share that sober satisfaction today, great though the problems still are which such transformations inevitably create.

27 | The Duncan Report

1969

I should have left Germany in October 1967 on my sixtieth birthday. But George Brown had some difficulties in deciding who was to be my successor, with the result that I was asked to stay on for another six months. I had been asked to join Unilever, where I became an advisory director, and also Lloyds of London as their first adviser on foreign affairs, mainly in Europe. Both of them were fortunately patient, and I started my new life as an 'amateur' businessman in the spring of 1968. I had dreaded not having enough to do in retirement, and soon found that I had been provided with an ample insurance policy against this.

A third major British company, Dunlop, then entering into what proved a difficult partnership with Pirelli, invited me on their board as a non-executive director. Through these business contacts I became involved with the work of the International Chamber of Commerce, particularly on multinational companies and in the United Nations, and also under Lord Shawcross's chairmanship in drawing up guidelines against bribery and extortion in international business. I also represented Unilever on a small group of senior international business leaders with the strange title of APPI, under Dr Abs's chairmanship. The letters stood for the Association for the Promotion and Protection of Foreign Investments. Our apparently most successful intervention on behalf of an American company expropriated in Peru unfortunately provoked a military takeover! These business connections took up about half of my time. I had an office and a most charming and efficient secretary, Jean Shepperd, at Unilever, who were most generous in allowing me to profit from both in my other activities not strictly concerned with Unilever. The Unilever connection was for me a particularly pleasant one, especially looking back to 1905 when my father was starting what became the Unilever businesses throughout Latin America.

The other half of my time was taken up in voluntary activity connected mainly with Germany, NATO and the Soviet Union. My NATO background led to my becoming the President for many years of the British Atlantic Committee, and this in its turn to my becoming President for the prescribed period of three years of the Atlantic Treaty Association, which links together the BAC and the national voluntary bodies supporting NATO in the other member countries. I also found myself Chairman and then President of the European Atlantic Group, and for many years was a member and chairman of the political committee of the Atlantic Institute for International Affairs, on the Council of the Royal Institute of International Affairs and also a member of the Trilateral Commission.

My German background led to my becoming, immediately after my retirement, the Chairman of the British steering committee for the Anglo-German Königswinter Conference. For nearly twenty years I had this privilege, which carried with it some hard and delicate work, more especially after the decision was taken in the early Seventies, on my initiative, to arrange and find the financial support for meetings every other year in the United Kingdom. The fortieth-anniversary meeting took place in Cambridge in 1990 in the presence of its founder, Dame Lilo Milchsack, then in her eighty-fifth year, and with the participation of the German Chancellor and the British Prime Minister. It was, I believe, helpful at a difficult moment in Anglo-German relations. Another result of my German career was the invitation to be the first President (for three years) and later for many years Vice-President of the new German Chamber of Commerce and Industry in the United Kingdom, promoting British as well as German trade. This led on to an invitation to become a non-executive director of the British subsidiary of a major German multinational, Hoechst. As with Unilever, Hoechst have been most generous in the facilities they have provided to help me in many 'extra-mural' activities, above all, for which I am most grateful, in the writing of this book. This was followed by similar appointments with Mercedes Benz UK and later with the Amalgamated Metal Corporation, also under German ownership, in this case of Preussag. All three have provided equally happy, helpful and interesting personal relationships over many years.

The third main chapter in my non-business activities concerned another country with which I had been much engaged, the Soviet Union. As a Vice-President of the Great Britain-USSR Association I have been able to follow the ups and downs of Anglo-Soviet relations over the past twenty years and to benefit from many interesting contacts in the recent Glasnost period. I also became, on my retirement in 1968, a member of the West European Advisory Committee of Radio Free Europe and Radio Liberty which, apart from their very important broadcasts to the Soviet Union and Eastern Europe, which certainly made a major contribution to the remarkable developments of recent years, have provided the best available research on the Soviet Union and Eastern Europe.

I was also fortunate to get away a little from my international past and to see something of the British educational world, first as Chairman of the Governors of Bedales, and simultaneously, as President of the Old Rugbeian Society and the Old Rugbeian Trust. I was for many years the Chairman of the Trustees of the Fund for International Student Cooperation, and a member of the Council of the European Cultural Foundation. This in its turn led to a more recent connection with the media through membership of the Council of the European Institute for the Media at Manchester. To write at any length about these very disparate, but for me fascinating, activities would unduly prolong a book which is primarily a personal commentary on the great events and the great leaders in my diplomatic career.

There was, however, one major activity shortly after my retirement from Bonn about which I should say something because it did in a sense round off my Foreign Office career. This was an invitation in the summer of 1968 from Michael Stewart, once again Foreign Secretary after George Brown's resignation, to join the Foreign Secretary's Review Committee on Overseas Representation, better known as the Duncan Committee. This had been preceded earlier in the summer by an invitation from Ted Heath, then Leader of the Opposition, to join a less official group, also to look into our foreign representation, of which the secretary was Douglas Hurd. Ted Heath fully understood that my duty lay in joining the official inquiry. The experience under Douglas Hurd was most valuable when the Duncan Committee started its work. Once again my business employers were understanding and patient.

We were not a Royal Commission but a small group of three, our chairman Sir Val Duncan, the head of Rio Tinto Zinc, being the businessman, and Andrew Shonfield, then director of studies at Chatham House, the academic. I was, I suppose, a sort of watchdog for the Diplomatic Service. As we proceeded with our work, I was gratified but a little alarmed to find that my two colleagues began to acquire what at times I thought rather too high an opinion of the Diplomatic Service, although never, I am glad to record, of working conditions in the Foreign Office! It fell to me to explain from time to time that things were not really quite as good as they thought and that there was scope for reform. In these views I was in complete harmony with those held by colleagues in the Diplomatic Service itself. I have happy memories of this close collaboration with my two colleagues, alas now dead for some years, and with our two Secretaries, Robert Wade Geary from the Diplomatic Service and Gavin Dick from the Board of Trade.

The Duncan Committee had been preceded some years before by the Plowden Committee, which had done all the basic work on the structure and organization of a Diplomatic Service expanded, not before time, to include the Commonwealth Relations Service. It had put the flesh on to the bones of the original Eden–Bevin reforms at the end of the war. Our task was not so detailed or demanding but it was in some ways more difficult and controversial. The Labour Government of the day were anxious to make economies, particularly in foreign exchange, and although the budget of the Foreign and Commonwealth Office over many decades has not exceeded one per cent of our total budget, it did appear vulnerable when it came to foreign exchange. The main issue with which we were faced was the importance of promoting British trade and exports, and ensuring that our new-model Diplomatic Service was qualified and prepared to put the same emphasis upon this work as upon its traditional political and diplomatic activities. We also took it upon ourselves to look into the major changes in diplomacy arising from the growth of important multinational organizations such as the United Nations, NATO, the Organization for Economic Cooperation and Development, the Council of Europe and the European Community.

We were asked to complete our report in six months, and did in fact do so in nine, no mean feat, since all of us, and more especially our chairman, were busy people. We visited over forty countries and had over a hundred and fifty meetings in this country. Some people were a little shocked by the emphasis that we did in fact lay upon trade

271

promotion as an important diplomatic activity, but in my business world I found that my new colleagues there were impressed by the improvements which this brought for their cooperation with Embassies and Consulates abroad, more especially in the Third World and in the Communist countries, where Government support was most needed. Others, including one or two of my older diplomatic colleagues, resented our assumption that Britain was now 'a major power of the second order', although I hardly think many people would question that today.

The recommendation which brought the most criticism down upon us was our division of diplomatic posts around the world into two categories. The first was the new kind of large multinational diplomatic mission (for example, the United Nations, NATO, the European Community) covering also our bilateral missions in countries which were members of these organizations. Our academic, Andrew Shonfield, proposed that we should call these posts, 'the area of concentration'. We were then tempted, very foolishly as it turned out, to follow Marxist thinking and to find an antithesis to these areas of concentration. We had to do much of our work late at night, and I think it was about one in the morning that someone proposed, 'the outer area'. I have since kicked myself for not having at once seen the trap. 'Outer area' was widely interpreted as covering second-class posts in countries which were regarded as of little or lesser importance. In fact, all we meant was that the kind of diplomacy conducted in these posts was different – as indeed it was and has remained – and by no means necessarily less important or less rewarding for the diplomats involved. The Soviet Union, Brazil or Saudi Arabia could in any case never have been considered as of lesser importance. Had we been, as Ernie Bevin occasionally accused the Foreign Office of being, 'Machivellic' in our thinking, this might have seemed a very 'Machivellic' proposal which diverted attention from many other possibly controversial proposals in our report!

Although the Duncan Committee proved to be valuable in protecting the Diplomatic Service from ill-considered economy proposals, such as five per cent or ten per cent cuts across the board, and we were determined not to suggest savings where we thought this would interfere with essential activities, we did not forget that our remit was based upon economies. The areas where we thought we could find them with least disadvantage were in our Services representation in the whole area east of Suez, from which Britain under the Labour

Government was then withdrawing, and also in the Government information services. These, as I recalled from my recent experience in Germany, were of high quality, but we felt – and I still hold that view today – that the picture of the country given by less official organizations such as the British Council and the BBC External Services was more likely to be accepted in the outside world than that from specifically Government information services. Our recommendation was that the funding and the high standards of the BBC and the British Council should be maintained. Had we felt it possible, we should have recommended increases in their funding, more especially in such areas as ensuring audibility for the BBC's External Services worldwide. I was shocked, although not entirely surprised, to find that the BBC, far from thanking us for our efforts, were dismissive of what they regarded as a group of amateurs expressing views on matters where they themselves were the experts.

Looking ahead to the Think Tank Inquiry some seven years later under Sir Kenneth Berrill, where much emphasis was laid upon the role of experts rather than generalists in the Diplomatic Service, I should perhaps record that the Duncan Committee strongly favoured what they called professional generalists, a conclusion which still guides our diplomatic practice.

We were unlucky in some of our efforts to save money. One of our ideas, strongly supported by the incumbent diplomats, was to give up old-fashioned and large Embassy residences in by then inappropriate locations. But our first attempts to do this in Athens and then in Istanbul came up against the unexpected hurdle that each of these splendid mansions had been the gift, in the one case of the widow of the former Greek Prime Minister, Venizelos, and in the other of a nineteenth-century Ottoman Sultan. Were we to cease to use them, they had to be returned to the original donors or their heirs. Another effort, based on Canadian experience, to save about £100,000 a year by introducing 'limp' passports instead of our large, hard British passports, which could not be put into typewriters or easily computerized, also came up against strong romantic prejudice. At a lunch at Lloyds at which I was present, one of the Foreign Office Junior Ministers was greeted with acclamation when he explained that he was late because he had been persuading our then Foreign Secretary, Lord Home, to have nothing to do with these 'terrible' limp passports. I believe that the EEC passports now being issued are in fact 'limp'.

273

On balance, I think that our report was on the right lines, as indeed it should have been, since we were really knocking on an open door and the Foreign Office itself was thinking on similar lines in regard to many if not all of our recommendations. Certainly, when seven years later the Think Tank under Sir Kenneth Berrill took their less sympathetic look at our overseas representation, my old department seemed happy to stand firm on what had emerged from the Duncan Report, and I was happy to have helped them to do so.

28 | Epilogue

It was the scale and rapidity of developments in Germany, Eastern and Central Europe in 1989–90 which impelled me after more than twenty years to set down in this personal record some of the background to German unification in 1990, to Glasnost and Perestroika under Gorbachev in the Soviet Union since 1985 and to the collapse of Communism in Central and South Eastern Europe in 1989. I should therefore perhaps attempt, however briefly and inadequately, and at the risk of being overtaken by developments in the next few months, to draw some of the threads together, if only to emphasize not only the magnitude of what has been achieved so far but also some of the problems and possible dangers ahead.

I begin with the Soviet Union, since the key to German unification and to freedom in Eastern Europe was always in Moscow and was only turned in the lock by Gorbachev. There had never been any prospect of it being turned by Stalin, nor even by Khrushchev, who, for all his 'liberal reforms' at home, was responsible for the bloody repression of Hungarian liberty in 1956, for the Berlin Wall in 1961 and the Cuba missile crisis in 1962, still less by Brezhnev, who extinguished Dubcek's Prague Spring in 1968 and laid down in the doctrine which bears his name that no country which had become a member of the 'socialist' community should be allowed to relapse into Western democratic institutions. Under these three leaders the Soviet Union hung on to its wartime gains in Eastern Europe, including the German Democratic Republic, although with the exception of Czechoslovakia in 1948 no further Soviet advance was made in Europe; indeed, Yugoslavia was lost to the Eastern bloc.

Throughout a period of adversarial East-West relations lasting
some three decades, the West built up its strength and unity – and its
economic prosperity – under American leadership, with a major
contribution, above all in NATO and in Germany, from Britain. The
illusions of 1945 about post-war cooperation with Stalin's Soviet
Union were abandoned for more realistic policies based upon strength
and firmness successfully pursued in all major crises, for example, the
Berlin Blockade, Korea and the Cuba Missiles. But these policies were
coupled with understanding and readiness for East-West discussion
and negotiation. Pursued consistently for forty years, they have led to
the transformation of Europe in 1989–90. They began with the policy
recommendations from the American and British Embassies in
Moscow in 1946 leading to the major decisions of Truman, Marshall
and Acheson in Washington and of Attlee and Bevin in London in the
late Forties. The Atlantic Alliance of 1949 was the essential instrument. Although originally conceived as primarily a military and
defence organization, it was already in the mid-Fifties preparing for
détente as well as defence and deterrence and for its eventual political
role in facilitating consultations within the Alliance, in preparing
negotiations with the Soviet Union and as a factor of stability. This
was eventually recognized by Soviet acquiescence in 1990 in continued membership of NATO by a united Germany and in a wide
consensus that NATO still has an important role to play in stabilizing
and consolidating the new East-West relationship of closer understanding and even cooperation.

Paradoxically, although Gorbachev has since 1985 led the way
towards the liberation of Eastern Europe and the unification of
Germany, the Soviet Union remains far behind in many respects.
Glasnost or openness has indeed transformed Soviet society and inter-
changes between East and West. But Perestroika or economic reform
is still far from achievement. Indeed, by the end of 1990 there were
few signs that the injection of elements of the free market into what
was still basically a Communist command economy could succeed and
more radical reforms still had to prove themselves. Economic
conditions have got worse rather than better; nationalism has been
gaining ground in all the republics of the Union, including the two
most important, the Russian Federation itself and the Ukraine. But
even if all fifteen republics were to go their own separate ways, which
seems unlikely, there would remain a Russia of some 150 million
people stretching from the Pacific to the Baltic, with a strong army and

nuclear weapons, probably in a dangerous nationalist mood. Alternatively, there could be chaos, which all Russians, recalling earlier times of trouble, most fear, or simply the indefinite prolongation of the current critical and uncertain situation. These dangerous possibilities provide argument enough for the maintenance of Western unity and strength in an Atlantic Alliance which should still be based upon nuclear deterrence, which still needs the presence of American troops in Europe and a Germany still committed to the defence as well as to the political goals of the alliance. It should also be an alliance which, whatever its strict treaty obligations, looks beyond Europe and the Atlantic to dangers overseas, for example in the oil-rich Middle East, and does not leave the USA as the sole world policeman.

The developments in the whole area between the Soviet Union and Germany have at long last taken us away from Yalta. The Yalta agreements were on paper to have given freedom and democracy to those 'liberated' countries. Stalin saw that they were placed instead in a Communist straitjacket. Now as a result of popular pressures and Soviet weakness they have the opportunity to resume their European role and to adopt the free market economies of the West. But with the exception of Czechoslovakia none of them have had much experience of democracy, although they have had much more experience of the free market than the Soviet Union or its predecessor the Russian Empire. Hungary and Poland, as well as Czechoslovakia, are obviously better placed than the Balkan countries, Roumania, Bulgaria and even Yugoslavia, to cope with current difficulties, but there is no assurance of success, even with support from the West and potentially from a united Germany. So the great achievements of Solidarity in Poland or Charter 77 in Czechoslovakia cannot yet be assured of final victory and there will be many and serious problems in reintegrating these historic European nations into a broader Europe than that of the existing Community of twelve. Some political strain and stress seems probable. Once again, the strength and unity of the Atlantic Alliance and the attraction of the European Community remain of great importance.

The only sure and final achievement so far would therefore seem to be German unification, and even this is subject to some doubts and even disquiet. It is in itself a great success story, which should not be dimmed by the existence of such doubts. From 1945 on, German unification has been the goal of Western policies. Division only came in 1948 when it proved impossible to restore the German economy, for the same reasons that it is proving at best exceedingly difficult to try to restore the Soviet economy, by a mixture of Western social free market methods and of the Soviet command economy in the east. The Berlin Blockade and Airlift led on to the Cold War and to division between two German states, one in NATO and the European Community prospering greatly, the other in the Warsaw Pact and Comecon at best at the head of a relatively backward Eastern class. Attempts to unite the two German states in the Fifties could not overcome the Soviet rejection of genuinely free elections on their side of the divide and of freedom of choice in its international relations for a unified German state. But the goal of unity was never given up. The three Western allies committed themselves by treaty when West Germany was admitted to NATO and WEU in 1955 to supporting the West German Government in any negotiations for reunification, although there was general acceptance in the West that this should not be based on neutrality. German unity had the support of Churchill, who wrote in his memoirs that 'the artificial division of Germany is a tragedy which cannot endure'. But unity seemed increasingly a far-off dream before Gorbachev came to power in 1985.

Meanwhile, following the lead given by Adenauer, West Germany anchored itself in the West, in NATO, in WEU and in the EC. Willy Brandt proclaimed that these firm ties with the West alone gave him the security to complete in the Ostpolitik of 1971 reconciliation with Germany's eastern neighbours following reconciliation in the west. After the Berlin Wall in 1961 it had been increasingly accepted by West Germans that ending the division of Germany could only come with the ending of the division of Europe and not, as had previously been claimed, vice versa. The immediate results in Germany itself were restricted to improving human contacts between East and West Germans and to ensuring the stability of Berlin. In this process the Communist East Germany of Honecker almost achieved respectability!

The rejection of their Communist state and society by the population of the GDR, first by emigration on a large scale and then in peaceful demonstrations, the determination of East Germans to share in the material advantages and free institutions of the Federal Republic, the help given to those leaving the GDR by Hungary, Czechoslovakia and even Poland, and finally the refusal of Gorbachev to give the green light to Honecker to stop all this by force, all came as a great surprise within and outside the Federal Republic. But in less than a year the many domestic and international obstacles were all overcome. The Wall came down in Berlin – free elections in the GDR were followed in a few months by the currency and economic union of July 1990 and by the final political unification of 3 October, all this with the agreement of the Four Allied Powers responsible for Berlin and for all-German questions. The Soviet Union's original objections to a united Germany rejecting neutrality and remaining in NATO were overcome through special military arrangements covering the territory of the former GDR, with limitations upon the size of the future German armed forces and with the alluring prospect of German economic assistance. Throughout all these negotiations the West German Government have firmly maintained their Westward orientation in the European Community and in NATO and have given the necessary reassurances over frontiers to Poland. Further reassurance lies in the probable maintenance of the capital, at least for some years, in Bonn rather than Berlin. There is also reassurance even in the method of unification, which has been the absorption of the reconstituted provinces of the former GDR under the Western Basic Law in the federal framework and democratic institutions of the Federal Republic. All in all, a great success story in which both German states, the Soviet Union and the three Western 'Protecting Powers' can take legitimate pride and pleasure. The policies consistently pursued by successive West German Governments in building up not only the strongest economy in the European Community but also a model system of social security and a stable and highly effective federal political structure and in displaying a high degree of international responsibility have borne fruit, as have the policies of the three Western 'Protecting Powers' in resisting Soviet pressures in Berlin and on all-German questions.

Why then should there still be doubts and disquiet? They arise partly of course from history and the role of united Germany in two World Wars. I have not, however, seen any traces of Hitler's Reich or even of the Kaiser's Germany in today's model bourgeois democracy, even when I hark back to the fears and concerns of the pre-war Foreign Office. Denazification, demilitarization and democratization were indeed successfully accomplished after 1945. What cannot, however, be dismissed is the relative size of a united Germany of 80 million in the heart of Europe. The Germans themselves are well aware of this. A former Chancellor, Kiesinger, spoke, as have many other German leaders, of the sheer size and geographical position of Germany as an inevitable source of concern to her neighbours. Chancellor Kohl and German political leaders of all parties remain fully conscious of this today, and are careful not to throw German weight about. But a strong Deutschmark and a strong economy could perhaps achieve for a united Germany hegemony in the Community and in Europe generally, even though the Deutschmark and the West German economy will be largely occupied for a few years at least in coping with the major problems as well as opportunities of the bankrupt East German system. All present signs, however, are that a united Germany will continue to behave as a responsible and not an over-dominant member of the European Community. Also, in a world where there are such major economic powers as the United States and Japan, with even bigger populations and economies, a Germany of 80 million can hardly look to play a much more influential role than that already achieved by the Federal Republic of 67 million on its own.

My own concern, and it does not keep me awake at night since it is shared by many influential Germans, lies more in the field of security and East-West relations. However sincerely anxious the leaders of a united Germany are to maintain the Western orientation of the Federal Republic with its capital at least for the time being in Bonn, it will lie in the centre, not the west of Europe. Once the Russians and Allied troops have left the GDR and Berlin, there will be very natural pressures to move the capital back to Berlin, itself a highly democratic Western city. A united Germany will inevitably become increasingly involved with its eastern neighbours, in itself not an undesirable development. In the long run there could be a revival of traditional concepts of a special relationship with Russia or with a Russian Confederation of the future, although my German business friends are always quick to remind me how very much more important are Germany's economic links with the West and the world overseas.

In the short term, it seems to me that there are more likely to be problems in the security field, affecting Germany's position in NATO. There are many elements in German public and even political opinion which, while anxious to remain in the Atlantic Alliance, already see it more as a political than a military necessity. This tendency may grow with the departure within three to four years of Soviet troops from Eastern Germany, coupled with the absence of any immediate threat from the east. The next stage could be to question the need for Allied troops on German soil and more especially of troops accompanied, as US forces would necessarily be, by nuclear weapons. This would risk undermining the Alliance itself, the main purpose of which remains to link the United States with Europe, a link which would be hard to maintain if American troops and nuclear weapons were completely withdrawn from Europe. There are, however, many Germans as conscious of these dangers and as determined to prevent them as are their partners and allies in Europe and in the Atlantic Alliance.

This is indeed the note on which I would like to conclude these random thoughts for the future. It is indeed paradoxical that doubts and disquiet about German unification should centre, at least for me, not on a united Germany showing nationalistic and potentially militaristic tendencies or flexing its economic and financial muscles, still less on a united Germany looking to the east for expansion, but rather on a Germany which might be tempted to underrate military requirements and, however unwittingly, to weaken NATO, while remaining one of its key members. Prophecy is a dangerous pursuit, which all diplomats are advised to avoid, but I would still expect a united Germany to continue the responsible, sensible policies which have ensured the economic success and the political stability of the Federal Republic in the West. We are lucky indeed that German unification, to which Britain has long been committed, which could have been a highly explosive event, came first in the form of a most restrained and bloodless 'revolution' from a united population in East Germany. Secondly, that it was supported by Germany's nearest Eastern neighbours in Hungary, Czechoslovakia and even, although to a lesser extent and with reservations, in Poland. Thirdly, that it was accepted and even 'promoted' by a wise Russian leader, Gorbachev, and facilitated by Soviet preoccupation with problems nearer home. Fourthly, that it was carried through by leaders in West Germany, supported by German public opinion, who are fully conscious of its wider repercussions, well aware that German unity is more than a German question, anxious to meet legitimate outside concerns and to ensure that a united Germany remains anchored in such Western institutions as the European Community and the Atlantic Alliance. It remains for Germany's Western allies to show understanding and support in the many problems ahead, which concern us all.

Index